Visions of Education in India

Visions of Education in India

Edited by
Muchkund Dubey
Susmita Mitra

AAKAR

Visions of Education in India
Edited by Muchkund Dubey and Susmita Mitra

First Published 2019

ISBN 978-93-5002-604-5 (Hb)

Published by
AAKAR BOOKS
28 E Pocket IV, Mayur Vihar Phase I
Delhi 110 091 India
aakarbooks@gmail.com

Laser Typeset at
Sakshi Computers, Delhi

Printed at
Sapra Brothers, Noida

Contents

PART III : INEQUALITY IN EDUCATION

PART IV : ROLE OF PEOPLE'S MOVEMENT

PART V : IMPACT ON EDUCATION OF GLOBALIZATION AND NEOLIBERAL ECONOMIC POLICIES

PART VI : RTE ACT AND ITS IMPLEMENTATION

Introduction

Muchkund Dubey and Susmita Mitra

Education is presently seen primarily as the means of earning a livelihood and making students fit for the market where they can be sold and purchased. This commoditization of education is a relatively recent phenomenon brought about by the dominance of neo-liberal thinking, reinforced by the latest phase of the phenomenon of globalization commencing approximately from the early 1980s.

Earlier, education was seen in a much broader prospective. There was an emphasis in it on inculcating values. The term 'learning', which is currently regarded as the principal outcome of education, was meant not only to acquire the three R's, i.e. Reading, Writing and Arithmetic, but also to comprehend and develop critical thinking in order to be able to separate the substance from the chaff. It was meant to help in cultivating the faculty to cast an intelligent and critical eye on the world around the learner. With the recent ascendancy of the concept of fundamental rights and people's movements to secure them, the word "comprehend" has been extended to embrace "contest" and to acquire the urge to seek the transformation of institutions and society to make them just and equitable.

In the later phase of the 18th century and in the 19th century, education was primarily used as a tool of nation-building in societies consisting of diverse socio-economic classes and cultural and religious communities. This happened particularly in the United States and several of the European countries, particularly

Germany. In these countries, children from diverse socio-economic conditions and cultural and religious backgrounds were brought under the single roof of a school to understand and live with each other and to develop a common understanding of basic values and objectives as the organizing principles of the nation. The school thus became one of the most important places for socialization. These objectives were pursued mainly through a common school system funded, built and operated by the state.

The instrumental value of education is at the core of the human capital theory advanced in the early 1960s by Theodor Schultz and other economists. This theory gave rise to a series of country and cross-country studies to calculate private and social returns on investment in education. An overwhelming number of these studies proved that education, particularly at the primary level, contributed significantly to the enhancement of private earning and growth of national GDP. The human capital theory was expanded significantly by Amartya Sen's emphasis on both the instrumental and intrinsic values of education. Amartya Sen's intention was not to replace the human capital theory but to incorporate it in the wider framework of the "capability" approach.

The notion of education as a basic human right, which has acquired traction recently is implicit in the concept of the intrinsic value of education. Yet another form of the intrinsic value of education, which has become salient recently with the spread of democracy, is education for inculcating democratic norms or education for citizenship.

The Right to Education approach underlines the importance of universalization of education which is necessary to ensure that every child, particularly children belonging to the poor and marginalized sections of the population, is given an equal opportunity for education for a minimum number of years. The opinion is veering around to the goal of the state universalizing education for a minimum of 10 years, but preferably 12 years.

Even if we see education from its instrumental value perspective, a country can derive maximum benefit from education for development purposes only if all or the vast majority of its children, and not only a few who come from well-to-do families, have the opportunity of contributing to the human capital of the country. This underlines the importance of making education inclusive for the purpose of optimizing human capital formation and for reaping the demographic dividend for which a window of opportunity is open for India during the next 15-20 years.

The four pillars of learning, i.e. 'learn to know', 'learn to do', 'learn to be' and 'learn to live together and with others' highlighted in the Report of the International Commission on Education for the 21st Century, also known as the Delors Commission Report, ideally combines both the instrumental and intrinsic values of education in the context of the challenges of the 21st century. The Report in this context very rightly emphasizes the importance of 'learning throughout life' and suggests changes of a structural nature in the present educational systems, in order to realize this objective.

The book revisits the visions of education of some of the great Indian philosophers, thinkers and leaders of the Indian cultural renaissance and of the movement for political freedom. These include, in particular, Rabindranath Tagore, Mahatma Gandhi and Sri Aurobindo. The volume then deconstructs seminal documents on education in India, particularly the Kothari Commission Report (1964-66), National Education Policies of 1968 and 1986 and the revision of the 1986 policy in 1992, the Report of the Commission on the Common School System, Bihar, (2007), and the Right of Children to Free and Compulsory Education Act (2009). The book also seeks to review education through a matrix of nation-building, democratization process, identity, power, social and economic divisions, and social hierarchies—all in the overall framework of globalization and neo-liberalism. There are also chapters devoted to the analysis of the very significant role played by the people's movement in shaping education. The volume also deals with trends and progress in the implementation of educational programmes and policies and suggests the way forward for achieving the goal of universalizing school education.

Indian Education in Ancient Time

Right from the ancient times, India had a rich tradition of education. It was mostly moulded by the religious values of truth, non-violence, peace, cooperation and self-fulfilment. Some of the distinguishing features of education in the ancient times were:

(i) Holistic learning acquired in the midst of nature under the supervision of a teacher. Close association between the teacher and the student was regarded as the real way of acquiring education.

(ii) Importance of arguments and debates as a means of arriving at truth and advancing knowledge.

(iii) Well established eco-system to support education.

Students resided in a place far enough from the nearest bustling towns or cities in order to ensure peace and tranquillity, and yet near enough for them to go to the city to seek financial and other assistance for running their institution, for remaining in close contact with common people and in the process acquire the knowledge of their practical problems. This practice was followed also to make them aware of the contribution of society to their education so that they felt obliged to return to society the benefits of their education.

(iv) Education was not confined to the bookish level. Equal importance was attached to acquiring skills and practical knowledge required for discharging social obligations. For this purpose, the students were also trained in agriculture, animal husbandry, dairy farming, martial art, etc.

(v) Education was the same for both boys and girls.

Education During the Buddhist Period

Indian education in the ancient period reached its pinnacle in the Buddhist period. Education in this era was divided into the primary and higher level. At the primary level, the emphasis was on learning reading, writing and arithmetic. Religion, philosophy, military science, medicine and other subjects of higher learning were taught at the next level. Some of the important centres of learning during this period were Takshashila, Nalanda, Valabhi, Vikramshila and Odantapuri. There is evidence of several foreign students coming to India to acquire higher education in these reputed institutions (Singh 2017)[1].

Education in the British Period

By the time the British came to India, the institutions of higher education had been demolished completely. However, the primary level indigenous education was well spread in the entire country. Education at this level was carried out in *pathshalas, madrassas* and *gurukuls*. Several survey reports completed in the early 19th century by British experts indicate extensive existence of such educational institutions in different parts of India. For example, there were around 100,000 village schools in Bengal and Bihar around the 1830s. Similarly, every village had a school in the Madras Presidency. Spread of education in the Punjab around 1850 was of a similar extent. According to those reports, in terms of the content and proportion of students attending institutions of school education, the situation in India in the early 19th century was superior to the one in England. The content of studies was better, the duration of study was more prolonged, and the method of teaching was superior. According to Dharampal (1983)[2], the only aspect where Indian institutional education seemed to have lagged behind was with regard to the education of girls.

(a) Between 1813 and 1835

The Charter Act of 1813 was a turning point in the history of Indian education. The Charter mandated the inclusion of education among the duties of the Company, and substantial funds got secured annually for educational activities. However, there were debates among two groups—the Orientalists who favoured the promotion of Indian education through existing media of instruction, i.e. Sanskrit, Arabic, and Persian; and the Anglicists who were in favour of promoting Western education in India through the medium of English. This controversy sharpened the ambiguity as to whether education should be for all or a selected few. The allotted funds were kept unspent till 1823. However, throughout this period, the indigenous educational system remained in operation without interruption.

The teaching of English started in several government schools and colleges after the establishment of the General Committee of Public Instructions (GCOPI) in 1823 to look after education in India. A radical change occurred in the education policy when Thomas Babington Macaulay became the Chairman of GCOPI following the 1833 Charter of the Company. Macaulay advocated a more aggressive policy of teaching English as a substitute for teaching Sanskrit, Arabic, Persian and regional languages, and prohibiting the publication of books related to oriental learning.

(b) Between 1835 and 1853

After Macaulay's proposals were approved by Lord William Bentinck on March 7, 1935, schools and colleges teaching English and European knowledge and science became entitled to receive government aid. This inevitably had an adverse effect on the traditional educational system. Thus, from this time onwards, the modern system of education in India got established at the cost of the traditional indigenous system.

In line with Bentinck's Resolution (1835), Lord Hardinge proclaimed in 1844 that for services in public offices, preference would be given to those who were educated in English schools. It implied that education was imparted with the limited objective of turning out clerks. This proclamation gave rise to a new division, that is, between English-knowing and non-English-knowing, in Indian society which was already divided by castes and religion.

During this time, the British rulers adopted the downward filtration theory of education. Macaulay thought that it was impossible to educate the masses with the limited resources available for this purpose. Therefore, he found it expedient to educate the upper classes mainly in order to fulfil the requirement of educated employees to run the commerce and administration, and leave it to them to spread elementary education among the masses. This approach and the attitude reflected in it, have continued till today in spite of the rhetoric of mass education and equality in the education system.

(c) Wood's Despatch (1854) and After

A landmark development in the effort to spread English education and teaching Western knowledge and science was Charles Wood's Despatch of 1854. Some of the salient features of the Despatch were:

(a) The purpose of education in India would be the inculcation of European knowledge and science.

(b) Asiatic learning is not necessary for progress; however, vernacular education would continue to get government aid because people had faith in it.

(c) English would be the medium of instruction in higher classes.

(d) The character of the vernacular schools would be gradually transformed by bringing in teachers from outside and introducing an appropriate syllabus.

(e) Government grants would be available to only those schools which provided secular education and which were under government inspection.

Wood's Despatch set the framework for expenditure on formal education in India. An immediate outcome of this Despatch was the passing of the three University Acts of 1857, establishing universities at Calcutta, Madras and Bombay and the establishment of an Education Department in each province of British India.

The period between 1859 and 1882 witnessed slow progress in the spread of education and there was no significant change in the education policy. On February 3, 1882, the then Viceroy Lord Ripon by a Resolution of the Government of India appointed the Indian Education Commission under the Chairmanship of William Hunter. The Commission recommended complete withdrawal of government from running of schools and the transfer of all primary schools to the control of local self-government bodies such as municipalities. Regarding secondary schools and colleges, the Commission was of the opinion that the government should withdraw as early as possible from their direct management.

(d) Education in the 20th Century Before Independence

In 1901, Lord Curzon, the then Governor General of India summoned the convening of an educational conference in Shimla. Following the conference, in 1904 the government passed a Resolution on Indian Educational Policy, commonly known as Lord Curzon's Educational Policy. The Resolution expressed grave concern regarding the shortcomings of the existing education policy, such as the objective of higher education being an entry into government jobs exclusively, dominance of examinations, overemphasis on memory training and neglect of the vernaculars, among others. The Resolution called for paying special attention to primary education as mass education, introduction of diversified courses to meet the demands of industrial development, and strengthening of secondary education by laying down certain conditions for recognition, funding, affiliation, etc. The Resolution also recommended mother tongue-based instruction till the age of 13 at least.

(e) Alternative Educational Visions Developed by Indian Personalities

In the early 20th century, alternative objectives and methods of imparting education were experimented by leaders and philosophers like Tagore, Gandhi and Aurobindo, among others. They proposed alternative visions and approaches for the design of a new system of education, which was different from the traditional, colonial and Western education systems.

The chapter by Susmita Mitra gleans Tagore's vision on education from some of his own writings. She brings out how Tagore in his experiment on education, pioneered ideas and practices which are taken for granted in the world today. Tagore wanted modern education to reach the masses and to be imparted in the mother tongue at least in the initial years. According to him, schools should not be like a factory to provide education in order to produce a homogeneous set of students. Each child is unique and his/her talent should be acknowledged and nurtured by competent teachers. He wanted education to be rooted in students' own history and culture. Moreover, children should learn through natural processes, i.e. intermingling with persons and things rather than only through books. In a crux, the ultimate purpose of education, according to Tagore, is not to teach us how to make a living but how to live.

The chapter by Sudarshan Iyengar examines the evolution of Gandhiji's ideas on education from his early days in South Africa up to the formation of the Gujarat Vidyapeeth in 1920. The chapter revisits his philosophies such as values of liberty, simplicity and spirit of service in education. Gandhiji believed that education mends society and not the other way round. For Gandhiji, inculcating values was the foundation for building character and personality. His ultimate mission was building a non-violent society. Gandhiji conceived the Gujarat Vidyapeeth as a fountainhead for teaching the theory and practice of education which could lead to building a non-violent society. Gandhiji wanted to establish an educational institution that would stand as an alternative to the system of education that prevailed under the British. The chapter by Sudarshan Iyengar also discusses the relevance of Gandhiji's ideas on education in the contemporary context.

The chapter by Anant Kumar Giri explores the vision of integral education of Sri Aurobindo and his followers. Giri emphasizes that a major crisis of contemporary education is the neglect of the goal of integral development of individuals and societies through education. Education should go beyond the dualisms of life and society—that between individual and society, between body and mind, mind and soul, the technical and artistic, the utilitarian and spiritual and, head and heart. The chapter also refers to similar educational initiatives inspired by Grundtvic and Kristen Kold in Denmark and Rudolf Steiner in Austria.

Evolution of Education Policy and State of Education in Post-Independent India

In the famous *Tryst with Destiny* speech delivered by Jawaharlal Nehru in the Indian Constituent Assembly on the eve of India's independence, he set very lofty goals for the nation. These included goals to be achieved in the social sector. Some of these goals were: "ending of poverty, ignorance, disease and inequality of opportunity"; and "to create social, economic and political institutions which will ensure justice and fullness of life to every man and woman". A major step in pursuance of these goals was the provision in the Constitution of India adopted three years later, for universalization of education up to the age of 14 years within a period of ten years of the commencement of the Constitution. However, this provision was included in the chapter on the Directive Principles of State Policy and not that on Fundamental Rights.

The first three decades after independence saw a phenomenal expansion of the education sector. The number of schools built, colleges and universities established and students attending these institutions multiplied manifold in quantitative and absolute terms. Side by side, institutions of higher learning for experiment and research, including national laboratories, institutions for education and research in science and technology, including Indian Institutes of Technology, and those for the development of art and literature were established by the state. Several economists attribute the spurt in the growth of the Indian economy during the last 20 years, in no small measure to the institutional infrastructure for research and education built during the early years after independence.

In the first Five Year Plan (1951-1956), elementary education received high priority. The Third Five Year Plan (1961-66) focused attention on children's health and education at the pre-primary stage. In the Fourth and Fifth Plans, concerted efforts were made to remove the deficiencies of the education system in order to achieve higher enrolment, reduce drop-out and improve the quality of education. For this purpose, among others, free supply of textbooks and midday meals were introduced.

Beginning from the early 1980s, neo-liberal economic thinking gained ascendancy worldwide. This led to an attack on the role of the state and encouragement of policies to give free play to market forces. This attack was led by major developed countries, the World Bank and the International Monetary Fund. This had an impact on India's development policy, including its education policy. From the early 1980s onwards, education was replaced by literacy. It resulted in the side-tracking or neglect of the traditional and more fundamental goals of education and their replacement by the learning of three R's. This along with learning of science, was regarded sufficient to make students fit for the marketplace.

The most disconcerting consequence of this shift in education policy was that these were meant only for the children of parents coming from the marginalized sections of the population. The children of the well-to-do sections continued to be sent to high fee-charging private schools. This accentuated the discrimination and inequality prevailing in the existing education system.

The World Bank and The United Nation Educational Scientific and Cultural Organization, the UN specialized agencies in the field of education, played an important role in promoting the neo-liberal education system in India. The Government of India not only went along with it but also facilitated it by its own policy measures. It was after all the Government of India which included in the 1986 National Education Policy, the component of non-formal education at the school level.

One of the arguments deployed by these international agencies, which the government also used, was that in the situation of shortage of resources, there was no scope for universalization of education in schools with inadequate infrastructure and other facilities, and, hence, the focus could be on less expensive means of imparting education and on market determined narrow norms and objectives of education.

This neoliberal shift in education policy also proved to be a major factor encouraging privatization of education and mushrooming of private schools and colleges, particularly those for educating teachers and medical and other professionals. It goes without saying that the standards in these institutions are abysmally poor. A rough estimate is that 80 per cent of graduates in India, mostly trained in such private institutions are unemployable.

Partly as a result of the progressive withdrawal of the state from the education sector and dominance of private institutions of education, the institutions for education, training and research built in the early post-independence period have rapidly declined. There has been a precipitous decline in the quality of education at all levels. Even the quantitative expansion which took place till the end of the 1970s, came to a halt after the neo-liberal shifts in education policy. In some states, such as Bihar and Jharkhand, no new schools were built and no new teachers' training institutions established for more than two decades after the mid-1980s.

After the adoption of the goal of Education-for-All in the Jomtien Declaration (1990), several governments of developing countries, including India, formally subscribed to the goal of universalizing education at the primary level. The Government of India launched the programme of *Sarva Shiksha Abhiyan* for this purpose. But this turned out to be mere window dressing. In retrospect, it appears that the government never had the political will to achieve this goal which remains unfulfilled till today.

Visions Projected and Roadmaps Drawn for Achieving Goals of Education in Post-Independent India

With the attainment of independence, a definitive provision on education was made in the Indian Constitution. This provision set a modest goal that was explicit and time bound, i.e. universal education up to the age of 14 within a period of ten years of the commencement of the Constitution. Meanwhile, commissions and committees were set up to make recommendations relating to secondary and higher education, presuming, perhaps, that the constitutional provision had taken care of elementary education. This was followed by the constitution in 1964 of the Education Commission headed by Dr. D. S. Kothari, with the mandate to outline the objectives and goals of education and draw up a roadmap for attaining them.

The Kothari Commission (1964-66) provided a template for education for national development, by means of a national system of education with 12 years of schooling, with science and mathematics as compulsory subjects till Class X and earmarking 6 per cent of GDP for expenditure on education. The Commission also made a powerful case for establishing a common school system (CSS) in India, though its recommendation on how to go about putting it on the ground was hesitant and half-hearted.

Sadhana Saxena in her paper explores some of the important national issues of the 1960s in the background of which the Commission functioned and made its recommendations. The burning national issues of that time were food insecurity, population explosion, illiteracy, slow industrial growth, unemployment, problems in agricultural modernization based on technology, resistance to land distribution and gathering momentum of resistance in the country, against the economic pressure from the World Bank and the United States.

Poornima M. in her chapter throws light on the processes followed by the Commission in organizing its work and arriving at its conclusions. She also discusses key recommendations of the Kothari Commission, particularly those related to school education and the problems encountered in implementing them in the contemporary context.

A National Education Policy was promulgated in 1968, based on the Kothari Commission's recommendations. This was followed by the National Education Policy of 1986. The Ramamurti Committee was constituted under the chairmanship of Acharya Ramamurti to review the 1986 Policy and the accompanying Plan of Action. Prof. Ramamurti instead of merely reviewing the 1986 Policy in the light of developments since then, challenged several of the basic assumptions behind the policy measures included in the Policy. This put the government somewhat in a fix, to get out of which it constituted another committee, namely, the Janardhan Reddy Committee whose report turned out to be a damage control exercise.

The late Vinay Kantha, in his chapter, provides an analysis of all the national education policies adopted in the post-independent era, with particular focus on the National Education Policies of 1968 and 1986 and the Ramamurti Committee Report (1992). In this chapter, Vinay Kantha examines whether the two national education policies were inspired by any vision and in the process projects a vision of his own on education. Vinay Kantha points out that the 1986 National Policy focused on technology-led, atomized, and prescriptive pathways for promoting education and lost sight of the holistic approach to education outlined in the Kothari Commission Report. The idea in the 1986 Policy, of non-formal schooling, in the name of flexibility of approach to education, led to the establishment of a parallel inferior system of education meant for the children of the neglected classes. It also resulted in a massive induction of untrained, poorly educated persons on a contract basis. These so-called para-teachers have had a corrosive impact on the regular cadre of teachers. This also marked the beginning of the neglect of government schools and consequent proliferation of private schools starting from the 1990s and continuing till today.

On July 22, 2006, the then Chief Minister of Bihar, Mr. Nitish Kumar, who also happens to be the present Chief Minister of the State, declared his government's commitment to establish a Common School System (CSS) in the state. Soon thereafter, the state government constituted the Common School System Commission, Bihar, under the Chairmanship of Prof. Muchkund Dubey to draw up a full-fledged plan for establishing CSS in Bihar. The Commission submitted its report in June 2007. This was the first and till now the only report in which concrete measures to be taken for establishing a CSS have been outlined, norms and standards commonly applicable to schools at different levels have been established, a price tag has been attached to each norm and standard and on that basis the total cost, both recurring and non-recurring, of establishing the CSS within the time frame of 9 years, has been calculated. The report gives a year-wise schedule and cost estimates of additional schools to be built and additional teachers to be recruited and trained. The report also gives year-wise plan and cost estimates for revamping existing teachers education institutions and for the new ones to be created. Within 3-4 months after the publication of the report, the State Government decided not to act on it and set it aside.

The chapter by Muchkund Dubey seeks to deconstruct the report of the Common School System Commission, Bihar. He points out that although the adoption of a CSS for India was strongly recommended by the Kothari Commission and subsequently endorsed by a number of other commissions and committees, and twice approved unanimously by the Indian Parliament, the support remained confined to the realm of rhetoric. The Bihar CSS report met a similar fate. Dubey states that the idea of a common school system was never taken seriously by the dominant class involved in educational policy-making and its implementation, because the parents belonging to this class sent their children to exclusive, mostly private schools with better infrastructure, better trained teachers and teaching standards and, therefore, have no stake in a common school system. Dubey refutes the argument that the implementation of a common school system is impractical in India because of the problem of mobilizing the additional resources and asserts that the additional resources calculated were not that colossal and that if all the suggestions made by the Commission for mobilizing resources had been pursued, finances would not have come in the way of establishing a CSS in Bihar. He further states that if the state had really made a sincere effort to implement the CSS, it would have set an example the emulation of which countrywide would have revolutionized the school education in India, education as a whole and hence the Indian society and polity.

The judgement of the Supreme Court in 1993 on the Unnikrishnan vs State of Andhra Pradesh resulted in the elevation of education from a Directive Principle of State Policy to a fundamental right. It took nine years after the Unnikrishnan judgement to amend the Constitution in 2002 to bring it in line with the judgement. The 2002 amendment provided that it would be implemented by a law to be enacted by the government. It took the central government another seven years to pass that law in the form of the Right of Children to Free and Compulsory Education Act, 2009 (RTE).

Archana Mehendale examines the RTE Act from the perspective of its significance for securing the fundamental right of children to education in the current context of privatization and globalization. She analyses the Act for this purpose by answering the important set of questions raised by Roger Dale (2000) in the context of globalization and education: "Who gets taught what, how, by whom and under what conditions and circumstances?"

Much was expected from the RTE Act but even eight years after its enactment, the Act remains largely unimplemented. This is a matter of great disappointment, if not a real let down, for the civil society which struggled for over a decade to get the right to education recognized as a fundamental right in the Constitution, and get the RTE enacted.

An important limitation of the RTE Act is that it leaves out children in the 3-6 year age group. Razia Ismail in her contribution, raises the pertinent point which we often tend to forget, and that is, the learning setting in early childhood. She argues that architects design the foundation before designing the rest of the building. But in education in India, we do not look at the foundation. We do not realize that learning begins at birth, if not before. We, thus, miss out a critical phase of the development and enlightenment journey of the child.

Prof. J.B.G. Tilak, in his chapter, explores the historical journey of the crisis in the educational policy, starting from independence and continuing till today. He cites various examples, namely moving target dates for the universalization of primary education, the target of devoting six per cent of the national income to education and those incorporated in the RTE Act. These goals were never met in large part due to the yawning gap between the allocations and requirements of resources.

On the other hand, the government's inaction to fully support the public schools resulted in the expansion and dominance of the private sector in Indian education. In fact, several of the measures taken by the government since the early 1980s helped the private sector engaged in educational activities in a big way. According to Tilak, the root cause of the policy crisis in education is that the governments, both the states and the Centre, let the education system evolve under the dictates of the market forces, forgetting the public good nature of education.

Tilak argues that education being a merit or public good with positive externalities, there is significant economic loss in leaving it in private hands. That is why in most of the advanced countries, primary education is provided free to all. But in India setting up of a private school has today become a lucrative business proposition, leading rapidly to the commoditization of education, constraining the realization of the goal of equality of opportunity, increasing per child expenditure and giving rise to another profit-seeking business, i.e. private tuitions. The increasing cost of education is one of the significant current trends in the Indian education system which has the effect of aggravating the inequalities prevailing in education and the society as a whole.

Inequality in Education

Equality in education matters at every level, from individual students who deserve to be treated fairly and have equal opportunity to realize their potential and achieve their aspirations, relating to the society at large because only a society having an equitable education system can be sustainable, as it can draw on the talents of all and not only the privileged few.

It is undoubtedly a positive sign that there is a rising demand for education in all classes, groups and communities in the country. This has been demonstrated by empirical studies carried out in recent years. This demand is driven by various factors. The most important and pervading among them is the ambition on the part of the neglected and downtrodden sections of the society to improve the material conditions of their lives and to get over their poverty, misery and deprivation. Another factor has been to gain a degree of social mobility, to move up in the ladder of social hierarchy. That is why we see that if a child of a peon, a clerk or a self-employed poor person competes to enter the higher services in India, it attracts unusually wide press and public attention.

A major feature of educational policy has been to provide assistance for enhancing access to education for the children of the targeted sections of the population in the country, mostly the poor and economically backward. However, the facilities provided under this policy have touched only the fringe of the vast magnitude of the problems facing the children from these sections. Besides, assistance is being provided to have access to an educational system which is inherently discriminatory and unequal. Finally, even the small amount allotted generally remains unutilized and quite often is utilized by the better off sections of society, mainly because of the problem of governance.

In her essay, Susmita Mitra documents the extent of inequality of educational opportunity in the country, by citing statistics drawn largely from the relevant report of the 71st Round (2014), of the National Sample Survey Organization (NSSO). The data show that even after prioritizing education after independence, today, on an average one person out of four is illiterate. Moreover, there are rural-urban disparities, those between the general population and scheduled castes, and between people of different income levels. Further, the education status of the female is worse than that of the male population in all the cases.

What should be the approach to resolving the problem of inequality in education? Should we wait for the social equality to be achieved before equality can be introduced in the educational system or should we take it that educational inequality is the source of the inequality in most social sectors and hence its removal can be the beginning of the redressal of inequality in the society as a whole?

Annie Namala, in her contribution underlines that education in India has maintained the existing social structure instead of contesting it. The universalization of education at the school level can, of course, reinforce the desire for acquiring more and higher level of knowledge and engender hope and confidence among the marginalized community. However, the real challenge is to build an educational system that can itself be a meaningful intervention to improve the quality of the life of the people, in a comprehensive sense of the term—including realization of their fundamentals rights and protecting their human dignity. She asserts that we often talk about physical access but there are also issues of social access. For education to promote social accessibility, we need to have an inclusive social system, a system which is non-discriminatory, and which respects the identity and dignity of all its citizens.

Annie Namala argues that education gets shaped by the larger forces of society and that there is a dialectic interaction between education and the real world, as social structures, forces, ideas, discourses and movements shape education. Unfortunately, these aspects of education are often ignored in the discourse.

Role of the People's Movement

Education has, for a long time, been used as a tool by certain sections of society to dominate other sections. In order to derive maximum gains from it, education should be owned by the society and taken forward by people's movements and their alliance.

Medha Patkar in her paper states that with the RTE Act, institutions of education are reaching out to the people in the periphery, but discrimination still persists in many forms, both old and new. If we actually want equity, then we should put in place a common school system with the neighbourhood concept. We also need to introduce in the curriculum, the knowledge of the culture and the lifestyles of those lying in the periphery. Providing a quota in the private schools for children living in slums can be useful, but what is more important is for the children of the elite to spend at least some time in the slums and understand the conditions in which children coming from different backgrounds live. This can be achieved only by a conscious effort of the parents, teachers, activists and state.

The paper by Kumar Rana documents how public deliberation and efforts based on various sets of collaborations—between parents, teachers, and educational professionals, can play an important role in translating the RTE Act into reality. In his paper, Kumar Rana cites the experiment under the Pratichi Trust, set up by Amartya Sen with his Nobel Prize money, which succeeded in bringing about remarkable changes in the functioning of schools in West Bengal, by working closely with parents and primary teachers' unions, irrespective of their ideological belief and political affinity. The Trust organized consultancy meetings and public discussions and teachers' workshops to find pathways of solving specific problems related to teaching and learning and improving school infrastructure and environment, through local level participation. This model can be usefully followed by educational practitioners across the country.

Ambarish Rai in his contribution highlights the need of linking the movement for implementing the RTE Act with other social movements. For, movements in the field of education which constitute a tool for social transformation, cannot work in isolation of other movements engaged in the same task. He believes that in a country like India with its segregated society, a common school system is the most appropriate instrument to bring about equity in education and society at large. But since there does not seem to be many takers for CSS, the RTE despite all its limitations, is the only ray of hope as it can pave the path for the introduction of CSS at an opportune moment.

Impact of Globalization and Neoliberal Economic Policies on Education

One of the major consequences of the current phase of globalization and the virtual triumph of the neoliberal economic policies has been the withdrawal of the state from the provisioning of education. This has led to the privatization and commercialization of education—a process facilitated by the state creating space for the entry of the private sector by introducing such methods as public-private-partnership and the voucher system for providing education.

Prabhat Patnaik in his contribution emphasizes that a fundamental change in the sphere of education has been the commoditization of education which has come in the way of equality of opportunity in this field. It has also pushed into the background some of the major objectives of education such as its being a source of questioning and stimulating rational thinking and the inculcation of social sensitivities among those who are being educated. Patnaik asserts that if education is to serve its social purpose, then it must be socially financed, maintained and operated and not based on private profit-making. If we have a large number of schools which are there to make profit then it becomes incumbent for society to regulate them in respect of their infrastructure, curriculum, fee structures, etc., in order to ensure that the fundamental social goals are not threatened or jeopardized by their unregulated operation.

G. Hargopal, in his chapter, brings out the various facets of the neoliberal attack on higher education in India. He analyses two initiatives of the Government of India which were in the offing a few years ago. They were the introduction of a Four-Year Under-graduate Programme in Delhi University and the tabling in the Indian Parliament, of a number of bills to facilitate the entry of foreign providers of education services. Mainly due to the strong public resistance to these moves, these initiatives were rolled back by the government. However, the effort to change the character of higher education in India has continued in different forms. Hargopal's chapter throws interesting light on the nature and implications of these efforts and forces behind them.

Education for the 21st Century

The Report of the International Commission on Education for the 21st Century (1996), set up by UNESCO, examines the main challenges facing education world-wide in the light of the changes that have taken place and are still in progress. The major changes the Commission took into account in its work were the increasingly crowded planet, globalization of human activities, universalization of communication, multi-dimensional global inter-dependence and the uncertainty and complexities brought about by these phenomena. The chapter by Muchkund Dubey brings out the main points of the analysis and the principal recommendations of this Report. The two defining features are:- 'learning throughout life' and the four pillars of learning. Another important feature of the Report highlighted by Muchkund Dubey, is the link between education and democracy, and tolerance for the views of others as a prerequisite for democracy. Schools should facilitate the daily practice of tolerance by helping pupils to appreciate the point of view of others and by encouraging discussion of issues and practical problems involving rational and ethical choices.

Ram Pal Singh, in his chapter, discusses the reasons behind the low quality of education. He states that over the last two to three decades, brain research has brought a significant shift in our thinking on the nature of learning. Each child constructs knowledge on his or her own by experiencing things and by reflecting on those experiences. The role of the teacher is to support the students in the construction of knowledge rather than to provide them information. While in India teachers are still teaching content, teachers in advanced countries are helping students to construct knowledge themselves and to develop creative and critical thinking and capacity for problem solving. According to Ram Pal Singh, for ensuring quality education, we must overhaul the objective of education, create an enabling learning environment and improve the quality of teachers by training and professional development. He also stresses that a major objective of education should be to promote peace, security and equality and transmit universal and local cultural values to future generations.

Conclusion

In the complex pluralistic society like ours it is very difficult, if not impossible, to choose a single vision of education that satisfies all our needs and aspirations. There are different visions of education coming down from the past and advocated at present. What is important is to be able to reconcile the differences to the extent possible and bring the best elements of these visions within a unified policy framework. In this book, an attempt has been made to elaborate the contours of the various visions—those coming down from the past and those of recent vintage. The challenge is to decide on the best framework in which they can be reconciled. At the school level, the common school system is the best framework for this purpose. It is the only system where equity and quality can be pursued simultaneously and where equity can be deployed to achieve quality. It is also the only system which can ensure the inculcation of constitutional and democratic values as a matter of course in the scheme of the education system. It is also the only system which can lead to the universalization of quality education within the shortest period of time. Almost all developed countries, particularly the Scandinavian ones, other European countries like Germany and France, USA, Canada, Cuba, China and South Korea have achieved universalization of quality education with state-funded, regulated and operated common school system. In India, however, we are travelling in the reverse direction by pursuing a policy of handing over the school system to private operators. This will prove the biggest constraint to universalization and hence achieving sustainable development and reaping the demographic dividend which is fast diminishing and is likely to be available not for more than another 15-20 years.

ENDNOTES

1. Singh, S. (2017). *The Educational Heritage of Ancient India: How an Ecosystem of Learning Was Laid to Waste*. Notion Press.
2. Dharampal (1983). *The Beautiful Tree: Indigenous Indian Education in the Eighteenth Century*. Biblia Impex.

Part I
Visions of Education

1

Tagore's Vision of Education and Its Relevance Today

Susmita Mitra

Tagore, the first Asian Nobel Laureate, was a man of myriad gifts. He wrote poems, short stories, novels, plays and essays on philosophy, religion and education; composed music, painted, acted in plays and got actively involved in major issues confronting the nation and human civilization. His ideas on education can be gleaned from some of his writing. But primarily they came from his own experience of childhood and of the then run-of-the mill education system. He recalls in his 'My Reminiscences' how one of the servants named Shyam applied an effective method of keeping the young innocent boy under control:

> He would put me into a selected spot and, tracing a chalk line all round, warn me with solemn face and uplifted finger of the perils of transgressing this ring. Whether the threatened danger was material or spiritual I never fully understood, but a great fear used to possess me.[1]

Even while growing up as a young boy he was forbidden to leave the house and even within the house there were many rooms where he was not allowed to enter:

> We perforce took our peeps from behind the barriers. Beyond my reach there was this limitless thing called the outside, of which flashes and sounds and scents used momentarily to come and touch me through its interstices. It seemed to want to play with me through the bars with so many gestures. But it was free and I was bound—there was no way of meeting.

> So the attraction was all the stronger. The chalk line has been wiped away but the confining ring is still there. The distant is just as distant, the outside is still beyond me.[1]

Tagore's philosophy of education can be analysed as a lifelong journey to wipe out the chalk circle, to rupture the boundary of 'the confining ring', in order to reach 'this limitless thing called the Outside'. Throughout his life, he vehemently opposed ongoing educational practices of encirclement of the childhood. Finally, he tried to implement in practice his ideas and philosophies in his experiment with education in Shantiniketan, to make it a 'poet's school' in sharp contrast to a 'parrot's cage'. In his own words:

> I know what it was to which this school owed its origin. It was not any new theory of education, but the memory of my school days.[2]

The main emphasis of the colonial education system was to make *brown sahibs* out of Indians in order to serve the British companies as clerks or as petty officials. In this process, Thomas Babington Macaulay made his well-known contribution by introducing a tailor-made education policy at the cost of the pre-British traditional education system. Tagore captured this transition in his writings:

> The report published by Ram Mohan Roy's friend Padri Adam Sahib shows that there were more than one hundred thousand primary schools (*pathshalas*) in Bengal and Bihar, and every village had an arrangement to provide a minimum education to its people. Apart from this, almost all the wealthy people maintained *pathshalas* in their own public place for worship (*Chandimandaps*), as their social responsibility, and the teacher (*guru*) would receive his salary and lodging from them. My first encounter with alphabets took place in our own building, with the neighbouring children..... Quite similar to drying up of our canals and rivers as a result of the negligence of the state, the pre-colonial arrangements of providing basic education for our masses have also become ramshackle.[3]

According to Tagore, Indian education in the pre-British period was not only the property of the educated ones, but also a social asset. However, in the colonial period, on the one hand, the flow of traditional education got stopped resulting in a permanent drought of knowledge and, on the other hand, the flow of modern education did not reach the common masses. Tagore had this to say about the British introduced education system:

> These days what we call education has its existence in cities. It is expected to bring business and jobs. However, this foreign education is just like the light of a moving train. The train compartment is lighted bright, but the miles and miles of stretches it crosses through, is immersed in darkness..... Only a group of urban people get entry in this education system and manage to become respected, rich and enlightened. Behind this light, the rest of the country remains in eclipse.[4]

Tagore believed that every child should have enough proficiency in the mother tongue, to have the cognition of vocabulary and sense of expression. If a child is taught in English or any other foreign language instead of his/her mother tongue, a split occurs in his/her sense of perception between the subjects taught in school and his or her everyday practical life. Tagore stated:

> I emphasize mother tongue-based education from my own experience....My parents started my education from an ordinary school. I learnt Geography, History, Mathematics, and Natural Sciences in Bengali.....Due to that my entry in the Bengali vocabulary was unrestricted even from childhood. Although my stock of words was limited, that was enough for nurturing a child's mind. .... I feel fortunate to have been admitted in an ordinary school.......So I got the enjoyment of expressing my own thoughts in my own language from the very beginning. I also realized that after getting used to write in vernacular, it becomes so easy to learn and use other languages courageously.[3]

Tagore found the main problem of the so-called 'modern' education in colonial India to be its complete domination by the English language. According to him, except India there has been no country where there has been such an alienation between the language of the study and that of the student[5]. However, while giving due importance to the mother tongue, Tagore never underestimated the importance of the English language. He only wanted that the medium of teaching should not be English or any foreign language, rather it should be the child's own language. For that purpose, he himself wrote two English grammar books in Bengali, viz. *Ingreji Sopan* (Steps to English) and *Ingreji Srutisikkha*

(Audition in English) for the beginners. However he never underestimated the importance of the English language, and had no problem with English education *per se*, as that was one of the windows to reach out to the Western civilization. He wrote:

> In this context I want to confess that in our universities the honoured seat of the English language cannot be unsettled. The reason is not simply that its role in our present life is inevitable, but also due to the fact that knowledge of Europe today has received the respect of all. It will be harmful if we deny that because of our national vanity. The role of this language is very important not only for self-defence in financial and state affairs, but also for releasing our mind and attitude from obtuseness.[5]

Tagore vehemently opposed the run-of-the-mill conventional schools which only taught children to learn by rote, partly by understanding, and even without understanding if needed. He felt that passing an examination by simply memorizing is not less than burglary. He said:

> It is strictly against the nature of human beings to live in the cage of only requirement....It is true of education as well. If children are forcefully confined to only essential education then their thought process cannot develop enough.....But our education system is such that we want children to pass the exams by learning the English language as fast as possible in order to get employment. Therefore students are left with no other option than running without looking at left and right, by memorising essential texts in the syllabus from their very childhood.....as a result, although we are getting BA, MA degrees by swallowing books of huge volume, our intellectual capacity is not getting ripened. We are not able to absorb anything firmly, and thus, not able to create anything concrete. Our opinions and attitudes hardly reflect maturity.....The main reason behind all these is simply the fact that since childhood there is no pleasure or delight attached to learning. We only memorize what is necessary.[6]

Tagore was also not fond of the idea of children being raised according to the wish and role model of their parents, in order just to realize their failed dreams. According to him, each child is unique and his or her talent should be acknowledged and nurtured. In his words: "Children have their subconscious mind more active than their conscious intelligence. It is not like a lantern that can be lighted and trimmed from outside, but it is like the light that the glow-worm falls for by the exercise of its life process."[2] And this enlightening process can only be managed by a competent teacher. Tagore had a strong conviction that for quality education it is the teacher who plays the prime role:

> I know it for certain, though most people seem to have forgotten it, that children are living beings—more living than grown up people who have built their shells of habit around them. It is absolutely necessary for their mental health and development that they must not have mere schools to go for their lessons, but a world whose guiding spirit is personal love.[2]

Teachers are highly paid and respected in the Scandinavian as well as in almost all other developed countries. It is indeed unfortunate that in the country of visionary legends like Tagore, there is today a mixed perception on the role of teachers. On the one hand, there is the traditional feeling of a teacher as the nation builder; on the other hand, studies have shown that the wider public does not respect and value the work of teachers.

Tagore questioned the teaching of national ideas because education based on such ideas tended, among others to dominate the minorities and underclasses. In this way, education became an instrument of communal or class domination. Tagore writes:

> If someone says 'national' feeling will be taught, then the question will arise, what is meant by national ideas or feeling in education? There is no definite boundary for the term 'national' ; moreover, it is even difficult to construct one. What is 'national' and what is not is defined by different people differently, according to their education, opportunity and prejudices.[7]

According to Tagore, schools should not be like a factory to provide education. This form of education only produces a homogeneous set of students.

> What we understand by school is basically a factory to provide education. The teacher is a part of this factory. At half past ten, the factory opens with the ringing of the bell. The machine starts and so does the mouth of the teacher. At four o' clock the factory stops along with the mouth of the teacher-machine. Students return home with a few pages of machine-chiselled

> education. During exams, this kind of education is weighed and the brand is stamped. The advantage of the machine is that the order is delivered in the right shape and fitting. There is not much difference between the products produced by different machines, so it is easier to give marks.[7]

In many developed states, particularly the Scandinavian countries, no uniform curriculum is imposed on the schools. Individual institutes prepare their own programme for themselves. Tagore had the vision of not only thinking about such a programme but also introducing and practising it in Shantiniketan.

India is a country of 'Unity in Diversity'. At a time when nationalism of a particular character is being sought to be imposed in the country, this diversity is under a major threat. It is, therefore, opportune to hark back to Tagore's vision and start cultivating respect for the socio-cultural diversity of this largest democratic country, from the very beginning of a child's thought development process, i.e. school education.

Tagore believed that to live a meaningful life at present we have to know the past well and the process should start as early as possible in life. Familiarity with the traditions, the folktales, the riddles and the rhymes of a particular culture has a deep influence on the mental growth of a child. He criticized the so-called modern education not rooted in culture.

> One thing which has been detached from modern education is culture. We have ignored the treasure of the heart and emphasised material success. But can this success be truly achieved without culture?[8]

Knowledge about the history of one's own country was fundamental according to him. That is why he took the responsibility of teaching history himself in his school in Shantiniketan. He wanted to inculcate through education the best of both the East and West. He stated:

> It is my earnest desire that the education system of our country should become a platform to unite East and West.....The house-owner who wants to stay only with his or her family, and is a miser in terms of providing hospitality to the outside guest, is a person with a beggar-like soul.[9]

Tagore attacked the male-dominated debate over education of women. His remarks on this subject were really profound:

> One group of people say, there is no need for education among women, because if they get educated men will have many problems. Educated wives do not consider their husbands to be God. They don't give much attention to them since they keep busy with education. On the other hand, according to another group of people, educating women is very important, because educated men's life partners should understand and realise their ideas. However, both the groups are judging women's education from their perspective. None of the two groups realises that women have their own identity.... and have their own fulfilment of life.[10]

He adds:

> If education is the way to humanity, and if it is a basic right, then I don't understand by which logic a woman should be deprived of education....whatever is worthy to know, has to be known by men as well as women, not merely to employ knowledge for practical purposes, but for the sake of knowledge itself....I believe, if women study Kant or Hegel they will still love children and not neglect men.[10]

According to Tagore, good education not merely gives us information but also brings our life in harmony with all existence.[2] He argued this point in his characteristic literary style. He wrote that the process of breastfeeding helps children find their food and their mother at the same time. Not only is the child's need of nourishment met, but in the process the child is brought into its very first relationship.[2] In his vision, this is the way education should function, providing what is necessary for our survival and at the same time connecting us to the ultimate source of our sustenance.

He admitted that underrating the advantages of the book would be foolish, but at the same time we must concede that the book has its limitations. During the early period of education, children should come to their lessons of truth through natural processes, intermingling with persons and things, rather than books. He wrote:

> We don't realize that books are simply convenient support to education, but we have come to consider reading books to be

> the only way of education.... We can deliver lectures based on bookish knowledge, but with that we cannot communicate with the audience.....children should not be allowed to be drowned in the superstition that reading books is the only means of education.[11]

As an escape from this trap of bookish knowledge he advised:

> Children should be reminded at every stage that books are nothing but compiled forms of the surrounding world and nature...they should be made aware from the very beginning how these books are produced so that they can feel the process within their mind with their own imaginations....Only then will they be able to benefit from the knowledge captured in a book, and at the same time they will be free of the burden of bookish knowledge.....[11]

He gives an excellent example of how he applied this philosophy in his school:

> My boys are able to make the best possible use of the tree in gathering fruits, resting and hiding from undesirable pursuers.... I consider it as a part of education for my boys to let them fully realize that they are in a scheme of existence where trees are a substantial fact, not merely as generating chlorophyll and taking carbon from the air, but as living entities.[2]

Tagore believed that "the young mind should be saturated with the idea that it has been born in a human world which is in harmony with the world around it. And this is what our regular type of school ignores with an air of superior wisdom"[2]. In his 'My Reminiscences', he illustrated the difference between a bad and good school by means of the metaphor of 'cage' and 'nest'. He considered the prototype school to be a cage, however ornate and rich it might be, it forbids communication with whatever lies outside. By contrast, the nest is open to the sky.

He explained in practical terms how teaching and research can take place in harmony with nature:

> If we want to establish an ideal school then it has to be built away from densely populated localities, within open space among trees under the vast sky. There, the teachers will live in solitary pursuit of knowledge and students will grow up within this surrounding of research and knowledge. If

> possible, there should be some agricultural land attached to the school. The necessary food for the school will be produced in that agricultural land, and the students will also help in this process...During breaks from education, if students are engaged in planting, fencing and watering of trees then they develop not only an emotional attachment with nature but a working relationship also.[7]

Conclusion

In a crux, the ultimate purpose of education, according to Tagore, is not to teach us how to make a living but how to live. This philosophy has been summed up very ingeniously in the Delors Commission Report (1996), which recommended an integrated vision of education, i.e. 'learning throughout life'; based on the four pillars of learning—learning to know, learning to do, learning to be, and learning to live together.

Even the revised National Curriculum Framework (NCF 2005) of our country begins with a quotation from Rabindranath Tagore's essay, 'Civilization and Progress', in which the poet reminds us that a 'creative spirit' and 'generous joy' are critical in childhood, both of which can be distorted by an unthinking adult world.

Even though Tagore's vision of education may resonate in many of the educational documents adopted by India after independence, the record for implementing them has been dismal. Tagore felt sad that although the country had common administration and common rules, owing to the narrow mindedness of the rulers at that time, widespread discrimination was practised in applying these rules to the common people. It is indeed unfortunate that the scenario, particularly with reference to the education system, has not changed in independent India. The inherited and growing socio-economic inequality is noticeably getting imprinted on the education sector. The rich parents' lobby often protests against getting their children study with poor children. In this context, it is relevant to recall Tagore's words:[5]

> Should we not admit that poverty is the school in which man had his first lessons and his best training? Even a millionaire's son has to be born helplessly poor and to begin his lesson of life from the beginning. He has to learn to walk like the poorest of children, though he has means to afford to be without the

appendage of legs. Poverty brings us into complete touch with life and the world, for living richly is living mostly by proxy, thus living in a lesser world of reality. This may be good for one's pleasure and pride, but not for one's education.[2]

Summing up Tagore's vision on education, the supreme goal of education is to attain the ultimate freedom by wiping out the chalk circle drawn by societal norms, prejudices, and myopic narrow-minded self-interest. He captures all these admirably in his poem 'Where the Mind is Without Fear', which is worth re-uttering to conclude this essay:

Where the mind is without fear and the head is held high
Where knowledge is free
Where the world has not been broken up into fragments
By narrow domestic walls
Where words come out from the depth of truth
Where tireless striving stretches its arms towards perfection
Where the clear stream of reason has not lost its way
Into the dreary desert sand of dead habit
Where the mind is led forward by thee
Into ever-widening thought and action
Into that heaven of freedom, my Father,
Let my country awake.

—*Rabindranath Tagore*

REFERENCES*

1. Tagore, Rabindranath (1917). *My Reminiscences*. London, Macmillan and Co. Limited.
2. Tagore, Rabindranath (1917). *My School Included in Personality* (pp. 135-180). New York, The Macmillan Company.
3. Tagore, Rabindranath (1936). 'The Connection to Education' (*Sikkhar Shaangikoron*).
4. Tagore, Rabindranath (1933). 'The Radiation of Education' (*Sikkhar Bikiron*).
5. Tagore, Rabindranath (1937). 'Addressing Students' (*Chhatro Sombhason*).
6. Tagore, Rabindranath (1892). 'Versions of Education' (*Sikkhar Herfer*).

7. Tagore, Rabindranath (1907). 'Problems of Education' (*Sikkha Samosya*).
8. Tagore, Rabindranath (1935). 'Education and Culture' (*Sikkha O Sanskriti*).
9. Tagore, Rabindranath (1921). 'Coalescence of Education' (*Sikkhar Milon*).
10. Tagore, Rabindranath (1915). 'Education of Women' (*Stree-Shikkha*).
11. Tagore, Rabindranath (1905). 'Cover' (*Aaboron*).

All the essays on Education 3. to 11. have been retrieved from the following link

http://www.tagoreweb.in/Render/ShowBook.aspx?ct=Essays&bi=72EE92F5-BE50-4047-9E6E-0F7410664DA3

* All the quotations under reference No. 3. to 11. have been translated into English by the author.

2

Gandhiji's Ideas on Education and Its Relevance Today

Sudarshan Iyengar

Gandhiji's ideas on education can be viewed in two ways. One way is to analyse Gandhi as an educationist. Second is to review how Gandhiji's ideas on education evolved during his lifetime and what they were. An erudite article has already been written for UNESCO by Krishna Kumar on Gandhiji as an educationist.[1] Hence, I propose to take the second way and examine the evolution of Gandhiji's ideas on education. This approach too is not a maiden attempt as scholars and practitioners have preceded me well in the effort. Nevertheless, there are two reasons for attempting the exercise. One is to present in brief the case of Gujarat Vidyapith, the university founded by Mahatma Gandhi and his associates in 1920 and examine its status today. Second is to revisit and discuss the relevance of Gandhiji's ideas on education in present times.

Experiments in South Africa

Gandhiji's engagement with education formally began in South Africa. He had taken two of his children and another child from the extended Gandhi family. Although his reputation as a practising barrister would have facilitated his children's admission to schools for English, European and rich and influential Indians' children, he was firmly against his children attending such schools. Marjorie Sykes, an accomplished teacher who came from England to then Madras and later worked at Sevagram's Nai Talim School, notes that in the initial times in South Africa, Gandhiji believed in three things: children should live at home and not be sent away to residential schools; they should learn through the medium of their mother tongue, and his children should not have any privilege that other Indian children did not have.[2] He had taken upon himself to teach his two children and a nephew, but his engagements in public life gave him little time. He engaged a governess for some time to teach English to children, but soon discontinued her as he was not satisfied with her work. In his autobiography he has noted that his initial experiments in educating children were inadequate. It had left the eldest son Harilal dissatisfied. When he came of age he broke away from his father and returned to India to enrol himself as a regular student in a high school. Gandhiji's remaining three sons and the children of Satyagrahi parents in South Africa received non-formal education in the improvised schools he had started in Phoenix Ashram and Tolstoy farm. It should be noted that he and his associates in those settlements could not provide adequate formal and literary education. But, Gandhiji considered the formal education system consisting of public schools in South Africa as artificial and distant from the Indian community's culture. However, he admitted that he acted upon half-baked knowledge and indulgence. He had also this question to self that what harm it did to the children. He wrote[3]:

> What right had I to clip their wings? Why should I have come in the way of their taking degrees and choosing their own careers?

Gandhiji had an answer too. In the context he made a profound observation.

> But the ultimate result of my experiments is in the womb of the future. My object in discussing this subject here is that a student of the history of civilization may have some measure of the difference between disciplined home education and school education, and also of the effect produced on children through changes introduced by parents in their lives.

Gandhiji considered formal education for his children not suitable. Commenting on it he noted in a chapter in his autobiography:

> The purpose of this chapter is also to show the lengths to which a votary of truth is driven by his experiments with truth, as also to show the votary of liberty how many are sacrifices

> demanded by that stern goddess. Had I been without a sense of self-respect and satisfied myself with having my children the education that other children could not get, I should have deprived them of the object-lesson in liberty and self-respect that I gave them at the cost of the literary training. And where a choice has to be made between liberty and learning, who will not say that the former has to be preferred a thousand times to the latter.

Gandhiji had tried to uphold values of liberty, simplicity and spirit of service as paramount in education. For him education mends the society and not the other way round. His education was educating in values.

An important component of education for children imparted at home dealt with lifestyle. Gandhiji had significantly altered his lifestyle in South Africa from the English European model to a life of utmost simplicity, and tried to inculcate the same in children. About the language used for educating children, he noted:

> Polak and I had often very heated discussions about the desirability or otherwise of giving the children an English education. It has always been my conviction that Indian parents who train their children to think and talk in English from their infancy betray their children and their country. They deprive them of the spiritual and social heritage of the nation, and render them to that extent unfit for the service of the country.

Polak did not agree. His contention was that if the children were to learn a universal language like English from their infancy, they would easily gain considerable advantage in the race of life. Interestingly, both the views continue to prevail today and debated. Educationists however, are almost unanimous that primary education (implying learning from infancy) should be based in the mother tongue. This view is supported by a study conducted and reported by UNESCO.[4]

Inculcating values for Gandhiji was the foundation for building character and personality. For him, the primary objective of education was character building. In the January 9, 1909 issue of *Indian Opinion,* Gandhiji wrote at length about the school in Phoenix. He noted the following on objective:

> The main object of this school is to strengthen the pupils' character. It is said that real education consists in teaching the

> pupil the art of learning. In other words, a desire for knowledge should grow in him. Knowledge, however, is of many kinds. There is some knowledge which is harmful. If, therefore, the boys' character is not formed well, they will acquire the wrong kind of knowledge. Because of lack of proper planning in education, we observe that some persons grow to be atheists and some, though highly educated, fall a prey to vices. It is therefore the main object of this school to assist in building the moral character of boys.[5]

Gandhiji had been intensely experimenting and thinking on education. His ultimate mission was building *ahimsa samaj*—a non-violent society. The foundation of a non-violent society was love force or soul force. To educate the soul, he presented his philosophy of education in a chapter in *Hind Swaraj* in 1909.[6] Gandhiji begins the chapter by raising a query as to why the necessity of education was not discussed until then? Illiteracy was very high in India in those times. The Maharaja of the princely state of Baroda had made education compulsory. His efforts were highly appreciated and he was considered progressive by the British and other enlightened people. In the chapter on education in *Hind Swaraj* Gandhiji discusses this point only to respond. He responds by commenting on the laudable efforts made by the Maharaja of Baroda in Gujarat in making modern education compulsory for all the citizens in the state. However, he warns that the education promoted by the Maharaja would lead to adverse results that he had described in the previous chapters. Because, the so-called modern education understood and used ordinarily comprised of three R's: reading, writing and arithmetic. At higher levels it comprised different subjects such as Geography, Algebra, Geometry, Astronomy, etc. Gandhiji thought that the three R's which equip persons in gaining knowledge of letters was mostly abused and only a few made good use of it. Mere knowledge of letters would lead to more harm than good. He appeared to correspond with the ideas of education expressed by well-known philosopher Thomas Huxley. Gandhiji quoted the following from his essay, *A Liberal Education: and Where to Find It:*

> That man I think has had a liberal education who has been so trained in youth that his body is the ready servant of his will and does with ease and pleasure all the work that as a mechanism it is capable of; whose intellect is a clear, cold, logic(al) engine

> with all its parts of equal strength and in smooth working order, whose mind is stored with a knowledge of the fundamental truths of nature ... whose passions are trained to come to heel by a vigorous will, the servant of a tender conscience ... who has learnt to hate all vileness and to respect others as himself. Such a one and no other, I conceive, has had a liberal education, for he is in harmony with nature. He will make the best of her and she of him.[7]

The knowledge of letters or what was obtained as education was not acceptable to Gandhiji as it did not help him to control his senses. Regulating behaviour for inner growth of self could come only when an individual was educated for handling freedom. In the absence of this core education, civilization would head for disaster. Gandhiji's conceptualization of education was thus clear. In order to build a non-violent society, where there is harmony with self, among selves and with nature, education had to be for regulating one's behaviour for inner or spiritual growth helping to form a moral and harmonious society. Such an education would augment truth force, love force and soul force.

Experiments in India

Gandhiji has been assessed as a pragmatic idealist. Before affirming or rejecting any idea, he would put it into practice. His experiments in education in South Africa had helped him to conceptualize it. He returned to India in January 1915, initially staying at the Kochrab village and shifting to the Sabarmati area in 1917. The community abode came to be known as Sabarmati Ashram. The paramount objective was spiritual growth of every inmate committing the bodily self for social service. The worldly duty of the Ashram's inmates was offering *Satyagraha* for independence. Gandhiji could sense the need for education including formal literary education for women, children and the illiterate who had become inmates of the Ashram. In a document that he prepared[8] on Ashram observances, Gandhiji wrote a section on education.[9] Gandhiji clearly stated that education should consist of manual training in some livelihood skill under the supervision of an educationist. He recognized that each child's aptitude should be examined before determining the work and skill to be taught. Reading and drawing had to precede writing. The child should be exposed to general knowledge. Nothing should be taught by force. Teaching should be in the mother tongue but Hindi or Urdu and English should be taught to every child. Household work should be taught to each child irrespective of the gender. The text on the chapter on education in the *Ashram Observances in Action* consists of 27 specific points. Sabarmati Ashram became a centre where Khadi and village industries including animal husbandry and leather work prospered and the education for the Ashram inmates was through vocation. In 1920, Gandhiji launched a major experiment by founding a nationalist university Gujarat Vidyapith, which experimented with school and higher education. More about the Vidyapith will be discussed in a section to follow.

Ideas Expressed

Gandhiji made a major impact on education in the country in 1937. He presided over a conference on education held during October 22-23 on the occasion of the Silver Jubilee of Marwari Shiksha Manda, Wardha. He had been commenting on the issues related to education in the periodicals he published for some time. The role of the state in education was being debated among the Congress elite. Gandhiji was of the opinion that education should be undertaken by civil society institutions and the role of the state should be limited. A substantive reason to keep education outside the state purview was his lack of faith regarding literary education for an individual and also for social development. He wrote:

> By education I mean an all-round drawing out of the best in child and man—body, mind and spirit. Literacy is not the end of education nor even the beginning. It is only one of the means whereby man and woman can be educated. Literacy in itself is no education. I would therefore begin the child's education by teaching it a useful handicraft and enabling it to produce from the moment it begins its training. Thus every school can be made self-supporting, the condition being that the state takes over the manufactures of these schools.[10]

In the July 1931 issue of *Harijan*, Gandhiji addressed the issue relating to mobilization of financial resources for school education. He argued that there were means of raising revenue other than tax on alcoholic beverages as was suggested by economists such as K.T. Shah and Khambhatta. In any case Gandhiji thought that the massive scale of problems of education in the country was beyond the capability of the state's tax regime. Therefore, he thought that the problem had to be approached differently. He wrote:

> But as a nation we are so backward in education that we cannot hope to fulfil our obligations to the nation in this respect in a given time during this generation, if the programme is to depend on money. I have therefore made bold, even at the risk of losing all reputation for constructive ability, to suggest that education should be self-supporting.[11]

Gandhiji's insistence on beginning the child's education by teaching a handicraft might at first sight appear as his fad, fancy or recommendation for ensuring building physical production capabilities and skills in a child. It was indeed so, but he also could clearly see that educating through a handicraft or physical productive work had potential to develop mind and soul. He observed:

> I hold that the highest development of the mind and the soul is possible under such a system of education. Only every handicraft has to be taught not merely mechanically as is done today but scientifically...I am not writing this without some confidence, because it has the backing of experience...I have myself taught sandal-making and even spinning on these lines with good results...One imparts ten times as much in this manner as by reading and writing...This is a revolutionary proposal...[12]

He continued his thought process in the direction, arrived at ideas and principles and expressed it in different places. Ruskin's thesis of the ideal society and ways to conduct life had convinced Gandhiji of earning one's livelihood through bread labour. Thus the physical and productive work had become an essential component of the education of children in the Phoenix Ashram and Tolstoy Farm. Agriculture, horticulture and the printing press work (necessary for publication of *Indian Opinion*) also generated product and income. With confidence gained by the experience, he could debate with conviction about financing education through production. Besides the principle of self-reliance, further reflection revealed the superior way of learning through a craft or a vocation than only classroom literary education. Marjorie Sykes notes:

From the beginning he had seen that the vigorous manual work to meet the needs of a family or community was the basis both of physical health and of an ethic of generous sharing and mutual respect. But the link between the skills of hand and eye, and the development of the mind, was not so clear to him in those earlier days..."I must confess," he wrote in 1937, "that up to now all I have said is that manual training must be given side by side with intellectual training. But now I say that manual training should be the principal means of stimulating the intellect." This meant that the manual training must be "scientific"... There must be full appreciation of the chosen handicraft in all its points of contact with natural science and human history, its standards of accuracy and beauty, the part it plays in the well-being of the people who practise it and in the enrichment of human life as a whole. Handicrafts taught in this way, far from being mindless drudgery, could stimulate endless intellectual curiosity on a great variety of topics. They opened the door wide for research and discovery".[13]

Prelude to *Nai Talim*

Shri Shrimannayaran Agrawal[14] the then Secretary of the Marwari High School, Wardha (renamed as Navabharat Vidyalaya) approached Gandhi to preside over a Conference on Education on the occasion of the Silver Jubilee of the School. Gandhiji set the agenda for the Conference and made it public in *Harijan* of October 2, 1937. He invited interested individuals to contribute. He suggested four propositions for the consideration in the Conference.[15]

First, the prevalent system of education did not meet the requirements of the country in any shape and form. Excessive importance to English and absence of vocational training were the key weaknesses and rendered the expenditure incurred by the state in primary education almost useless. True even today!

Second was to impart primary education for seven years in the mother tongue through a substantial productive vocation.

Third was making education self-reliant for the student and the institution. Occupations and vocation requiring less capital and more human power should be chosen for teaching and production.

Finally, higher education should be left to private enterprise and for meeting national requirements whether in the various industries, technical arts, belles-lettres or fine arts. The state Universities should be purely examining bodies, self-supporting through the fees charged for examinations.

Gandhiji claimed that if the whole scheme was accepted, it would solve the question of the greatest concern to the state: educating its youth for rebuilding society.

Birth of *Nai Talim*

Gandhiji's agenda for the Conference was accepted. In the inaugural session, he made it clear that his ideas were for education as a whole, for school and college education both with emphasis on the former.[16] In school education (primary and secondary levels); his focus was on rural boys and girls who were almost illiterate. He criticized the prevailing education system and observed that the children who passed through the system were lost to their parents, their vocation and imbibed a value-set that was socially irrelevant and perhaps harmful. Mahadev Desai had recorded thus:

> He was deliberately of the opinion that the present system of primary education was not only wasteful but harmful. Most of the boys were lost to their parents and to the occupation to which they were born. They picked up evil habits, affected urban ways, and got a smattering of something which may be anything else but not education.

The way out according to Gandhiji lay in educating by means of vocational or manual training. Gandhiji had argued that this way was relevant, useful and perhaps a scientific way, time tested in the Phoenix settlement and Tolstoy Farm in South Africa. Mahadev Desai noted:

> The core of his emphasis was not the occupations but education through manual training—all education, of letters, history, geography, mathematics, science, etc., through manual training...In this age those born to certain professions had forgotten them, taken to clerical careers, and were lost to the countryside...The remedy lay in imparting the whole art and science of a craft through practical training and there through imparting education. Teaching of *takli-spinning*, for instance,

> presupposed imparting of knowledge of various varieties of cotton, different soils in different provinces of India, the history of the ruin of the handicraft, its political reasons which would include the history of the British rule in India, knowledge of arithmetic, and so on. He was trying the experiment on his little grandson who scarcely felt that he was being taught, for he all the while played, laughed and sang.[17]

The other point raised by Gandhiji was about financing of education. With more than five lakh villages, India required at least one school per village. Gandhiji had a practical solution. He wanted the teachers and students to be productive. The goods produced in schools were to be purchased by society and government. He was advocating education that would also bring dignity and self-reliance. He said:

> This system was to be common to all—Hindus, Muslims, Parsis, Christians. Why did he not lay any stress on religious instruction, he was asked. Because he was teaching them practical religion, the religion of self-help.[18]

Gandhiji in this historical address proposed an education system with content and method to help build a society based on non-violence. Concluding he observed:

> We have communal quarrels—not that they are peculiar to us. England had also its Wars of the Roses, and today British Imperialism is the enemy of the world. If we want to eliminate communal strife and international strife, we must start with foundations pure and strong by rearing our younger generation on the education I have adumbrated. That plan springs out of non-violence… this education would be a *sine qua non* if we did not want to urbanize our boys… Europe is no example for us. It plans its programmes in terms of violence because it believes in violence. I would be the last to minimize the achievement of Russia, but the whole structure is based on force and violence. If India has resolved to eschew violence, this system of education becomes an integral part of the discipline she has to go through… we have no alternative but this plan of education which is based on non-violence.[19]

Krishna Kumar has pointed out that Gandhiji also had a political agenda in his education philosophy. He says:

> The idea was not simply to introduce handicrafts as a compulsory school subject, but to make the learning of a craft the axis of the entire teaching programme. It implied a radical restructuring of the sociology of school knowledge in India, where productive handicrafts had been associated with the lowest groups in the hierarchy of castes. Knowledge of the production processes involved in crafts, such as spinning, weaving, leatherwork, pottery, metal-work, basket-making and book-binding, had been the monopoly of specific caste groups in the lowest stratum of the traditional social hierarchy. Many of them belonged to the category of 'untouchables'. India's indigenous tradition of education as well as the colonial education system had emphasized the skills (such as literacy) and knowledge of which the upper castes had a monopoly. In terms of its epistemology, Gandhi's proposal intended to stand the education system on its head. The social philosophy and the curriculum of 'basic education' thus favoured the child belonging to the lowest stratum of society. This is how it implied a programme of social transformation. It sought to alter the symbolic meaning of 'education' and thereby to change the established structure of opportunities for education.[20]

The Conference deliberated for two days to craft a nationalist education for the country. At the end the following three resolutions were adopted.

1. That free and compulsory education should be provided for seven years on a nation-wide scale.
2. That the medium of instruction should be the mother tongue.
3. That the process of education throughout this period should centre around some form of manual and productive work, and all other activities to be developed and training to be given should as far as possible be integrally related to the central handicraft, chosen with due regard to the environment of the child, that the products of tile handicraft should gradually be able to cover the remuneration of the teachers.[21]

A committee chaired by Dr. Zakir Husain drafted a report which was submitted to Gandhiji in December 1937. A revised and final version was prepared in 1938. The curricula included education through agriculture, spinning, and weaving and other handicrafts prevalent in the region. The concept of *Nai Talim*—Basic Education was formulated not only to strengthen the spirit of nationalism and *swadeshi*, but also to establish a scientific approach to learning and teaching. Gandhiji's ideas on education thus evolved and took concrete form in *Nai Talim*.

The initial enthusiasm in introducing *Nai Talim* was short-lived. The experiment in *Nai Talim* was undertaken in Wardha from where the all India Nai Talim Samiti worked. The principal governments ruled by Congress tried to introduce the concept and opened *Nai Talim* schools, but soon reverted to mainstream. After independence, the education system in the country continued on the British line and remained largely confined to literary education. The Wardha experiment also faded with time. Marjorie Sykes documented the 50 years' *Nai Talim* story in 1987 and analysed the rise and fall of it.[22]

Gujarat Vidyapith

Gandhiji and his close associates in Gujarat founded Gujarat Vidyapith in 1920 in Ahmedabad and called it a nationalist university. Gandhiji conceived it as a fountainhead for theory and practice of education leading to building of a non-violent society. He wanted to establish an educational institution that would stand as a strong alternative to the system of education that prevailed under the British. In the Issue of *Young India* of September 1, 1921 he wrote:

> In my opinion the existing system of education is defective, apart from its association with an utterly unjust government, in three most important matters:
>
> 1. It is based upon foreign culture to the almost entire exclusion of indigenous culture.
> 2. It ignores the culture of the heart and the hand, and confines itself simply to the head.
> 3. Real education is impossible through a foreign medium.[23]

Gandhiji said that the curriculum and pedagogic ideas that formed the fabric of modern education were imported from Oxford, Cambridge, Edinburgh and London. They were essentially foreign and till they were repudiated there never could be national education. The nationalist education should be one which educated the new generation in preservation and development of original culture that promoted harmony and non-violence.

In the first three decades of the Vidyapith, outstanding scholars and teachers such as Choithram Gidwani, J.B. Kripalani, Kaka Saheb Kalelkar and J.C. Kumarappa had joined. Most of them entered public life and were outstanding freedom fighters. Since the teachers were nationalists and were engaged in the freedom struggle, the students were also drawn to it. In the process, the Vidyapith was sealed by the British Government in the early 1930s, post Dandi March. During the Quit India movement, university authorities declared it closed *sine die*. The normal academic activities were resumed in right earnest only after 1950. Besides its political existence as a nationalist institution, the Gujarat Vidyapith followed the principle of education through vocation. Many of the Ashram observances were followed in the Gujarat Vidyapith as part of curricula, co-curricular activities and community living. Agriculture, animal husbandry and cloth making—*vastra vidya*, were the main vocations around which education was imparted. Education through vocational skill building and production was supplemented with literary education in the humanities and social sciences, basic sciences and commerce. Before higher education was discontinued after 1931 and resumed in 1950, slightly above 1,000 students had enrolled.

Character building was and is the most essential objective of education at the Gujarat Vidyapith. Leading a simple life and education for bread labour was the next important value to be inculcated. The knowledge building, scholarship and innovation had to be followed to accomplish the first two objectives. Thus, the essence of *Nai Talim* that was formalized in 1937 at the Wardha Conference was being experimented at the Gujarat Vidyapith since its foundation. It was education for heart (character building), hand (education for bread labour) and head (literary education) in that order.

After independence, higher education commenced as Mahadev Desai Samaj Seva Mahavidyalaya was opened and students were enrolled for graduation studies. A pass out was called *Snaatak*. A student was supposed to take a minimum of 39 courses that included languages such as Gujarati, Hindi, Urdu and Sanskrit; agriculture and animal husbandry; spinning, weaving;

various smithies and carpentry. The orientation was completely rural. The *snataks* were expected to settle in villages and undertake rural reconstruction with *Gram Swaraj* as their goal. The year 1963 was a watershed in the history of the Gujarat Vidyapith. It was recognized as a deemed university by the University Grants Commission (UGC). Government grants began to flow and by the mid-1970s, the higher education programme of the Gujarat Vidyapith was almost fully supported by the Government of India. Between 1947 and 1963, more than 1,200 *snatkas* passed out and a significant number of them settled in villages. Their main contribution has been in the field of school education. Sizeable civil society organizations in Gujarat owe their origin to the Gujarat Vidyapith. A notable feature of the Gujarat Vidyapith during 1920-63 was: Vidyapith *snataks* or graduates did not look for jobs.

From 1963 till the turn of the millennium, higher education at the Gujarat Vidyapith followed the traditional university path with some exceptions. Prayer and spinning remained as symbolic activities of *Nai Talim*. The science and commerce streams were discontinued. The courses offered were limited to the humanities and social sciences. Nevertheless postgraduate and M.Phil. and Ph.D. courses were introduced. The Master's programme in Social Work was introduced and it became popular and a flagship postgraduate course at the Vidyapith. It should be noted here that after Gandhiji's departure from the scene, the Gujarat Vidyapith was virtually deserted by the thinkers and practitioners. From 1963 onwards the UGC norms pushed the Vidyapith administration to hire teachers from mainstream universities and since the medium of instruction was Gujarati the choices became limited. The university attracted Dalit and Adivasi students in large numbers and reservations in government and public sector jobs made it easier for the pass-outs to get jobs as teachers, village-level revenue and development workers and with non-government organizations. The objective of educating youth for rural reconstruction was lost sight of. Nevertheless, Vidyapith graduates were preferred over graduates from other universities by the civil society organizations and the government because of two distinct characteristics. One, a Vidyapith graduate was sound in character and two, she/he was willing to live and work in rural areas. Gandhi's ideas continue to live partially. Before the turn of the century, the Vidyapith had taken some distinct initiatives in mainstream education. It became the first university to introduce postgraduate diploma and degree courses in computer application. Later, an undergraduate course in microbiology, and Masters in Rural Management were also added.

From 2001 onwards the management of the Vidyapith started inviting relatively young individuals on its Board of Management and by 2004 a revival phase began. The motto was 'back to basics'. From 2006 all the degree courses were made residential. Life skill education, literary education and vocational education formed three pillars of higher education. Khadi as a vocation has been revived and some village industry products including crafts are added. Fresh orientation has begun towards rural reconstruction. The *Gramshilpi* scheme has been introduced to help the young pass-outs to settle in villages and work for village development. The new orientation has till date met with limited success as the mainstream trends are contrary and strong. The Vidyapith in the past fifteen years has also tried to revitalize the *Nai Talim* schools in Gujarat. But the state and the society look elsewhere.

The Tandon Committee set up by the Ministry of Human Resources Development, Government of India in 2009 to review the performance of the private universities initially found Gandhiji's 'idea of university' worthy only of 'F' grade! However, later a committee sent by the UGC concluded that the Gujarat Vidyapith was one of the rare universities in the country that was addressing the core of the higher education problem upfront and hence deserved more support. Later in 2015 the NAAC team also found the Vidyapith to be an institution with great potential and relevance for the present times and accredited it with 'A'. Despite the recognitions the struggle continues.

Relevance of Gandhiji's Views

Education in India today is in a crisis. At all levels of schooling and university, absence of value education is seriously felt. Private schools, that have access mainly to the rich and the privileged, claim to incorporate value education in their curricula. The government and municipal schools are almost being written off by the people. Most of them lack everything: infrastructure, content, pedagogy and value education. Most grant-in-aid colleges and universities turn out graduates who are not worthy of even employment let alone value education. The students in the higher education stream severely lack skill and training in vocations. The government is trying hard to skill the Indian youth. The National Skill Development Corporation has been set up and it aims to skill 400 million persons by 2022. The mission is to fulfil the growing need in India for skilled manpower and narrow the gap between demand and supply of skills. It further aims to upgrade skills to international standards through significant industry involvement and develop necessary frameworks for standards, curriculum and quality assurance, enhance, support and coordinate private sector initiatives for skill development through appropriate Public-Private Partnership (PPP) models, and strive for significant operational and financial involvement from the private sector.

However, the approach is partial and piecemeal. It has no relation with the challenge education faces in the country. A major problem faced by the Indian society today is the growing alienation of children from their cultural roots. The education system is playing a central role in aggravating and accelerating the process. The National Focus Group on Work and Education set up by the NCERT[24] noted in its Report in January 2007 that the exclusionary character was founded on the artificially instituted dichotomy between work and knowledge. Those who work with their hands and produce wealth are denied access to formal education while those who have access to formal education not only denigrate productive manual work but also lack the necessary skills for the same. Over a period of time and through systematic practice, such a notion of education has come to be embedded in the knowledge system, representing the dominant classes/castes/cultures/languages with gender in each of these categories. The education system has tended to 'certify' this form of knowledge as being the only 'valid' form. In the process, the knowledge inherent among the vast productive forces along with the related values and skills has been excluded from the school curriculum.

Emphasizing the relevance and need for introducing Gandhiji's view on education, the Group noted that the Gandhian proposal of *Nai Talim* (Basic Education) challenged the dichotomy by placing productive manual work at the centre of the school curriculum itself. Participation in productive work under conditions approximating to real life situations is pedagogically linked to learning and simultaneously becomes the medium of knowledge acquisition, developing values and skill formation. Engagement with work will promote multidimensional attributes in the cognitive, affective and psycho-motor domains in a holistic manner, i.e. by integrating 'head, hand and heart'. Such attributes are admittedly missing in the education system. In this sense, placing productive work at the centre of curriculum will act as a powerful corrective to the 'book-centred', information-oriented and generally unchallenging character of school education and, in turn, helps to relate the latter to the life needs of the child. Pedagogical experience in using work is thus viewed as an effective and critical developmental tool at different stages of childhood and adolescence.

The essence of Gandhiji's views on education and its relevance for present times may be summarized by quoting the man himself. Addressing the teacher trainees from all over India at Wardha in February 1939, Gandhiji said:

> Our education has got to be revolutionized. The brain must be educated through the hand. If I were a poet, I could write poetry on the possibilities of the five fingers. Why should you think that the mind is everything and the hands and feet nothing? Those who do not train their hands, who go through the ordinary rut of education, lack 'music' in their life. All their faculties are not trained. Mere book knowledge does not interest the child so as to hold his attention fully. The brain gets weary of mere words, and the child's mind begins to wander. The hand does the things it ought not to do, the eye sees the things it ought not to see, the ear hears the things it ought not to hear, and they do not do, see or hear, respectively what they ought to. They are not taught to make the right choice and so their education often proves their ruin. An education which does not teach us to discriminate between good and bad, to assimilate the one and eschew the other is a misnomer.[25]

Gandhiji's views on education beckon. Mission possible.

ENDNOTES

1. Interested readers should refer to Krishna Kumar, 1993. Mohandas Karamchand Gandhi, in *Prospects*, the quarterly review of education (Paris, UNESCO: International Bureau of Education), Volume 23, No. 3/4, pp. 507-17.

2. Sykes Marjorie, 1988. *The Story of Nai Talim: Fifty Years of Education at Sevagram (1937-87)*. Gandhi Seva Sangh, Sevagram, Wardha, 2014 Reprint.
3. For quotes and other details interested readers are advised to refer to, Gandhi, M.K. 1927. *An Autobiography or the Story of My Experiments with Turth*, Navajivan Publishing House, Ahmedabad. 1976, Reprint, pp. 149-51.
4. Dörthe Bühmann and Barbara Trudell, 2008. *Mother Tongue Matters: Local Language as a Key to Learning*. Section for Inclusion and Quality Learning Enhancement Division for the Promotion of Basic Education, Education Sector UNESCO, Paris.
5. *Collected Works of Mahatma Gandhi* (CWMG), Vol. 9, pp. 138-9. Publications Division, GoI, April 1963.
6. The reader may be reminded that *Hind Swaraj* is written in a dialogical form where there is a reader and there is an editor.
7. *CWMG* Vol. 10, p. 54. Publications Division, GoI, September 1963.
8. Gandhiji was not satisfied with the writing and wanted to revise. He could not do so during his lifetime. A copy of the typed script was with Kakasaheb Kalelkar. It was published in a book form in 1948. The publication was titled as *Satyagraha Ashramno Itihas*. It was latȩr translated into English and published in 1955. The title is *Ashram Observances in Action*.
9. Readers interested to read in detail should refer to *CWMG* Vol. 50. Publications Division, GoI, March 1972, pp. 188-236.
10. Ibid., p. 450.
11. *CWMG* Vol. 65. Publications Division, GoI, August 1976, p. 450.
12. Ibid., pp. 450-1.
13. Sykes, op. cit., p. 23.
14. In later days he had dropped his family name and was known only as Shrimannarayan. He was a Gandhian and a senior Congressman. He served as Governor of Gujarat between December 1967 and March 1973.
15. Readers interested in details may kindly refer to CWMG Vol. 65. Publications Division, GoI, July 1976, pp. 194-5.
16. Mahadev Desai, Gandhiji's well-known Secretary and an erudite scholar in his own right had taken notes on Gandhiji's inaugural speech. He wrote an article based on it titled

The Primary Question. Excerpts are reproduced in CWMG Volume 66. Publications Division, GoI, October 1976, p. 263.

17. *Ibid.*, p. 264.
18. *Ibid.*, p. 265.
19. *Ibid.*, p. 266.
20. Krishna Kumar, op. cit.
21. Sykes, op. cit., p. 20.
22. Sykes, Marjorie, op. cit.
23. *CWMG* Vol. 21. Publications Division, GoI, August 1966, p. 38.
24. The Committee was chaired by Anil Sadgopal. For details one may go to http://www.ncert.nic.in/new_ncert/ncert/rightside/links/pdf/focus_group/workeducation.pdf Accessed December 26, 2016.

3

Learning the Art of Wholeness: Sri Aurobindo's Philosophy of Education

Ananta Kumar Giri

Children are not the people of tomorrow
But are people of today
They have a right to be taken seriously
And to be treated with tenderness and respect
They should be allowed to grow into
Whoever they were meant to be—
"The unknown person" inside each of them
Is our hope for the future.

—Janus Korzack (1999), In *A Voice for the Child*, p. 4.

We should not ask: what does a person need to know or be able to do it in order to fit into the existing social order? Instead we should ask: what lives in each human being and what can be developed in him or her? Only then it would be possible to direct the new qualities of each emerging generation into society. Society will then become what young people, as whole human beings, make out of the existing social conditions. The new generation should not just be made to be what present society wants it to become.

—Rudolf Steiner (1985), *The Renewal of Social Organism*, p. 71.

Almost all over the world at present, as people are becoming more and more aware of the gods that have failed them, the heroic in them is searching for alternatives, an alternative in science and technology, alternatives in political and economic

> patterns, and also an alternative in education. Man everywhere has never been so rude and ruthless in throwing away the old idols as he is now. It seems there is going to be a total leap, a decision in direction of the vertical.
>
> And in the direction of the vertical, lies the spiritual, the integral, the intrinsically human. Education must have a spiritual base; in other words, it must start from the basic faith that what is intended to be brought about is already involved within. In actual practice, this faith will mean freedom, love and commitment. Only those who are free can help others in the right way to grow with freedom.
>
> —Chitta Ranjan Das (1980), "Searching for an Alternative," p. 14.

> This cannot be taught; it has to be stimulated. It can arise only out of the affective attachment of children or adolescents to a reference group who makes them feel deserving of unconditional love, and confident of their capacity to learn, act, undertake projects and measure themselves against others—who gives them, in a word "self-esteem." The subject emerges by virtue of the love with which another subject calls it to become a subject and it develops through the desire to be loved by that other subject. This means that the *educative* relation is not a social relation and is not socializable. It is successfully achieved only if the child is an incomparably singular being for the person educating him / her, a being loved for him / herself and to be revealed to him / herself by that love as entitled to his / her singularity: that is to say, as a subject-individual.
>
> —Andre Gorz (1999), *Reclaiming Work: Beyond the Wage-Based Society*

Introduction and Invitation: Education as Learning the Art of Wholeness

Our educational systems are in a crisis now. This is evident at all levels of education—from the primary to the higher. A major part of the problem lies in our education lacking a soul dimension and striving for realization of wholeness as pedagogical methods lack a relation of love, mutuality, care and creativity among the partners and fellowtravellers and educational objectives lack the goal of integral development of individuals and societies. Our conventional educational systems reflect the fragmentation and mechanical closure of modern subjectivity and society and it is mainly confined to rudimentary aspects of skill-training and mental education and it does not touch all the dimensions of life and society.

Education for wholeness nonetheless has been a yearning of humanity from its very dawn. The Greek root for education means to evolve and this does embody a process of evolutionary realization of wholeness. Education for wholeness is a perpetual journey; it is not a linear one but nonetheless despite complex turns and cycles and circles of learning it does embody certain learning of insights which is preserved as evolutionary knowledge and wisdom. Education for wholeness is not a holistic education in a literal, conventional, superficial, *a priori*, and determined sense as it realizes that wholeness is a journey of self and social transformation—it is a perennial journey from fullness to a different fullness realizing on the way an integral emptiness. Education for wholeness realizes that wholes to be realized are made up of many holes but these holes are neither dark nights of the soul nor dark spaces but spaces of energy and light. These holes and different fragments of life do embody an integral yearning for connectedness and being part of a garland of togetherness, a symphony of wholeness. Education for wholeness strives to go beyond varieties of dualisms of life and society such as the individual and society, body and mind, mind and soul, technical and artistic, utilitarian and spiritual and, head and heart. It embodies a multi-valued logic of living and a movement learning across positions embodying transpositional learning and a multi-*topial* hermeneutics where our interpretation of the world emerges by walking and meditating across different domains and terrains of self, culture, society and the world (see Giri 2016a; 2016b). Hermeneutics here presents us a different vision and pathways of becoming subject other than the ones proposed by the state (cf. Foucault 2005).

Education as learning the art of wholeness also interrogates the available understanding and organization of education as a top-down activity. It challenges us to realize that education is first of all an activity of learning in which all the engaged participants are learners. Education is an activity and process of learning and co-learning in which the so-called students and teachers are first of all learners and co-learners. This is at the core of Sri Aurobindo's vision of integral education as he says that nothing can be taught and the teacher is an aid in the process of learning. A similar attitude also permeates other initiatives in learning the art of wholeness in our present-day world, for example, the Bifrost School in Denmark, where teachers are not called teachers. But education for wholeness is not student-centred in a naïve sense as it is also not teacher-centred. It is a learning-centred education which continuously decentres a taken-for-granted conception learning and learner.

Learning the Art of Wholeness: Integral Education

There have been different visions and experiments with education for wholeness in our modern world. Integral education is one such, the other two, among many others, are the Steiner-Waldorf schools in Germany and around the world and the Grundtvig-Kold free schools in Denmark. Integral education strives for integral, not fragmentary, development of self and society. It draws inspiration and insights from the vision, experiments and works of Sri Aurobindo and the Mother and as a humanistic and spiritual pedagogy is in tune with the *gestalt* and integral educational movements of the 19th and 20th centuries pioneered by such educational visionaries as Kristen Kold, Rudolf Steiner, Rabindranath Tagore, Mahatma Gandhi and others. Integral education is a social, cultural and educational movement in a state like Odisha with more than fifty years of continued striving to build on and now around six hundred schools in different parts of the state—rural, urban and tribal. In this essay we shall describe the ideals and hopes that animate this striving.

These schools say that they provide a soul-touching and child-nurturing education from pre-nursery to the high school level (up to Standard X). Probably for the first time in the country, these schools achieved autonomy in terms of having their own syllabi and methods of examination up to the 7th Standard. After the Right to Education in 2009, examinations have also been abolished in many schools across the country for primary and secondary education. The first effort in integral education in Odisha began with the establishment of the Institute of Integral Education in the state capital of Bhubaneswar in 1970 which was inspired by the Sri Aurobindo International Centre of Education of Sri Aurobindo Ashram, Pondicherry established in 1943. In Odisha, now integral education has attained a level of grassroots mobilization but integral education is striving in many other parts of the country as well. For example, the Mirambika School run by the Sri Aurobindo Ashram, Delhi also strives to put into practice the vision of integral education from kindergarten up to the 10th Standard (Pathak 2002).

The Vision of Integral Education

Integral education submits a radical and evolutionary challenge before humanity that education is not only for children but for all of us, the adults, and it is for our entire life. Thus declares Mother, Mira Richards, the spiritual fellowpilgrim of Sri Aurobindo: "The education of a human being should begin at his very birth and continue throughout his life" (Mother 1956: 96). She adds: "Education to be complete must have five principal aspects relating to the five principal activities of the human being: the physical, the vital, the mental, the psychic and the spiritual. Usually, these phases of education succeed each other in a chronological order following the growth of the individual, this, however, does not mean that one should replace the other but that all must continue, completing each other, till the end of life" (ibid: 96-97). For this, Sri Aurobindo enunciates three principles of education:

1. "The first principle of true teaching is that nothing can be taught. The teacher is not an instructor or task-master, he is a helper and a guide. His business is to suggest and not to impose. He does not actually train people's minds, he only shows them how to acquire";
2. "The second principle of education is that the mind has to be consulted in its own growth"; and
3. "The third principle of education is to work from the near to far, from that which is to that which shall be" (Sri Aurobindo in Mother 1956: 20-21).

The Mother describes for us the further contours of integral education as the integral development of body, mind, the vital, the psychic and the spiritual. Physical education is a core dimension of integral education as it seeks to create a supple and healthy body which becomes an instrument of the Divine here on earth.[1] Mental education or education of the mind has five aspects:

(i) "Development of the power of concentration, the capacity of attention";

(ii) "Development of the capacities of expansion, wideness, complexities and richness";

(iii) "Organization of ideas around a central idea or a higher ideal or a supremely luminous idea that will serve as a guide in life";

(iv) "Thought control, rejection of undesirable thoughts, so that one may, in the end, think only what one wants and when one wants it"; and

(v) "Development of mental silence, perfect calm and a more and more total receptivity to inspirations coming from the higher regions of the being" (The Mother 1956: 114-115).

The Mother further writes about mental education "[..] learning is only one aspect of mental activity; the other, at least, as important, is the constructive faculty, the capacity to give form and therefore prepare for action;" and for her, "control over the formative activities of the mind is one of the most important aspects of self education" (ibid: 118).

The education of the vital is an important part of integral education which involves education and development of the senses. "The child must be taught to observe himself, to note his reactions and impulses and their causes, to become a clear-sighted witness of his desires, his movements of violence and passion, his instincts of possession and appropriation and domination" (ibid: 112). In integral education, art, songs, painting, music and drama play a pivotal role in the education of the vital. While psychic education is the recognition of the psychic force in one's life and it helps one to pull out of the "barriers of egoism" (ibid: 124), spiritual education helps one to realize life as "light and balance, beauty and joy." Spiritual education also enables seekers for a radical universality where one recognizes the Divine in each and all: "The Divine is the fourth dimension. The Divine does not come and go. He is there, always, everywhere."

Integral education according to Sri Aurobindo and The Mother, is an aid in the integral evolution of humanity. For Sri Aurobindo, "Humanity in its education of children has chosen to thwart and hinder the rapidity of its onward march" (Sri Aurobindo 1956: 35). In this context, integral education aims at "not merely in a progressively developing formation of human nature but a transformation of the nature itself, a transfiguration of the being in its entirety, a new ascent of the species above and beyond man towards superman, leading in the end to the appearance of a divine race upon earth" (Mother 1956: 131).

To this core of the vision, the participants of the integral education movement of Odisha have added their nuances and emphases. For many of them, integral education is a method and a field of *yoga*. Where the conventional methods of yoga, spiritual union and spiritual realization had visualized individuals sitting cross-legged and doing *yoga*; in Sri Aurobindo's path of spiritual striving, yoga has to be *karmayoga* and integral education is a method and field of *karmayoga*. Integral education is a *sadhana* for the participants in which one tries to realize the divine in oneself by establishing a loving and life-elevating relationship with one's students. For the participants of integral education, the school is itself an embodiment of Divine Mother and many of them have a literal conception of school as Divine Mother. This view of integral education became clear to me during the annual meet of integral education activists in Matrubhavan, Cuttack in October 2000. At this meeting Lambodara Bhai, a longtime activist of integral education, said: "Earlier the *rishis* were going to the forest and were doing their *tapasya*. In integral schools, we are doing *tapasya* through our children. Unless we realize this, our education cannot fructify itself."

Chitta Ranjan Das (1923-2011) was a devoted participant and engaged leader of the integral education movement of Odisha. Das himself was an experimenter in many efforts in child-nurturing and soul-touching education and in order to understand different dimensions of integral education we should do well to get to know his elaboration of the agenda of integral education. In his educational practice, Das combines the best source of inspiration in the world—Kristen Kold, Gandhi, Janus Korchak, Tagore—bringing all these rich sources to have a dialogue with the pathway of integral education. Twenty years before joining the integral education movement in Odisha as the first Director of the Institute of Integral Education in Bhubaneswar, Das had himself started a new school in the forests of Anugul, Odisha, called *Jeevana Vidyalaya*—School for Life (see Das 2006; Das 2013). Das brings a loving and life-affirming relationship with children and creating proper environment—outer and inner—for the integral development of the human person to the heart of the vision and experiments of integral education. In the words of Das: "[..] The object of concern in integral education is the total child, the whole person in him that waits to be attended and unfolded. The stress is on each individual child with a style, a rhythm and a pace of his own and no effort is made arbitrarily to groom every budding soul to a uniformity that the adults around him have decided to hold as very significant and sacred. Integral education assumes that a really alive, alert and awakened person has a child within him and it is the business of all good education to perpetuate it" (Das 2003: 239-240). For Das, "Integral education deals with the human child as an emerging person, not as a thing. A person is never a thing, he is a totality, a unity as multiplex, with a dimension of depth suggesting the innumerable possibilities latent in him and divinely decreed to unfold in its own way" (ibid).

Earlier we have listened to Mother's elaborations of the fivefold processes of integral education—physical, vital, mental, psychic and spiritual. Das adds his own originality while elaborating these dimensions. On vital education he writes: "Vital education will engender in the child the penchant to develop a discipline of his own which would further his growth and take care of distractions and deviations. This education rules out all coercion and compulsion and aims at making the child willing to collaborate in his own growing up process, cultivating in him the right taste, right sensibilities and the right awareness of the fulfilment and joy that will be his if he is able to listen to the best in himself and cooperate with it" (ibid). Furthermore, "Vital education takes care of the vital emotional surplus in the child as a being that grows, that discovers and establishes the many threads of relationship that invisibly govern the development of the part in him that gives itself to others and shares in order that he can more wholesomely live" (ibid: 241). In the integral schools, mental education provides the child with the "clues to inherit the legacy of knowledge that is man's, to organize it around and aim that one has chosen for oneself." Mental education makes "the head equipped and ready to serve the heart, the real heart of man. The spontaneous love to learn, to know and to be linked with the world in a sense of genuine concern are the aims mental education has in view" (ibid: 242). For Das, "Psychic education brings the human person to himself, to the centre that unites him with the whole universe." But Das urges us to realize: "[..] Psychic and spiritual education in the total plan of integral education is not a separate segment in it [..] it is the total climate that pervades everything that is done in an integral school, and characterizes the quality of rapport that exists in all its educational and human situations" (ibid). Recently there is a relational redefinition and reworking of spirituality where spirituality refers to the quality of relationships and institutions rather than a thing (Giri 2008, 2016; Wuthnow 1998). Das's interpretation of spiritual education makes spirituality an aspect of our relationship and urges us to be aware of the quality of it. Das therefore writes: "There should be a total feeling of involvement and togetherness that should permeate everything that is meant and taught in the entire gamut of the school programme and the quality of that feeling will be spiritual, recognizing the truth that is in everyone and that is being explored in the daily relationship between person and person" (Das 2003). The new relational matrix that integral schools strive to create is not confined to either the classroom or the school. For Das, "The integral school tries to incorporate much of the child's home within it and also tries to incorporate a bit of itself to the child's parental home situation" (ibid).

Das now describes for us the special methods of teaching in integral schools and integral education. These are:

1. All teaching is primarily a learning situation. In integral schools, "encounter between the pupils and the teachers are not confined to the formal classroom teaching only. Even the so-called formal teaching tends not to be formal at all."
2. "The class is a group situation where the teacher gets an occasion to learn more about the child as well as about his capacity to really come close enough to the child in order to be able to really impart something useful to the child and where the child makes himself more and more exposed to the available occasions of learning without being abhorrently conscious that he is being taught."
3. "The various subjects are introduced to the child not as abstractions and soulless scraps of foreign matter, but as mysteries waiting to be discovered and made one's own."

4. "The aim of all methods in integral schools aspires to create an attitude of affirmation, towards life and towards the world, towards knowledge and its incumbent challenges" (ibid: vi). For Das, methods of education, including integral education, are "meant to help the children to find their own inherent way to learning, never to fit the child brutally to adult formations of methods."
5. An alternative educational practice which seeks to recognize the many-sided potentialities of children needs to have an alternative method of assessment and evaluation. For Das, "The Integral education centres in Odisha have already made a beginning towards change in the traditional pattern of assessment because they are convinced that a new education ought to have a totally new approach to this also." It must be noted here that Integral education schools in Odisha have got autonomy of internal evaluation and assessment up to Class 7 and they are not required to go through the state examination board for this purpose. In his introduction to the Comprehensive Syllabus of Integral Education, Das writes about the method of assessment which would be gradually adopted in all schools: "[..] Tests will be throughout the year and the cumulative results will tell us how a child has fared in a particular subject and in the aggregate." Furthermore, "Besides the so-called academic performances, a pupil's performance in the so-called non-academic fields has to be taken into account. [..] Thus, our pupil's performance in games, sports, music, painting, occasions of leadership, his cheerfulness, capacity for endurance and even his sense of humour and an attitude of non-complaining non-exhibitionistic equanimity will all be taken into full account in assessing him. Personality and attitude tests can be made use of to make the teachers more scientific in their judgments" (Das 2003: 244-246).[2]

Other Related Visions: Free Schools of Denmark

The vision of integral education finds a resonance in other related movements notably in the educational initiatives inspired by Grundtvig and Kristen Kold in Denmark and Rudolf Steiner from Austria. Grundtvig and Kold in Denmark inspired formation of folk high schools where children of peasants studied about life.

These schools got established around the 1840s and they are also active today. These schools drew inspiration from the following thought of Grundtvig, "No one has lived and has knowledge about something that has not loved it." Grundtvig-Kold also inspired formation of free schools for education at the primary and secondary levels.

Free schools are an important part of educational reality of Denmark. Many school-going children from kindergarten up to the 9th/10th grade go to free schools. These schools are free in this sense that they have emerged out of initiatives of parents and not controlled by the state though the state is constitutionally obliged to financially support the expenses of the school. But the state educational department also ensures that the free schools provide quality education to the children and in the name of freedom do not abuse it and fail in their responsibility to the children. Recently some free schools started by Muslim parents and religious associations have been closed in Denmark for reasons of standards and pedagogical quality including issues of dignity and democracy which are a part of the free school tradition of Denmark. This tradition was envisioned and cultivated by Grundtvig (1783-1872) and Kristen Kold (1818-1864). Grundtvig was the poet, pre-eminent pastor and thinker of Denmark who contributed to a new Danish awakening and strove for transformation in religion, education and society. Kristen Kold was an experimenter in new ways of education and learning and he established the first free school in 1851 for children where he taught by telling stories. Instead of rote learning Kold strove for co-learning with telling of stories. Both, Kold and Grundtvig contributed to transformation of landscape of learning and self-formation in Denmark. Folk high schools were built for adults which provide an opportunity for adults to learn about life in new ways. Free schools are for school-going children. There are also After Schools for students who would like to spend one year after their 9th grade, or the 9th grade, only before gymnasium which consists of grades 11, 12 and 13. There is also one inspiring teacher's training college, Den Free Laererskole (DFL)—The Free Teacher's Training College—in Ollerup which prepares aspiring students to be teachers embodying the poetic spirituality of Grundtvig and the child-centred pedagogy of Kristen Kold. According to Thorsten Balle, the Principal of DFL: "The school that Kold founded in 1851 has become the foundation of a school tradition that today encompasses hundreds of independent schools for children, young people and adults. A tradition still kept alive in over 260 children's schools called free schools, 260 boarding schools for young people called continuation schools [or after schools] and finally 85 schools for adults, called folk high schools" (Balle 2007: 5-6).

The Grundtvig-Kold Paths of Learning for Wholeness

Free schools began with the initiative of Kristen Kold but over the years there have been free schools established from many different sources of inspiration and emphasis. For example, in contemporary Denmark there are free schools initiated from a Catholic background, there are also Muslim free schools. There are also free schools with specific pedagogical emphases such as Steiner-Waldorf pedagogy. But of these many free schools the ones inspired by Grundtvig and Kold are the most widespread and most influential in Denmark. Their vision and practice over the last one hundred and fifty years have also influenced the making of government Schools in Denmark which are called folk schools.

Grundtvig (1783-1872), a clergyman, poet, theologian and educationist, inspired new ways of learning and awakening in Denmark. Grundtvig was a contemporary of two other eminent Danes—Hans Christian Andersen (1805-1875) and Soren Kierkegaard (1813-1855). As Pedersen writes: "Andersen and Kierkegaard are both far better known in the world at large than Grundtvig. But Grundtvig from a Danish point of view has left the most reliable mark on Danish culture until today, although it is a matter of discussion, whether or not his influence has a future in the age of globalization"(Pedersen 2008: 1).

Grundtvig strove to establish schools of life in place of Latin Grammar Schools which he termed as schools of death. In 1838, coinciding with political changes in Denmark and pleading for people's enlightenment and the need for establishing schools for life where all interested especially peasants could come and learn, Grundtvig wrote: "I maintain that if the school is really to be an educational institution for the benefit of life, it must first of all make neither education nor itself its goal but the requirements of life, and secondly it must take life as it really is and only strive to shed light on and promote its usefulness" (Grundtvig 1838:71). Grundtvig also wrote: "[..] only as far as the use of words in the teaching becomes a dialogue or conversation the enlightenment succeeds."

Grundtvig inspired many in Denmark especially to establish schools of life and be engaged in new experiments in education. Grundtvig inspired formation of folk high schools where boys and then later girls of peasants came and studied.

Grundtvig was a visionary. His vision inspired many including Kristen Kold. Kold came from a humble background and in his journey of life went on to become a teacher (Das 2007). While studying in his teacher's training college one day he heard from one of his teachers that God loves all. This was a turning point in his life. He brought the spirit of love to his teaching and could feel the pain and suffering of young children trying to memorize prescribed textbooks. It must be noted here that in Denmark then children had to memorize a textbook for religious confirmation. Even if one did not want to study such a book memorized knowledge was a must for getting confirmation. Kold once said the same thing that children were memorizing it as a story and could remember it easily. Being taught in this way children could also answer all the questions from the priest. But the authorities both in the Church and state education board did not accept Kold's innovative educational method. Kold did not get a regular job in the state education department. He worked in different private houses as a home teacher. He also followed a missionary in his journey to Turkey. He stayed there for five years and after the initial days with the missionary, Kold worked as a book binder. He had a flourishing trade in this new place but he remembered the children of Denmark and came home. But during his return he chose to walk on foot. He purchased a cart, put all his belongings and walked his way back to Denmark. Upon return he founded a folk school in Ryslinge for the adult sons of the farmers. Shortly after, in 1851 he established a free school for younger children also in Ryslinge. This was the first free school which then inspired many such schools. Now there are over 260 free schools around Denmark building on the Gruntdvig–Kold tradition.

Kold was an experimenter in new initiatives in learning. He had not written much except one text, "Thoughts on the Primary

School."[3] In this Kold pleads for teaching oriented towards children's abilities and needs. Kold begins his thoughts on children's school: "Primary school teaching is guilty of the fact that it has attempted to speak almost exclusively to reason and only partially to the feelings. While imagination and perception has been almost completely left out." For many followers of the path of Kold's way of educating such as young people I met in DFL, Ollerup Kold was a visionary and more than a hundred and forty years ago Kold's prophetic thoughts about different kinds of intelligence are at the cornerstone of much of child-centred pedagogy today. At DFL, students aspiring to be teachers in the Grundtvig-Kold tradition told me about current work on emotional intelligence and the need to work with children with their different kinds of intelligence. For Kold: "[…] far too little attention has been given in teaching according to the child's abilities, through focusing on developing the intellect, which has not yet reached maturity, instead of working through the *imagination*, which is *already* present. The reason for this can probably be found in the conscious or unconscious mistaken belief that the child is an animal, which, through disciplining and education will turn into a human being --- instead of encouraging and developing those abilities which the child already has" (Kold 2003: 48).

In his work on the children's school, Kold discusses two approaches to teaching children—the systematic/catechistic, and story-telling. In the systematic method one teaches a subject in a systematic way and in the story-telling method one teaches children by telling stories. For Kold, "We can easily find out how our children want to be enlightened; we only have to ask them. The answer is 'Tell us a story!' We know from our own childhood the many voluntary teachers who, with the loving care for the children undertook to teach them through telling stories and sagas […] The beneficial and joyful influence that the gentle work has had is invaluable […]" (ibid: 48). But Kold does not follow an either or approach: systematic or story-telling. For Kold: "We use the catechistic method where it has its rightful place: in teaching mathematics, geometry and simple arithmetic, which consist of definite solutions. Bible teaching, however, and the history of the fatherland and everything else that has the purpose of elevating human beings into living members of the spiritual as well as the civic community, is in my view and from my experience most certainly and most easily facilitated through story-telling" (ibid: 50).

For Kold, for young children, oral teaching and teaching through story-telling should be the primary concern of the teacher and the school rather than being preoccupied with teaching them to write. For Kold, "The over emphasis on reading, is to a great extent, the cause of our corruption. If it were just enough to read, why would we need school teachers? [...] learning from books belongs to a more mature age and has to be prepared through oral teaching: but if this is found wanting, the desire to read will also be lacking" (ibid: 58). For Kold, "We are in such a hurry to teach children to read as if the whole secret to learning was buried there. We start with this before there has been any significant development of their spiritual capabilities" (ibid: 62). Kold here makes a profound internal cultural criticism of fixation with the written form:

> [..] Luther and others like him turned to the written word as a means of finding the truth themselves. [..] In this way one discovered the need to be able to read, and have fully and firmly believed that it was no longer possible to be fooled. However, this belief was mistaken: daily experience proves it. In building one's faith on the written word, one merely builds one's own or on someone else's interpretation, and what we end up with is a new papacy (ibid: 64).

Kold also believes that examinations are not suitable for children in the primary school. For Kold, "the adults now asked about what they knew already, and the little ones boldly answered what they did not understand. Through this questioning by the wise and the answers of the simple, the darkness naturally increased the longer this carried on, and finally it turned into a completely Egyptian darkness" (ibid: 82). For Kold, "The school has much more important things to do, namely: to develop the children's spiritual capabilities, which is done most easily and safely through oral teaching. When this has been properly accomplished, the child will, on its 13th or 14th year, have developed its capabilities and scope for perception, easily enabling it to learn to read as much as it will have need for the rest of its life. If it should turn out to be the case that a child used an hour to spell its way through one page of a book, which understood as the end of it, then we would be better off than now, where children read 10 pages in an hour without understanding one line" (ibid: 65).

Kold is against dead formality and bondage in the schools. The teachers and the school should focus on developing the spirit of the children and teach through heart-to-heart communication: "Only that which comes from the heart is received by the heart. Everything, good as well as bad, which is to have any real impact must be prepared from the depths of the heart, and be transformed into word and deed from there. A surface life only produces appearances and shadows; to the uninitiated it looks as though it exists, but it does not however"[4] (ibid: 74). For this the teacher must have sufficient knowledge of "the child's spiritual capabilities" and work with her "imagination and feelings" and not only through "intellect" (ibid: 75). For Kold, even developing intellect calls for work on and with imagination: "[...] if one wants to develop the child's intellect successfully, it has to happen with *the aid of the imagination* otherwise the concept will remain dead" (ibid: 54).

Kold takes great pain to explain that one must have infinite patience with children and move step by step in accordance with natural and spontaneous development of children's capacity to learn. What Kold writes deserves our careful consideration:

> When one deals with children, one ought to remain close to their own situation. So that they can get a taste of leading a meaningful life early on and to learn to realize the necessity for enlightenment that they are receiving, through finding it *immediately* useful or pleasurable. If one ventures beyond this, and belittles the importance of enlightening the child according to its *existing* life experience in order to illuminate situations which will arise in adult or old age then one will not be understood [...] Putting enlightenment too far in front of life experience are the most dangerous rocks a skilful and earnest teacher must try to avoid: one needs a great deal of knowledge of people in order to be able to judge to what extent life has advanced, and thereby to what degree one should convey light, as well as having the patience to wait; since both teachers and parents certainly wish to see the children advance. The teacher's love for children, and an over estimation of his influence on them, may also lead him to assume that they have

> come further than they actually have. However, these have to be avoided because they have very dangerous consequences for the children, and most of the time these lead to a total shipwreck. The more skilful a teacher is the more he is able to paint a natural, clear and lively picture of the kind of life he is promoting, and more his goal will be oriented towards the spiritual depths of the child's soul (ibid: 76; emphases added).

Kold further says: "One has to be careful not to force onto the child some definitive mark through our teaching. One has to leave it up to the child what and how much it will receive from it" (ibid: 78). Furthermore,

> It is bad practice to ask the child to account for what it has learned either immediately, or shortly following the teaching. A wise man once said that that would be like a mother demanding her child to throw up the food it had just received, in order to show her how much or what it had eaten. In this way the child would be deprived of the means of supporting its body... One would certainly think it right to let the child keep the food till the body had absorbed the necessary nourishment from it. However, this mistaken procedure is probably caused by the fact that one aims at remoulding the child, therefore wanting to know how many parts of metal there are, in order to melt the mixture. Even though this chemical investigation looks thorough enough, I nevertheless do think that its impact on living beings will be far too violent and it will undoubtedly lead to a quick and abrupt death [...] (ibid: 78-79).

But Kold is for the school of life not only for the children but also for adults. Kold himself established a folk high school in Ryslenge in 1850 and then one at Dalby later on. Taking inspiration from Kold there are also after schools where children come to spend a year or two for their 9th year or after finishing their 9th year one year before moving on to the last three years of gymnasium. In all these schools there is a continued striving to embody the Grundtvig-Kold vision of soul-nurturing education and school for life. For Kold, just learning to read is not the goal of the school of life, rather it is awakening of the spirit.

Along with these schools of different levels—Free Schools, After Schools, and Folk High Schools, there is also a Teachers' Training College which tries to train aspiring teachers in the Grundtvig-Kold tradition. This is called Den Frie Laererskole

(The Independent Teachers College) which is in Ollerup in the Island of Fuenn.

Grundtvig-Kold Free Schools in Contemporary Denmark

There are around 260 children's schools or free schools working in the Grundtvig-Kold tradition in contemporary Denmark.[5] Bordings is one of the most widely known free schools in Copenhagen. It has classes from kindergarten to the 9th Standard. In each of the classes there are 18 to 20 students while in government schools there are around 28 students. This small size of classes creates a facilitating structural condition in which teachers can spend time with students much more individually. Story-telling and other creative ways of teaching are also integral ways of teaching and learning in this school. In the school students learn different creative vocations such as stitching and making food.

I had spent a few days in the school in March 2007 as well as in January 2008. I had sat in Class 7 as well as Class 3. Viveke, the class teacher of 3b, told me: "We have a lot of story-telling from the first class to the 6th grade. Pupils like it very much. They love their stories not because they have to appear for the examination but because they love it." Forming a loving foundation at a young age through telling stories and team work gives the children the self-confidence to express themselves truly when they go to gymnasium, universities and professions in life. Says Viveke: "When they go to gymnasium they speak in their class because it is the way we teach them. You can feel that they like to come here. We have good parents who support the school. There is learning among the parents who support the school. They do things together. Children see that the grown ups can live together."

Free schools are characterized by greater involvement of parents and lively interaction between the teachers and the taught. Parents take responsibility for the affairs of the school and they also contribute to the continued maintenance and upkeep of the school through financial contributions and sharing of labour. This is also evident in the Bordings school as I had taken part in the parents' meeting at Bordings.

Coming back to the classroom dynamics children are fearless and able to express themselves. I attended a theatre production in Class 3. I also accompanied children going to a children's theatre in Copenhagen. In Class 7 (b), I attended both the Danish class and Mathematics class. In the Danish class children read a novel and then made a portrait of some of the characters in the novel. Helge, the class teacher, tells us about it: "We have to describe the character, write what we think about them. We would then put the portraits as an exhibition in the wall." In the Mathematics class the teacher Merton led to teaching by encouraging students around a table to work together: "When you interact with others you know more about yourself and more about others [...] I have some good students who are very good to help each other. Sometimes it takes twenty seconds to help and then move on. Initially they thought that they did not have time but now they are calm, they can solve the problem and help others." Helge, the class teacher teaching Danish, also says: "Our students are used to working together. They are not the cleverest but they are good at working in groups."

Merton, this young Mathematics teacher from the class gave me the example of two students from the class--Sarah and Esther: "Sarah is good in her studies while Esther is not. She moved from 7A to 7B and is behind in many subjects. She is learning little by little [..] She looks weak in the eyes of the others. She may miss a subject but for us it is most important that we have a happy Esther. Her parents want her to smile [...] You cannot teach children if they are not ready to learn. If they are sad or angry you cannot teach. Their personal welfare is our first priority: this is the unwritten rule. This is the way we do it here."

Merton continues: "I have a special eye for the students who feel that Maths is difficult. If you go by the book you spend equal time with every student. But some students are insecure and I spend more time with them. They want everything to be 100 per cent perfect. I sit with them and say: it is fine to make mistakes. They feel secure." During my time in the class, I observed that Jacob, a student, came and sat besides Merton at his table. Merton added: "Everyone can come to my table. I do not sit down. I walk around. They just come to my table, they do not need permission."

Bordings has around 30 teachers. I had a series of meetings with Morgens, the headmaster of the school. Morgens says that along with Kold's first initiative of establishing the free school, the origin of free school lies in the 1849 Danish constitution which says that children are obliged to receive education but not go to school. While the government schools belong to a system, free schools belong to a movement: "The public school is a system, we are a movement. Parents take the initiative to build these schools and the movement of the free school grows from below. Our basic principle of education is to develop as a human being. In the free school we have the freedom to develop our curriculum." Morgens adds: "We emphasize development of the individual as well as development of the community. The modern individual would be alone if the individual is at the centre. We stress social competence, the ability to cooperate. In our globalized world we are particularly keen that our children learn to live with different languages and cultures."

Free schools have autonomy but they have to ensure acceptable standards. In recent years partly because of globalization and European integration there is a growing anxiety on the part of the government for better performance by pupils in standardized tests. All over Europe and all over the world there is more stress on standardized tests and examinations by educational policy makers, educational bureaucrats, politicians, parents and pedagogues. Denmark which has given more space for alternative child-centred education because of the strong free school movement is also going through this contemporary European and global stress. The government wants schools to show better performance of their pupils in standardized tests. The anxiety is partly due to comparative European study on students' performance in standardized tests known as the Pisa Test. All over Europe educational discourse and policy making is influenced by one's comparative ranking in the Pisa Test. Teachers in Bordings free school as well teachers interested in giving creative autonomy to children told me: "Oh when our politicians see that our children do not do as well in the Pisa test as pupils of some other countries such as Finland they become nervous. They want our children to do better in standardized tests. They want schools to have more tests. They also want teachers to write detailed reports about individual children. A teacher spends more time in writing reports rather than spending time with the students."

Free schools feel the pressure to introduce tests. Earlier they did not have many tests. But individual free schools as well as the association of free schools in Denmark are exploring ways of doing tests which can be creative. They are trying to accept this challenge in a creative way. On an experimental basis a teacher in Bordings free school is trying to do tests in a different way. Principal Morgens during our conversation told me: "Test is one part of the evaluating process. It is possible to use tests but test have their limits. But many look at tests as if they are the result of the school as a whole." He suggested that the alternative to tests is observation, reflection and dialogue between the teachers about children and between teachers and the children. For Morgens: "I still feel the challenge. The future is a challenge. Examinations are a danger but the danger is we just continue as an old school or we have the strength to develop into future without losing the tradition." He says that even if the government wants us to be more concerned with performance we still have the freedom to use 30 weeks from 40 weeks period as the normal week and 10 weeks for spending time in a creative way: "You mix pupils from different ages. You put teachers in groups who do not cooperate. The basic faith in experiment is important."

Viveke Semstad is the class teacher of Standard 1 at Bordings who has taken the lead to have an alternative test. She tells us that in Standard 1, each student has made a file and s/he evaluates her own performance by putting a red or green smile. Then the teacher has put a file of his or her test and gives grades about the following themes:

1. Happiness in being in the class
2. Respect
3. Listening
4. Waiting for each other's turn
5. Honesty

This experimental teacher tells us: "The teacher also makes a file on each student and then we discuss. I set a goal for myself—the social and mathematical goals make me aware of what I am doing in the class; it has made me aware of the goal for each student." She further says: "Government has introduced the test. Instead of saying no we explore in what way we can use them [..]." She adds: "If you use testing to beat the children in the head then testing is bad. But through testing we can also build little steps for them." She uses what she calls a portfolio way of testing.

Four teachers in the school are working with the portfolio way of testing."

This willingness to experiment and participate is what is crucial to teaching in the free school. Says Helge, the class teacher of 7B: "In this school we work with rich spoilt kids. Their parents pay 1000 DKK per child to study here. Parents are allowed to phone you at home and you have a lot to answer for. At the same time parents also cooperate with us and there is a respect for each other's work."

During my work I also visited a Muslim free school in Copenhagen. This school was started in 1991. There are 117 students in this school from pre-school till the 9th grade. Along with fulfilling state minimum standards, learning Arabic and Islam is compulsory here. Says the headmistress: "In state schools they teach about Christianity. Here we would mainly teach about Islam." I had a discussion with the secretary of the school board. Dorthie Amzouru, the secretary, says: "We do not preach about Islam. We teach our children how to live in Denmark." The teacher of intercultural communication in the school says: "Our goal in this school is to meet both the Danish culture and Islamic culture. We try to involve the parents. Their presence is important for the children. Many parents think that because they cannot speak good Danish they cannot help." She also says: "In this school we do not have emphasis on music. It is a shame because in their homes there is a tradition of music. This is not a rich school so students cannot have excursions outside Denmark. Once we wanted to go to Prague. But two pupils were not allowed to go. Some of the girl students have difficulty in convincing their parents. But it was not so much being Muslim girls but lacking money."

I also had a discussion with the headmaster of a Catholic free school which is just adjacent to the Bordings free school in Copenhagen. This school is a hundred and fifty years old having been founded in 1858. He says: "We have 22 Catholic schools with 8000 pupils. In our schools only 20 per cent are Catholics while others come from Protestant and other religious backgrounds." The headmaster tells us that his free school is more open to tests than in a Grundvig-Kold free school such as Bordings. About the impact of the Grundtvig-Kold tradition in his school he says: "I am telling histories and stories like Grundtvig and Kold."

Steiner Waldorf Schools

Rudolf Steiner (1861-1924), the philosopher and educationist from Austria, has inspired many creative efforts in education, religion, science, social action, architecture, and agricultural initiatives such as biodynamic agriculture. He also founded a path of self-knowledge called Anthroposophy. In 1919 he founded a school in Stuttgart, Germany, in the factory of an industrialist named Waldorf for teaching children of the workers of the factory. This school came to be known as Waldorf School. Since then for the last ninety years or so many schools inspired by Steiner's vision and experiments have sprung up in Germany and other countries around the world and these schools are known as Steiner Waldorf schools. In countries like Germany and the Netherlands they are much more part of an alternative pedagogical and socio-cultural movement.

Waldorf Steiner schools are characterized in their emphasis on art and music in the class. Another distinctive feature of such schools is that in the kindergarten and in the early classes such as classes one and two there is minimal emphasis on reading and writing and more emphasis on story-telling, art and music which resonate with the spirit and practice in both integral schools in India and free schools in Denmark. Steiner and people inspired by him believe that early exposure to writing and reading hampers the smooth unfoldment of the holistic being of the child. In Steiner schools one class teacher follows the class from Class 1 to Class 8 and usually he or she teaches all subjects. For example, during my first visit to a Waldorf school near Chapel Hill, North Carolina, USA, in 2003 the class teacher taught many subjects during the course of the day, for example, music and chemistry and the mother of one of the students in the class had come to assist the teacher with his experiments during his teaching of chemistry in the class. This continuity creates a bond of intimacy and a constant loving frame of reference for children to grow. A teacher in a Waldorf school in South Germany where I had done fieldwork tells us: "Growing with children from class one to class eight I have become a mother to them." Though like any system, in Steiner Waldorf schools much also depends on the quality of the person concerned. If a class teacher does not have real love for the children and subjects them to mental abuse (if not visible verbal and physical abuse) then holding onto one teacher for the long period of eight years becomes a matter of deep anxiety and pain for the children. This was shared with me by some students and parents during my fieldwork in Europe.

Educational Vision of Rudolf Steiner and the Steiner Waldorf Schools

In Rudolf Steiner's vision, human beings are energetic beings as well as spiritual beings and they are spiritual (Marshak 1997). Steiner's vision of education is based on his vision of human becoming which has three epochs. The first epoch continues from the birth till the changing of the teeth in the seventh year. David Marshak describes Steiner's educational vision thus: "The child of this epoch learns best from imitation; he does not understand or learn as deeply from rule teaching or admonition. Nor should he be asked to learn other abstractions, such as reading or writing before the change of the teeth. Although many children are capable of such tasks, the learning of abstractions in this epoch misdirects energy that is needed for physical and spiritual growth" (Marshak 1997: 40). For Steiner, children who learn to read prematurely "age too early, are limited in their life of soul and spirit, and are predisposed to a materialistic outlook" (ibid).

In Steiner's vision, the second epoch begins from the seventh year with the changing of the teeth and continues through the onset of puberty till thirteen or fourteen. In this epoch, the child's "capacity for feeling broadens and deepens, as does his capacity for moral understanding. Through much of this epoch, the child seeks legitimate authority in an adult whom he can revere and love and whose guidance he can follow" (ibid: 42). Furthermore, in this period, "The child needs to experience story as living pictures to be visualized and understood inwardly. He also needs to experience beauty in all forms, for aesthetic feeling awakens during these years and must be cultivated. His proper activity lies in the creation and appreciation of beauty in music, colour, shape, and form. Also, memory awakens with the changing of the teeth. It is a soul activity that must be cultivated" (ibid: 44). In the second epoch there are two phases—one phase of emotional and artistic identification of the world and the other phase of beginning of questioning. As Marshak interprets Steiner's vision: "From the changing of the teeth through the ninth year, the child wants to experience all that comes to him through inner rhythms that correspond to his own rhythmic system [..] He learns best from that which is alive—plants and animals—or full of life—pictures and stories" (ibid: 45). But "Some time in the tenth year, a great but unarticulated desire may arise within the child, which he manifests as unusual restlessness. It is a question about the worthiness of his teacher. The child wants to know in some new way that this loved one is deserving of his reverence. When this questioning occurs, it is imperative that the teacher should respond with special care and warmth."

The third epoch of childhood and youth begins with the onset of puberty and continues through the twenty-first year. "The youth's puberty is marked by various physical changes that are material elements in a much larger transformation of his being. The focus of inner growth during this epoch is the unfoldment of the spirit" (ibid: 46). He "enjoys ideas as younger children enjoy pictures." "With this growth, the young person becomes a complete being, a self who no longer accepts external authority on its own terms but gains the capacity for critical questioning and independent judgment. He begins to examine and often challenge all that lies around him, both large and small. While the choice he makes during these years are not always wise and this epoch involves the learning of good judgment, the young person needs the opportunity to think on his own, make his own evaluations and decisions, and experience and learn from their consequences" (ibid: 47).

The vision and practice of education in Steiner schools is based on Steiner's vision of human becoming. In the first epoch, the parents are the main teachers and they have the primary responsibility to create safe and beautiful environments in which "the child can heed his inner teacher." In Steiner's pathways, children should spend time in families or family-like kindergartens. During my visit to the kindergarten in the Waldorf school in Walwies the kindergarten teacher observed: "We cook with children. We grind the wheat and then we break bread. We do not buy things: our children must see how things are. We do not buy dolls: we make the dolls ourselves. It is important that children do not just sit. It is important that children do not have fear." "The little child must be warm to be a child. We do not teach children to read and write. This is after 7 years."

In the second epoch beginning with 7 years the children are slowly opened to new worlds of learning but in Steiner schools in this art and music play an important role. Eurythmy is a special kind of dance developed by Steiner which children in Waldorf schools learn and practise. They are also taught history: first the Greek, then the Roman period and then the period of modern Renaissance. These stages correspond to the stages of development of the child. Though there is an Europe-centredness to this way of teaching history in Steiner schools, in other countries such as Thailand where I visited a school in Bangkok, they adapt it to local culture and history.

Learning the Art of Wholeness and New Horizons of Human Development, Social Transformations and Planetary Realizations

Primary and secondary education in India, especially in rural India, is in shambles now. The dismal situation in which we are in is movingly portrayed by A. Vaidyanathan and Gopinathan Nair: "Eradication of poverty and illiteracy figured prominently in the political rhetoric of the Indian nationalist movement even before independence. Achieving universal elementary education within 10 years was included as one of the Directive Principles of State Policy in the Constitution of the Indian Republic. The rhetoric continues but the goal remains elusive even after 50 years of planning. Governments, both at the centre and the states, irrespective of their ideology, have not pursued this objective seriously and with vigour. Resources allotted to education have been woefully inadequate, and with higher education absorbing a rising proportion of allocations, elementary education has remained on a semi-starvation diet. The idea of making education legally compulsory for all children has not evoked much enthusiasm. Some states have enacted the necessary legislation but they have not exerted themselves to get the law enforced. The prospects of a dramatic turnaround in this situation do not seem bright" (Vaidyanathan and Nair 2001: 23). The situation has not much changed after the introduction of the Right to Education in 2009. One was expecting that with the Right to Education, the government would be legally and constitutionally duty bound to provide the necessary financial and other support to initiatives in education, especially the experimental schools such as integral schools. But in turn government is tightening bureaucratic control on such schools. This is different from countries like Denmark where government provides support to any school that teaches children. In India, we need a comparative global perspective to understand the reality and possibilities of education.

Expansion of primary and secondary education for accelerating human development in India is on everybody's lips now. Amartya Sen has been one of the leading votaries of such an agenda of education and human development. For Sen, an expansion of primary and secondary education is critical to the realization of autonomy and well-being of millions of people. This expansion is not possible without political mobilization for primary education on the part of the poor and the underprivileged. As Sen and Dreze tell us: "The more privileged groups, who clamour for further expansion of higher education, are politically much more powerful and better organized in pressing for what they want. [..] To counter this resilient stratification, what is needed is more activism in the political organization of the disadvantaged sections of Indian society" (Dreze and Sen 1995: 95).

But what is the pedagogy of this desired expanded education? And is political mobilization, as important as it is, enough? Sen has not raised these questions and here the case of the integral education movement provides us important lessons. This has been a movement from within local communities and civil society and this movement has drawn inspiration and continues to function because of spiritual mobilization of individuals and communities. A commitment to a higher purpose of life in which one wishes to be an errand in the evolutionary transformation of humanity, an evolutionary engagement however concretely manifested in loving and caring relationships with oneself and one's students, is a primary motivation behind innumerable young men and women of Odisha who have given their lives to this pursuit without much material gain in the process. Their pedagogical strivings teach us that it is not enough to have schools, what is important is to build a school which would be a school for the subject, a subject who is not subjected to multiple determinations of society and history, but a subject who contributes to the making of this world as a more beautiful and dignified place of being, becoming and transformation. Alain Touraine (2000) has spoken about the need for establishing a school for the subject but in Touraine, the subject is a subject of reason. The schools that focus on education for wholeness strive to build such integral schools. Grundtvig-Kold free schools and the Steiner Waldorf schools are not only schools for the subject of reason but also schools for the integral human person whose full realization requires not only mental education but also physical, vital, psychic and spiritual. Our ethnography of these initiatives in education suggest that in each of these there are challenges but at the same time all these three initiatives make an important contribution to the development of a new education and a new pedagogy which strives for realizing wholeness in self and society.

But education as learning the art of wholeness calls for transformation of our prevalent vision and practice of human development, especially child development. It challenges us to have an integral view of the human person as well as society and not only to be imprisoned with the development of the mental and focus on those aspects of education which bring social conformity and technical success. Education as learning the art of wholeness does not dismiss science and technology, rather it strives for a new integration in which art, science and technology become part of ever-widening interpenetrative circles of realization. It also calls for transformation of the existing vision and organization of society. For example, it challenges us to transform our educational institutions into spaces of learning in which the fundamental identity of each participant in this field is that of learner rather than just teacher, manager, or student. It also calls for political, economic and social transformation that grants substantive autonomy to the space of learning.

But education as learning the art of wholeness is not just confined to a select few as is the case with all initiatives in alternative education. Most of these learning spaces are not accessible to socially and economically backward classes and here there is an epochal challenge of inclusion which calls for transformation of both the society as well as these initiatives of alternative education. For example, in Odisha as well as in SAICE (Sri Aurobindo International Centre for Education), Pondicherry it is difficult for the poor to study in these schools. Here learning the art of wholeness is confronted with the challenge of creating a space which is accessible to all no matter what their economic and social situation may be. In Denmark where Grundtvig-Kold free schools work, it is more inclusive of students from poorer backgrounds possibly because the state supports these schools. In Steiner Waldforf schools in Germany and around the world the ability of resource poor students to reach schools vary from country to country, dependent on state subsidy and other factors.

These three different experimental pathways with learning the art of wholeness suggest important pathways of rethinking the vision and practice of education in India. In all these schools there is a great deal of devotion, sacrifice on the part of the teachers as well as communities which have founded such schools. These schools challenge the prevalent systems of education of society but they are also affected by it, for example all these educational movements are now under pressure to have more result-oriented pedagogy. In this context, these educational movements need to create and be part of a wider socio-cultural movement which would create a new value of cooperation, collaboration and experimental creativity in self, culture and society. These movements call for social transformation and also related movements of planetary realizations where we realize that we are children of Mother Earth. Such realizations also call for integral development of self and society where we establish relations of beauty, dignity and dialogues between humans and non-human forms of life as well as go beyond existing logic of anthropocentrism and nation-state centred rationality.

ENDNOTES

1. The flexible body of integral education is different from the flexible body and body culture promoted by late capitalism where the body becomes a flexible and ready instrument for the valorization of capital (cf. Martin 1994).
2. This is an ideal set by Das and in some schools we find a much more dedicated striving towards it. Still, as a whole, much needs to be done for following an alternative method of evaluation and assessment.
3. According to Lars SkriverSvendsen, "Christen Kold was not a writer. His influence was based first and foremost on his personal commitment and his living world. He left us only

one written book--this pamphlet *Onbornenskolen* (Thoughts on the Primary School).

The occasion for Kold writing the pamphlet was a competition for the best paper on the education of children, sponsored by the literary society of the Funen Diocese. Kold finished writing his pamphlet on December 30, 1850 and submitted it in the competition. However he did not win. The pamphlet was published first in 1877 after his death" (Sverdsen 2003: 47).

4. Kold (2003: 74) further says:

> Life in our schools is like that of our prisons and corrective institutions. When one sees the little ones packed together on the school benches, unnaturally serious and quiet for their age, clearly as a result of fear, then one gets the uncomfortable feeling that slavery reigns. It ought, after all, to be the most delightful sight when the young gather around their teacher; they ought to be freer and happier and freer there than anywhere else. But mostly one only sees boredom reflected in their faces. The children are not allowed to behave in a way that is natural to them—and in the circumstances cannot be easily allowed to do so. They develop a spirit of bondage, which is expressed through the slyness and cunning with which they learn how to avoid the teacher's attention when carrying out their naughty tricks. The teacher is generally viewed as a prison guard, who it is a good thing to fool whenever one can get away with it.

5. This is the data based on my fieldwork, in 2007.

REFERENCES CITED

Balle, Thorstein. 2007. Paper on DFL presented at the Effe Conference.

Das, Chitta Ranjan. 2003. *Purnanga Siksha* [Integral Education].

Bhubaneswar: Siksha Sandhana.

2006a. *Letters from the Forest*. New Delhi: National Book Trust.

2006b. *Bira Jodya Kari* [Being a Heroic Warrior]. Bhubaneswar: Siksha Sandhan.

2007. *Kristen Kold: A Revolutionary in Education and Pioneer of Danish Folk High School Movement*. Delhi: Shipra.

2008. "Jamidari Nuhe Prayagosala [Not a Fiefdom But a Laboratory]." Suhrut 17 (2): 10-13, May.

Dreze, Jean and Amartya Sen. 1995. *India: Economic Development and Social Opportunities*. Delhi: Oxford University Press.

Foucault, Michel. 2005. *Hermeneutics of the Subject*. New York: Palgrave.

Giri, Ananta K. 2008. "The Calling of Practical Spirituality." In Makarand Paranjape (ed.) *Science, Spirituality and the Modernization of India*. Delhi: Anthem.

2016a. "Transforming the Subjective and the Objective: Trans-positional Subjectobjectivity." Paper.

2016b. "With and Beyond Epistemologies from the South: Ontological Epistemology of Participation, Multi-Topical Hermeneutics and the Contemporary Challenges of Planetary Realizations." Paper.

_____(ed.) 2016. *Practical Spirituality and Human Development*. New Castle upon Tyne: Cambridge Scholars Press.

Kold, Christen. 2003 [1850]. *Thoughts on the Primary School*. Edited and Slightly Abridged by Lars Skriver Svendsen. Copenhagen: Forlaget Vartov.

Korsgaard, Ove. No Date. "Free Schools in a More Multicultural Society." Paper.

Mahapatra, Madhusudan. 2009. *Purnamudachyate: Eka Aurnadoya* [Rising Fullness: A Dawn—A Collection of Essays in Oriya on Integral Education]. Patnagarh, Bolangir: Sri Aurobindo Pathachakra Trust.

Marshak, David. 1997. *The Common Vision: Parenting and Educating for Wholeness*. New York et al.: Peter Lang.

Martin, Emily. 1994. *Flexible Bodies*. Princeton: Princeton University Press.

Mother [Mira Richards]. 1956. *On Education*. Pondicherry: Sri Aurobindo Ashram.

Mukherjee, Jugal Kishore. 2005. *Principles and Goals of Integral Education*. Pondicherry: Sri Aurobindo Ashram.

Pathak, Avijit. 2002. *Social Implications of Schooling: Knowledge, Pedagogy and Consciousness*. Delhi: Rainbow Publishers. Pedersen, Kim Arne. 2008. "NFS Grundtvig: Human Life and Church Life." Paper. Grundtvig-Academy, Copenhagen.

Steiner, Rudolf. 1985 [1915-1921]. *The Renewal of Social Organism*. New York: Anthroposophic Press.

Touraine, Alain. 2000. *Can We Live Together? Equality and Difference.* Cambridge: Polity Press.

Vaidyanathan, A. and P.R. Gopinathan Nair. 2001. (eds.). *Elementary Education in Rural India: A Grassroots View.* New Delhi: Sage Publications.

Wuthnow, Robert. 1998. *After Heaven: Spirituality in America Since the 1950s.* California.

Part II
Deconstructing Seminal Documents on Education

4
Delors Commission Report (1996)

Muchkund Dubey

The International Commission on Education for the 21st Century, also known as the Delors Commission after the name of its Chairperson, submitted its report to UNESCO in 1996. As the Commission stated while forwarding its report to UNESCO, the principal purpose of the report was to "contribute to invigorating a debate that is indispensable, nationally and internationally, on the future of education". The Commission examined the main challenges facing education worldwide in the light of the changes that had taken place or were in progress at the time of the deliberations of the Commission. The major changes and factors that it took into account were an increasingly crowded planet, globalization of human activities, universalization of communication, multi-dimensional global interdependence and the uncertainty and complexities brought about by these phenomena.

Several of the Commission's predictions about globalization and the implications of the technological revolution which have triggered its current phase, are a fact of life in the new millennium. We shall turn to some of the prescient observations and recommendations of the Commission on globalization and technological changes, later in this paper. At this point, we are highlighting the two defining features of the recommendations of the Commission, i.e. 'learning throughout life' and the four pillars of education consisting of 'learning to know', 'learning to do', 'learning to live together and with others' and 'learning to be'.

Learning Throughout Life

In the report, the concept of learning throughout life "emerges as one of the keys to the 21st century" (p. 22)[1]. It is "the heartbeat of society". It goes beyond traditional distinction between initial learning and continuing education. It rather links up with other important concepts like the emergence of a learning society, learning as a fulfilment of one's full potential and learning as an essential tool to gain mastery over one's destiny. It is a means for each of us to establish an equilibrium between learning and working, for continued adaptation to various avenues of occupations in one's lifetime and for the exercise of active citizenship. The Commission advances powerful arguments to demonstrate why learning throughout life has become imperative. These include the following:

- Today, no one can hope to amass during his or her youth an initial fund of knowledge which will serve for a lifetime. The swift changes taking place in the world call for knowledge to be continuously updated. This is already happening in some of the very advanced societies. In this connection, the Commission cites the examples of Sweden and Japan where around 50 per cent of the population are at present involved in adult education (p. 103). Every third student in university and college in Sweden comes via municipal adult education (p. 104).
- The initial education of young people itself is tending to be protracted because of the induction in the curriculum of various subjects the knowledge of which is indispensable in the modern context.
- Education has become so varied in its tasks and forms that it covers all the activities that enable people from childhood to old age, to acquire a living knowledge of the world, of other people and themselves.
- The very idea of learning is changing from merely acquiring skills to developing competence, adaptability and capacity to interlink with people and environment. These characteristics can be acquired and are needed any time during the lifetime and stand good throughout life.

- The shorter working life, shorter working hours and longer expectancy of life are adding substantially to the time available for other activities, and nothing is more important among these activities than learning.
- More and more opportunities of learning out of school are arising in all fields. The spaces outside school that are now available for learning are home, workplace and the community.

The report brings out some of the important practical implications of moving towards learning throughout life. Learning throughout life "presupposes the existence of universal basic schooling of good quality and accessible to all, irrespective of geographical, material, social or cultural circumstances. It offers to all the opportunity of seizing fresh chances after the completion of the initial education cycle" (p. 175). Thus, a person 's further participation in educational activities is related to the level of schooling already received. Here there is clearly a cumulative effect: the more education you have, the more education you want. Second, for learning throughout life, education must become multidimensional. It should combine non-formal with formal learning and the development of innate abilities with the acquisition of new competencies. Third, for making learning throughout life a reality, talents of every sort should be encouraged and a broad variety of learning paths be opened up and all the resources existing in society should be mobilized for that purpose (p. 175). From this, the Commission also draws the inference that for learning throughout life, even the employment of para-teachers, particularly from the community, may become necessary. Fourth, as family has become a very important place of learning, mainly facilitated by technology giving ready information sitting at home, education given by the school should be backed up by education given at home. Fifth, the community as a place for lifelong learning has a powerful educational influence because of the opportunities it offers of learning cooperation with and concern for others and gaining active experience of citizenship. Sixth, learning at the workplace is important because it is a powerful force for socialization as well as specialization. Finally, there should be a dynamic relationship between the school and university on the one hand and different alternative spaces of learning on the other—a relationship involving complementarities and partnership.

Four Pillars of Learning

The Commission's second most important recommendation is the four pillars of education. Education throughout life is based on these four pillars, i.e. learning to know, learning to do, learning to live together and learning to be. In a sense, these four pillars constitute the four basic purposes of education. All the four pillars of learning apply to the entire duration of a person's learning process. The following is a brief explanation given in the report, of these four pillars along with their practical implications.

(a) *Learning to know:* Learning to know pre-supposes learning to learn, calling upon the power of concentration, memory and thought (p. 87). Under this, the human faculty of memory by association, which cannot be reduced to a form of automatic functioning, must be carefully cultivated (p. 88).

Learning to know calls for mastering the instruments of knowledge (p. 86). Such a process of learning should combine a sufficiently broad general knowledge with the opportunity to work in depth on a small number of subjects (p. 87).

Learning to know involves enabling each individual to understand at the very least enough about his or her environment to be able to live in dignity, to develop occupational skills and to communicate (p. 86).

It is vital for all children, wherever they may be, to acquire a knowledge of the scientific method in some appropriate form and become 'friends of science' for life. In secondary education, the initial training in science should be supplemented by instruments, concepts and references for scientific progress and contemporary paradigms (p. 87).

In teaching, right from the beginning, both the deductive and the inductive methods, i.e. the abstract and the concrete, should be combined.

(b) *Learning to do:* Learning to do is generally linked with the question of vocational training. The rationale for it arises from the fact that the future of industrial economies depends on their ability to transform advances in knowledge into innovation that generates new jobs (p. 89). The report underlines that learning to do includes not only acquiring occupational skill but also the competence to deal with many situations and work in teams. The ascendancy of knowledge and information as factors in the production system is making the idea of occupational skills obsolete and is moving personal competence to the fore. The employers are seeking competence not only through technical and vocational training but also through social behaviour, aptitude for team work and initiative and readiness to take risks. To these can be added the requirement of personal commitment on the part of the worker and his or her ability to become an agent for change (p. 89).

The dominance of the service sector in the economy has made it essential to cultivate human qualities that are not necessarily inculcated by traditional training and which calls for the ability to establish a stable and effective relationship between individuals (p. 90).

(c) *Learning to live together and with others*: This pillar or basic objective of learning calls for developing understanding of other people, a gradual discovery of others and acquiring experience of shared purposes throughout life. The Commission's report emphasizes that to know others, one must know oneself. The teaching of the history of religions and customs can serve a very useful purpose in this regard. Moreover, the formal education must provide enough time and opportunity in its programmes to involve the willing from the childhood in cooperative undertaking through participation in various cultural and social activities (pp. 93-94).

This pillar of learning should also include learning to manage conflicts in a spirit of respect for the values of pluralism, mutual understanding and peace. In this connection, the Commission recommends teaching non-violence in schools as a part of imparting such learning. The Commission also underlines that the spirit of competition and ambition inculcated by the present system of education militates against this pillar of learning.

(d) *Learning to be:* The purpose of 'learning to be' is to better develop one's personality so as to be able to act with greater autonomy in making judgements and assuming personal responsibility in life (p. 94).

The 'learning to be' enables each individual to discover himself and enrich his entire potential, i.e. "to reveal the treasure within each of us".

The report emphasizes that education through learning to be, must contribute to all-round development of each individual's mind and body, intelligence, sensitivity, aesthetic sense, personal responsibility and spiritual values. All human beings must be enabled to develop independent, critical thinking and form their own judgement, in order to determine for themselves what they believe they should do in the different circumstances of life. Essentially, it means giving people the freedom of thought, judgement, feeling and imagination. One of the specific suggestions made for inculcating 'learning to be' is teaching art and poetry in schools and attaching priority to oral cultural knowledge.

Broader Meaning and Purpose of Education

While elaborating its two most important recommendations, i.e. lifelong learning and four pillars of learning, the report makes some very perceptive remarks and far-reaching recommendation on the broader meaning and purpose of education. It says: "The central aim of education is the fulfilment of the individual as a social being". Education serves as a vehicle of culture and values, creates an environment where socialization can take place and is the melting-pot in which common purposes take shape (p. 53). The report continues: "Throughout the world, one purpose of education is to create social links between individuals on the basis of shared references" (p. 53).

Education "must enable people to understand themselves and to understand others through better understanding of the world" (p. 49). This purpose is served by education making individuals aware of their roots so as to give them points of reference that enable them to determine their place in the world. But it should also teach them respect for other cultures. Knowledge of other cultures leads to awareness of one's own culture as well as heritage common to all communities. "Understanding others thus makes possible a better knowledge of oneself" (p. 50). Education, therefore, must seek to engender a new humanism, one that contains essential ethical components and sets considerable store by knowledge of and respect for the cultures and spiritual values of different civilizations. The Chairperson's summarizing chapter highlights at some length, the moral aspects of education. It says: "There is every reason to place renewed emphasis on the moral and cultural dimensions of education, enabling each person to grasp the individuality of other people and understand the world's erratic progression towards a certain unity. But this process must begin with self-understanding through another voyage whose milestones are knowledge, meditation and the practice of self-criticism" (p. 19).

An important contribution of the report is the link it seeks to establish between education and democracy. It states that education has a very important role in fostering and giving deeper root to democracy. Tolerance and respect for other people is a pre-requisite for democracy. This should be a general and ongoing enterprise in educational institutions. Schools should facilitate the daily practice of tolerance by helping pupils to appreciate the points of others and by encouraging discussion of moral dilemmas or cases involving ethical choices (p. 60).

The report recommends that there should be civic education in the practice of citizenship. An essential part of it is instructing students in their rights and duties and also developing their social skills for team work (p. 61). Education should, therefore, prepare children for active participation in the life of the community (Ibid). The report states: "From an initial minimalist viewpoint the objective is simply learning to perform one's role in accordance with established sets of rules" (p. 62). This calls for civic instructions or imparting elementary political literacy as a part of basic education (p. 62). Thus, education for active and conscious citizenship must begin at school (p. 67).

In addition, the report makes the following important recommendations:

(a) Education systems must not lead to exclusion that happens when it is sought to be made merit-based, particularly at the primary level where the acquisition of minimum skills for every child is necessary (p. 57).

(b) The teaching system should be diversified in order to make it the primary base for continuing education (p. 58).

(c) Racial prejudices should be combated by exchange of information about the history and values of different cultures.

(d) Education systems should not emphasize only the development of abstract knowledge to the detriment of other faculties such as imagination, ability to communicate, leadership, a sense of duty, spiritual dimension of existence or manual skills (p. 56).

The Commission has grappled with some of the contentious issues which are at the centre of the debate on education for the new millennium. These include: basic education, role of teachers, the role of the state in education, globalization and education, and the implications of information and communication technology for education. In the following paragraphs, a brief summary of the findings and recommendations of the Commission is given on each of these issues.

Basic Education

Emphasizing the importance of basic education, the Commission states that "it is there that the spark of creativity may either spring into life or be extinguished, and that access to knowledge may or may not become a reality" (p. 115). In this context, the Commission establishes a link between learning throughout life and that at the stage of basic education. Elaborating on the foundation laid at this stage of education, the Commission states: "This is the time when we all acquire the instruments for the future development of our faculties of reason and imagination, our judgement and sense of responsibility, when we learn to be inquisitive about the world around us" (p. 116). The Commission recalls that it was indeed to this end that the international community pledged itself in the 1990 Jomtien Conference on Education For All. Given the importance of secondary education as a continuum of basic education, the Commission considers "that a similar commitment to secondary education should be written into the agenda of the major international conferences for the next century". However, while recognizing this continuum the Commission is backward looking when it comes to defining basic education. The definition given by it is "an initial education (formal or non-formal) extending in principle from around the age of 3 to at least age 12" (p. 118). Towards the end of the first decade of the new millennium, UNESCO convened an expert group to revisit the concept of basic education which defined it as an initial education preferably for 12 years and at the minimum for 10 years.

The Commission regards basic education "as an indispensable passport to life" that will enable people to choose what they do, to share in building their collective future and to continue to learn. Clarifying this further, the Commission states that basic learning needs "comprise both essential learning tools (such as literacy, oral expression, numeracy and problem solving) and the basic learning content (such as knowledge, skills, values and attitudes) required by human beings to be able to survive, to develop their full capacities and to live and work in dignity, to participate fully in development to improve the quality of their lives, to make informed decisions and to continue learning" (p. 119).

In its recommendations on this subject, the Commission urges the public authorities to examine a set of possibilities, including

- Careful school mapping to ensure that children do not have to travel too far.
- Establishing single sex schools or special facilities for girls in centers where parents keep girls out of school to prevent them from mixing with boys.
- Hiring more women teachers when the majority of the teachers are men.
- Providing school meals.
- Preparing school time-tables in such a way as to take into account children's family duties.
- Supporting non-formal programmes that involve parents and local organizations.
- Improving basic infrastructure, in particular access to clean water.

Moving to secondary education, the Commission focuses mainly on how education at this level can prepare citizens for lifelong education. Commission is emphatic in its view that such a preparation must begin at the stage of basic education itself. But, secondary education provides greater scope for preparing for lifelong education. A very important recommendation that the Commission makes in this regard is to universalize secondary education. In addition, the Commission discusses a few specific linkages between secondary education and lifelong education. These linkages should be established through diversity of courses, increased emphasis on the alternating of study and professional or social work, and attempts to improve quality (p. 126).

Teachers

The Commission makes some far-reaching comments and very important recommendations on the role of teachers in revamping the education system in order to meet the challenge of the new millennium. It states that the realization of the vision of learning throughout life will largely depend on teachers. For, teachers are instrumental in the development of attitudes to learning. They can awaken curiosity, stimulate independence, encourage intellectual rigour and create the conditions for success in formal and continuing education (p. 141). Jacques Delors in his summary states that for advancing to a learning society, "there is no substitute for the teacher-pupil relationship, which is underpinned by authority and developed through dialogue" (p. 21).

The Commission underlines that the role of teachers as an agent of change, promoting understanding and tolerance, has never been more obvious than today. And it is likely to become even more critical in the 21st century. "The need for change, from narrow nationalism to universalism, from ethnic and cultural prejudice to tolerance, understanding and pluralism, from autocracy to democracy in its various manifestations, and from a technologically divided world where high technology is the privilege of the few to a technologically united world, places enormous responsibilities on teachers who participate in the moulding of the characters and minds of the new generation (pp. 141-142).

The teachers face new challenges in the context of the changes taking place after the onset of the new phase of globalization. They have to make schools more appealing to children while implicitly providing them with a "user's guide' to the media. They have also to face the challenge posed by the fact that social environment can no longer be left behind at the school gates. Poverty, hunger, violence and drugs enter classrooms with the children, and can no longer be kept separate from the content of the curriculum (p. 143). Moreover, today communities increasingly expect to have a say in decisions concerning the organization of schooling. The Commission, therefore, recommends that teachers must adapt their relationship with learners, switching roles from 'soloist' to 'accompanist' and shifting the emphasis from dispensing information to helping learners seek, organize and manage knowledge, guiding them rather than moulding them. On the other hand, they need to display great firmness in relation to the fundamental values that should guide each individual's life" (p. 144).

The report highlights the fact that the teaching profession is one of the most highly organized in the world and teachers' organizations can and do play powerful roles in various fields. These organizations are, in many countries, essential participants in the dialogue between school and society. The report, therefore, considers that "it is possible and desirable to improve the dialogue between teachers' organizations and educational authorities" (p. 144). In this connection, the Commission asserts that "no reform has succeeded against teachers or without their participation" (p. 145).

While recommending that both distant learning and the new technologies and classrooms have proved to be effective, the report states that "the teacher remains the essential catalyst" (p. 145). The teacher's work is not confined simply to transmitting information or even knowledge. It also entails presenting that knowledge in the form of a statement of problems within a certain context and putting the problems into perspective" (p. 145).

"Teachers' great strength lies in the example they set, of curiosity, open-mindedness, willingness to put their assumption to the test and to acknowledge mistakes; most of all, they must transmit a love of learning" (p. 146).

One of the findings of the Commission was that for a variety of reasons, the quality of teachers has deteriorated. The reasons include, rapid increase in the world school population, limited financial resources, great deterioration in many cases of teachers' working conditions, and unpreparedness of the teachers, for lack of training and experience of teaching, to cater for pupils who have serious social and family difficulties (p. 146).

The Commission, therefore, recommended that, "improving the quality and motivation of teachers must be a priority in all countries" (p. 147). Moreover, special measures should be envisaged to recruit candidates from diverse linguistic and cultural backgrounds to enter teaching (p. 147). Further, closer attention "has to be paid to maintaining teachers' motivation in difficult situations" (p. 148) by improving their working conditions, training and self-education. Tthe Commission recommends that teachers' training "should at an early stage place emphasis on the four pillars of education discussed in the Report of the Commission". The Commission calls for upgrading of teachers' status, recognition by society of their position as masters in the classroom, recognition of the requirement to upgrade their knowledge and skills and the need for collaboration and partnership with families, industry and business, voluntary associations, people active in cultural life, etc.

The above observations and recommendations of the Commission on teachers are applicable to all societies and all economies—both rich and poor, developed and developing. At the same time, it must be recognized that some of the recommendations like training teachers from an early stage in the four pillars of education, though highly desirable, may not be relevant to the immediate problem of universalizing quality school education in developing countries.

Jacques Delors in his part of the report gives a very fitting reply to the current tendency to blame teachers for all the failures of the education system. He says: "We are asking a great deal, too much even, of teachers, when we expect them to make good the failings of other institutions which also have a responsibility for the education and training of young people. The demands made on teachers are considerable, at the very time when the outside world is increasingly encroaching upon the school, particularly through the new communication and information media" (pp. 29-30).

Role of the State in Education

The Commission in its report, particularly in the part written by its Chairperson, assigns the state a key role in spreading education among the people and preparing them for lifelong learning. The Chairperson asserts that "education is a public good and should be made available to all". He calls upon the policy makers to face squarely their responsibility in this regard. He says: "We cannot leave it to the market forces or to some kind of regulation to put things right when they go wrong" (p. 31). An important observation made by him in this regard is: "All the choices to be made should, in any event be predicated upon the fundamental principle of equality of opportunity" (p. 32). It is implied that the state alone can be held accountable for the application of this fundamental principle. This cannot be left to the vagaries of the market forces.

In the main report, the emphatic assertion made by the Chairperson, on the role of the state is somewhat diluted by mentioning such factors as the force of financial constraint, raising money from private sources, and involving the local community to meet a part of the financial requirement for school building and upkeep.

Globalization and Education

The report was written after the current phase of globalization had run its course for over a decade and a half and some of the negative sides of globalization had started becoming evident. The report graphically brings out these negative sides. It states that whereas worldwide economic, scientific, cultural and political interdependence is becoming ever more securely established (p. 39), because of economic interdependence, industrial crises of the most developed countries reverberate throughout the world (p. 41). Many countries are unable to participate in the process of globalization which makes the disparity between the winners and losers in the development game even more blatant (p. 42). Side by side, the knowledge gap is also widening which makes those deprived of knowledge cast adrift, far from where the action is (p. 42). Moreover, with economic globalization there is also cultural and social globalization; even crime is becoming globalized.

New technologies have brought humankind into the age of universal communication by abolishing distance. However, a very large underprivileged population remains excluded from these developments (p. 43). At the time of the writing of the Commission's report, large areas in the world were still without access to electricity and over half of the world's population had no access to various services available via telephone systems (p. 43). The report warns that "the major danger is that of a gulf opening up between the minority of people who are capable of finding their way successfully about this new world that is coming into being and the majority who feel that they are at the mercy of events and have no say in the future of the society, with the dangers that it entails of a setback to democracy and widespread revolt (p. 51).

Population growth, uprootedness associated with migration, breakdown of family life, uncontrolled urbanization, collapse of traditional neighbourhood solidarity and condemning many groups and individuals to isolation and marginalization in both developed and developing countries constitute the main components of the developing global social crisis. This crisis is compounded by a moral crisis and the spirit of violence and crimes.

The report also underlines that the nation state as it came to be defined in Europe in the 19th century is no longer the sole frame of reference.

In the above context, one of the essential tasks of education should be to help to transform *de facto* interdependence into a solidarity freely entered into. To that end, education must enable people to understand themselves and to understand others through better understanding of the world (p. 49).

The first step towards grasping the growing complexities of world events and combating the feeling of uncertainty it engenders is to acquire a body of knowledge and then learn to put the facts in perspective and adopt a critical approach to the flow of information (p. 49). There is obviously no way of understanding the world without understanding the relationship between human beings and their environment. Education should, therefore, seek to make individuals aware of their roots so as to give them a point of reference that enables them to determine their place in the world, but it should also teach them respect for other cultures (p. 49).

Information and Communication Technology has been one of the main drivers of the current phase of globalization. The Commission's views on this subject are bold and forward-looking. While recognizing the danger of its creating divides and disparities, it underlines that "The internet technology is vital for an understanding of our modern world as it is creating new forms of civilization and even new types of individual and collective identity (p. 64). It rightly anticipated that the negative side of the new technology can be exaggerated because progress in technology will itself enable the citizens of developing countries to link with the database and virtual laboratories in the developed countries. The Commission also anticipated that there would be a general fall in equipment costs which would enable developing countries to cross the infrastructural barriers. According to the Commission, the real difference will be between societies that will be capable of producing the content of information goods and those that will be merely receiving them. The Commission also anticipated that "the greatest cleavages are likely to occur within given societies." (p. 65). The Commission recommends that the full potential of the new information and communication technologies should be harnessed to serve education and training.

A Brief Critique of the Report

While analysing the main findings and recommendations of the report, it is important to bear in mind the setting in which the Commission was constituted and carried out its work. The Commission did its work mostly in the early 90s and submitted its report in 1996. It was the time when globalization and liberalization policies reflected in the Washington Consensus and other regimes set up during that period, had been widely accepted and reflected in the development strategies and policies adopted by most of the developing countries. That was also the time when as a part of the general trend of globalization and liberalization, the process of commodification or commercialization of education had started in several of these countries. In country after country in the developing world, under the influence of the Washington Consensus and the pressure of bilateral donors, education had been reduced to literacy; non-formal education imparted outside schools, had become common, and a large proportion of regular and trained teachers in schools had been replaced by para-teachers, part-time teachers or contract teachers. A number of the recommendations of the Commission, particularly in the areas of basic and secondary education, were influenced by this setting.

Another important characteristic of the report is that it is basically addressed to the challenges faced at that time—and continuing even today—by the developed countries in the field of education. Its main recommendations on lifelong learning and the four pillars of learning can be implemented only in those societies which have already laid the solid foundation of high quality basic and secondary education. This has been achieved mainly by developed countries. This essential pre-condition for lifelong learning does not prevail in most of the developing countries—the whole of South Asia including India, and the overwhelming majority of the African countries. The real challenge in these countries in the field of education is to universalize quality basic and secondary education. This calls for exercise of political will, reprioritization of public expenditure in favour of education, building of institutions, including legal framework, and massive mobilization of resources. The Commission has very little to offer on any of these burning issues of education in the developing world. All that it does is to go back to the Jomtien Declaration on basic education and recommend another Jomtien, in the form of a Declaration at the international level, on secondary education. The Commission does not ask the governments which have not so far universalized basic education, to do so within a time-bound framework and as a legal obligation. It does not try to make even a rough calculation of the resources that will be required for this purpose—overall, in terms of a percentage of GDP or percentage of public expenditure—and has not made any recommendation to the member states of UNESCO to commit themselves to make the resources in the required quantum available for universalizing quality school education.

For basic and secondary education where developing countries face the biggest challenge, the Commission has not thought it proper to lay down a set of minimum norms to be applied to all schools in this category. One of the toughest problems that developing countries face in education at this level is its extremely poor quality. And the problem of quality cannot be tackled effectively unless the countries concerned apply a minimum set of norms to all the elementary and secondary schools.

The Commission has undoubtedly made some specific suggestion as possibilities to be examined by the public authorities (p. 120). The norms implicit in these suggestions are meagre and fragmentary. Besides, these are made in a highly qualified manner in that the public authorities are urged "to examine a set of possibilities". The Commission has not brought its full authority to bear on these recommendations nor has it called upon the states concerned to undertake a commitment to apply a set of minimum norms within a time-bound framework. Moreover, some of the norms or the possibilities urged by the Commission, can really militate against universalization of quality basic and secondary education on a non-discriminatory basis. These include the Commission's support for non-formal programmes (p. 120) and using auxiliary teachers or para-teachers within the school system (p. 124). The Commission's recommendation that the school time-table should be adapted to take into account children's family duties (p. 120) carries the dangerous implication of justifying child labour for domestic services. On basic infrastructure, Commission has recommended (p. 120) only its improvement as though it already exists in all the schools in all respects. Under this recommendation, the Commission singles out access to "clean water" as though other items like provision of separate toilets for boys and girls, adequate sitting facilities, availability of laboratory facilities and teaching aides are already available in all the schools. These are of equal, if not greater, importance than access to clean water.

It is also not surprising and again a reflection of the trend of commercialization of education at the time when the Commission carried out its work, that there is not even a mention of, let alone a recommendation for the adoption of a common school system by developing countries, which has been mainly responsible for bringing developed countries to their present position of economic prosperity and power.

The Commission has not even taken a serious note of the fact that in most developing countries with pluralistic societies and unequal distribution of incomes and assets, the education system is characterized by the worst forms of discrimination which perpetuates the overall social inequality and discrimination. Under the influence of the World Bank, other international agencies and bilateral donors, the Commission has in fact recommended the continuation of practices like non-formal education, and para-teachers in the name of the involvement of the community, which have the effect of perpetuating and aggravating the prevailing social inequality and discrimination. For, they are mainly the children of the poor and the marginalized who are condemned to the very inferior non-formal education imparted outside school by para-teachers and part-time teachers.

Measures for International Cooperation

The Commission made mainly three recommendations for broadening international cooperation in the field of education. These are:

(a) A quarter of development assistance should be earmarked for investment in education.

(b) Debt swaps should be encouraged in order to offset the adverse effect of adjustment policies and policies for the reduction of domestic and foreign deficits, on educational spending.

(c) A UNESCO Observatory should be set up to look into the new information technologies, their evolution and their foreseeable impact on not only education systems but also on modern societies.

These recommendations are very limited and not of much significance in changing the educational scenario in developing countries. Moreover, it is more than 20 years when these recommendations were made and still none of them has been implemented except in a token manner. Foreign funding constitutes a very small proportion of the expenditure that developing countries are required to make for universalizing basic and secondary education. Even if the recommendation of earmarking 25 per cent of this funding had materialized, it would have made only a marginal difference to the availability of overall resources that developing countries need to invest in the field of education. It may be argued that the purpose of earmarking is to give an incentive to developing countries to attach higher priority to education in the allotment of their development resources. However, there is minimal evidence to show that sectoral earmarking of external resources for development has had any significant impact on changing development priorities in favour of these sectors. In fact, what the developing countries need from external sources is additional resources for development. Earmarking does not necessarily ensure additionality.

The experience with debt swaps for reduction of poverty and the protection of environment has not been encouraging during the past few decades when such swaps have been carried out. In fact, very few cases of such swaps have been taken up. Besides, as in the environment and other fields, debt swaps for education carry the danger of the intrusion of the private players including foreign private companies, in the field of education. This, among others, goes against one of the principal recommendations of the Report, that is, education is a public good and policy makers must face squarely their responsibility to make it available to all.

Distinction Between Information and Knowledge

The part of the report containing the Chairperson's summary underlines that information and knowledge are two different things. Unlike information, knowledge requires effort, concentration, discipline and determination. This very valid distinction between information and knowledge was brought out by Swami Vivekananda over a century ago in the following verse:

Yatha khar chandanbharwahi
Bharasyavetta,na tu chandansya

(Those who take information as knowledge are like the donkey under the load of sandalwood, who knows only of the load and not of the sandalwood).

ENDNOTES

1. All the page numbers cited in this paper are from the Report to UNESCO of the International Commission on Education for the Twenty-First Century, under the title, *Learning: the Treasure Within*, published by UNESCO in a pocketbook edition in 1998 and 2010.

5

Kothari Commission Report (1964-66)

Poornima M.

The destiny of India is being shaped in her classrooms and education determines the level of prosperity, welfare and security of the people.

—*Education Commission, 1964-66*

Introduction

As noted by the Education Commission of India way back in the 1960s, the well-being of people depends on the kind of education that is imparted to them. Thus education is an indispensable tool for personal and social development, thereby contributing to the holistic development of an individual and its nation. It is important to strategically design the powerful instrument of education because of the great prospects it offers for enhancing the quality of life. In view of the strategic importance of education, the Directive Principles of the Constitution included the provision to impart free and compulsory education to all children up to the age of 14 years. Further, India pursued its commitment to educational goals also by virtue of being the signatory to various international instruments on education right from the Jomtien framework on 'Education for All' to the recent framework of Sustainable Development Goals (SDGs). However, in spite of emphasizing the importance of education repeatedly, the successive governments of India have not displayed the required seriousness in bringing the constitutional obligation into reality.

In such a context, where there is an immense gap between the policy framework and action for implementing the vision, it is critical to revisit some of the seminal documents which have analysed the broader purpose and vision of education in the context of the current challenges. It is in this backdrop that this chapter revisits the landmark vision document, the Report of the Education Commission, 1964-66, popularly known as the Kothari Commission Report that made key recommendations for revamping the education system of India. To this day, the Report of the Commission holds a place of significance because of the long-term perspective in which it is set; the approach followed by the Commission in linking education with national development; its richness in drawing upon the experience and ideas of both national and international educational thinkers; and its coming up with comprehensive recommendations covering the entire education system at all levels.

Though the Commission made its recommendations on the different levels of education, in this chapter, the summary and analysis is restricted to school education. The chapter is divided into 4 sections: the current section setting the context for the paper, Section II presenting an overview of the recommendations of the Kothari Commission on school education, Section III containing comments on the implementation of the key recommendations over the years and Section IV reflecting on the reasons for the failure in realizing the educational vision projected in this document.

II

Overview of the Education Commission, 1964-66

The Education Commission was constituted in 1964 and it came up with its Report in 1966. The great significance of the Commission and its recommendation derives from the following factors. Firstly, this Commission was the first of its kind in India that made a comprehensive analysis of the education sector as a whole, while previous Commissions had focused only on specific areas such as University Education, Secondary Education, etc. The approach of the Commission in making a holistic analysis of education without segmenting it is really commendable (Naik, 1982). The report thus covered within its ambit, the entire system of education, though it did not cover medical and legal education. Secondly, the Commission looked at education mainly as an instrument of national development. This signifies that human resources as embodied in education must be developed if national objectives in the economic and social fields are to be realized. In this sense, the Commission reflects the views of Schultz (1971) who stated that investment in education would lead to human capital formation essential for economic development. In contemporary times, a linkage of this thesis can be found with the views of Dreze and Sen (1996) who have underlined that the intrinsic and instrumental values that education offers, directly contribute to socio-economic development and to the widening of choices and opportunities of individuals in a society. Thirdly, the analysis and the suggestions of the Commission are enriched because of its having pooled in the views of both national and international educational thinkers. In order to make a thorough analysis of various aspects of education, the Commission set up 12 Task Forces and 7 Working Groups[1], involving resource persons from various backgrounds and both from India and abroad. In this process, renowned educators from USA, UK, and Japan, France and USSR and experts from UNESCO were consulted by the Commission. Fourthly, as highlighted by Tilak (2007), considering the backdrop of political flux in which the Commission worked, its courage in coming out with far-reaching recommendations is really noteworthy. And finally, the most important feature of this Report is its emphasis on the 'equalization of educational opportunity' and in this context its approbation of the 'Common School System', which is best designed to eliminate the inequality and discrimination in the Indian school system.

The mandate of the Education Commission was to advise the government on the national system of education at all stages and in all aspects. The Commission did full justice to this mandate in its recommendations. The Commission's Report highlighted the need to bring about major improvements in primary education; introduce work-experience as an integral element of general education; vocationalize secondary education; improve the quality of teachers at all levels; and provide teachers in sufficient strength (Government of India, 1966).

The Report is divided into three parts. The first part of the report discusses the general aspects of education. The second part covers school education, higher education, agriculture, technical and vocational education and adult education. The third part deals with the problems of implementation which include educational planning, administration and finance. Table 1 gives a picture of the key aspects of school education covered by the Commission.

Table 1: Key Aspects Covered by the Education Commission (1964-66) on School Education

S. No.	Chapters	Key Aspects Covered
1.	Chapter 1: Educational and National Objectives	• Transforming education to meet the needs and aspirations of the people • Increasing productivity by focusing on science education, work experience and vocationalization of education • Mother Tongue as the medium of education in schools • Modernization of education to suit rapid change • Inculcation of social, moral and spiritual values in schools
2.	Chapter 2: Educational System: Structure and Standards	• Lengthening the duration of higher secondary by two years • Norms and standards related to education
3.	Chapter 3: Teacher Status	• Fixing of pay scales for teachers • Provision for teacher recruitment and promotional prospects • Parity in retirement benefits and work and service conditions of teachers • Employment of women teachers at all levels • Recognition to the professional organization of teachers and Joint Teachers' Council
4.	Chapter 4: Teacher Education	• Adequate financial provision for teachers' professional development • Removing isolation in teacher training in schools and universities • Improving the quality of teacher education by integrating general and professional courses in education, improving teaching and evaluation methods and revising curricula • Standardization of the duration of training

Contd...

S. No.	Chapters	Key Aspects Covered
		• Improving the quality and facilities of training institutions • Maintenance of standards in teacher education
5.	Chapter 5: Enrolment and Manpower	• National Enrolment Policy o Providing free and compulsory education of 7 years duration to every child; providing higher secondary education to those who are willing o Equalizing educational opportunities and eliminating glaring inequalities • Estimating manpower requirements for educated manpower and the corresponding development of vocational education • Enrolment policy in secondary education • Educational expansion based on manpower requirements • Employment to every graduate based on his degree or diploma
6.	Chapter 6: Equalization of Educational Opportunities	• Tuition fee free education and abolition of fees in government, local authority and private schools at primary level • Tuition fee free education to all needy and deserving at higher secondary level and free studentship to the extent of 30 per cent of enrolment • Free textbooks and writing material at primary level • Scholarships at all levels on an equitable and egalitarian basis • Development of educational tools to meet differential needs of handicapped children • Reducing regional imbalances by equalizing educational development in different states and districts • Education of women, backward classes (SCs) and tribal people, by reducing gender gap, expanding educational facilities, establishing ashram schools and adopting tribal language as the medium of education

Contd...

S. No.	Chapters	Key Aspects Covered
7.	Chapter 7: School Education : Problems of Expansion	• Development of pre-primary education by establishing pre-primary centres at district level, having play centres as part of primary schools, developing flexible programmes with play and learning activities • Expansion of primary education by providing free and compulsory education, reducing wastage and stagnation, providing short vocational courses • Providing a lower primary school within a distance of 1 mile and upper primary school within 1-3 miles from home • Improve retention and reduce stagnation by adopting play-way techniques and part-time education • Planned expansion of secondary schools and vocational education and accelerated expansion of girls' education at secondary stage
8.	Chapter 8: School Curriculum	• Freedom for schools to experiment with new curricula and formation of subject teachers' association to stimulate experimentation • Common curriculum of general education for 10 years with diversification of studies at higher secondary stage • Systematic teaching methods and enrichment programmes for talented children • Adoption of three-language formula • Teaching of mathematics, science, social studies, physical education and education in moral values and creative activities like art education and extra-curricular activities • Work experience—simple handwork at lower primary, craft in upper primary, workshop in secondary and work experience at higher secondary stage • No differentiation of curricula on the basis of sex

Contd...

S. No.	Chapters	Key Aspects Covered
9.	Chapter 9: Teaching Methods, Guidance and Evaluation	• Improvement in teaching and evaluation method by reducing the rigidity of the educational system • Diffusion of new practices to schools and skilled help to teachers to try innovations • Sophisticated forms of newer techniques should be tried out, for instance radio talks • Provision of guidance and counselling at primary and secondary stage • Attention on underachievers and remedial programmes for them • Focus on continuous evaluation process and adopting new approach to evaluation • Comprehensive internal assessment that evaluates all aspects of student growth • Right of selected establishments to establish experimental schools and frame their own curricula, textbooks and educational activities
10.	Chapter 10: Administration and Supervision	• Creation of common school system of public education • Measures to overcome weakness of government and local authority schools: engaging local representatives in schools and providing greater freedom to schools • Taking over or elimination of not so well-managed private schools • Adoption of the concept of neighbourhood schools at lower primary level • Improvement of physical facilities of schools through community cooperation • Separation of administration and supervision; the District School Board to deal with the former and the District Education Officer with the latter • Establishment of educational boards at the national and state level and prescribing the role of the central government • Legislation for compulsory registration of all educational institutions and the running of unregistered institutions, i.e. unrecognized schools, being declared an offence

Contd...

S. No.	Chapters	Key Aspects Covered
11.	Chapter 18: Educational Planning and Administration	• A redefinition of the role of different players, viz. Centre, state, private enterprise, local authorities, and other administrative units at the central, state and local levels. • Reflection on the role of NCERT, educational secretariat, Directorate of Education, Indian Educational Services, etc.
12.	Chapter 19: Educational Finance	• Proportion of GNP allocated to education should rise from 2.9 per cent in 1965-66 to 6 per cent in 1985-86 • Strategy on allocation of funds in the first two decades • Mobilization of resources from local communities, voluntary organizations and local authorities, apart from government funding • Grant-in-aid from state to zila parishads and municipalities • Role of Centre in financing

Source: Compilation based on Education Commission, 1964-66.

From Table 1, it can be observed that the Commission has made path-breaking recommendations on almost all the major aspects of education. The Commission had prepared a blueprint of education development, which was to be implemented in a phased manner in the next two decades. However, the different parts of the report elicited a different response. While some recommendations received wide recognition, there were others that were not given much consideration. J.P. Naik, the Member Secretary of the Commission, had later classified the recommendations of the Commission into 4 categories as: the recommendations that received wide attention, those that received limited attention, those that were opposed and finally, 'other recommendations' that were either ignored, rejected or were found to be useless. His classification also highlights the set of recommendations that were implemented imperfectly and others that had become outdated owing to the lapse of time (Naik, 1982). However, beyond all these good, bad or indifferent responses to the recommendations, they remain valid because of the vision and the commitment that inspired them.

III

Reflection on Key Recommendations of the Kothari Commission in the Current Context

(i) Common School System (CSS) of Public Education

The Commission highlighted the need to have a common school system mainly for the purpose of eliminating the prevailing inequality and discrimination in the school education system whereby the children of the masses received sub-standard education, while those of the rich and middle classes received education of their choice, thus increasing social segregation. Based on an analysis of the practice that existed in the USA, USSR and Scandinavian countries, the Commission recommended a common school system in India for the first time. The vision of the Commission on CSS was that:

- The schooling system should be open to all children irrespective of caste, creed, religion, community, social status, economic conditions, etc.
- The access to good education should depend on talent rather than on wealth or class.
- CSS will maintain adequate standards in all schools, in which no tuition fee will be charged and which will meet the needs of average parents, so that they do not feel the need to send their children to expensive schools.

(Government of India, 1966).

The Commission made a powerful case for establishing a common school system in India. However, this was not reflected in its recommendations on the subject. The Commission suggested the implementation of CSS in selected districts on an experimental basis. The outcome of this half-hearted approach was that when the National Education Policy came to be formulated, CSS did not find a place among the major components of the Policy. Later in the 1990s and the early 2000s, the objective of establishing CSS became a major theme of the movement for advocacy for reforming the school education, mounted by civil society organizations and public intellectuals in the country. A National Campaign Committee for a common school system was established which remained active till the end of the 2000s decade. A significant outcome of this campaign was the commitment publicly announced by the Chief Minister of Bihar for establishing a common school system in the state and his subsequent decision to establish a Commission on a Common School System in Bihar under the Chairmanship of Professor Muchkund Dubey, to prepare a phased plan for the implementation of such a system in the state. The Commission completed its task and submitted its Report within nine months after its establishment and recommended a year-wise plan for a period of nine years to establish a common school system in the state. However, the Government of Bihar could not muster the political will to implement the recommended system and the recommendations of the Commission, like those of several others on the subject of education, were quietly shelved.

(ii) Equalization of Educational Opportunities

The Kothari Commission in its report observed that "one of the important social objectives of education is to equalize opportunity, enabling the backward or underprivileged classes and individuals to use education as a lever for the improvement of their condition. Every society that values social justice ... must ensure progressive equality of opportunity to all sections....and this is the only guarantee for the building up of an egalitarian and human society in which the exploitation of the weak will be minimized" (Government of India, 1966). Contrary to the Commission's observation, the stark reality is that only a small privileged minority is able to access the education of their choice and live a parasitic life based on the exploitation of the masses, while the bulk of the people are deprived of education (Naik, 1982). While the children of the rich and the elite access good quality private and special type of public schools, the children of the vast majority of the poor, including the minorities and marginalized can afford only government schools which are in shambles. The preliminary findings of an ongoing study by the Council for Social Development in the states of Karnataka, Rajasthan, Tamil Nadu and Uttar Pradesh highlight the differential access to school education in terms of gender, social groups, religion and income status.

(iii) Universalization of Education

One of the key recommendations of the Commission was universalization of elementary education (UEE). Naik (1982) regards this measure as a programme of transformation, as its impact could be fundamental and far-reaching. The major reason cited is that it would break the *status quo* where education has been the privilege of only the upper and middle class. Interventions such as UEE can bring about a radical change in the situation, where the education system is taken to the masses instead of to the classes (ibid.). UEE has been on the agenda of the country right from the Fourth and Fifth Five Year Plan, partly due to India subscribing to UNESCO's goal of Education for All (EFA). Subsequently the government initiated the *Sarva Shiksha Abhiyan* (SSA) and much later the *Rashtriya Madhyamik Shiksha Abhiyan* (RMSA), ostensibly to universalise primary and secondary education. However, as observed by Dubey (2011), universalizing school education remains a distant goal due to the inadequacy of access, lack of quality, discrimination and underfunding of school education. For instance, regarding access, though there are progressively rising figures of gross enrolment ratio (GER), when the figures of attendance and drop-out rates are looked at, it becomes clear that a sizeable number of children are still deprived of education. Attendance is found to be at least 25 per cent below enrolment and the dropout rates are exorbitantly high. The net result is that a substantial proportion of children in the school-going age are still out of school (Dubey, 2011).

(iv) Free and Compulsory Education of Children

In line with the Constitutional commitment of the country to provide free and compulsory education to all children till they complete the age of 14 years, the Kothari Commission recommended that at least 7 years of free and compulsory education should be provided to every child, so as to equalize educational opportunities and eliminate glaring inequalities. The country could not implement the Constitutional provisions for 50 years after the promulgation of the Constitution. Ultimately the Union Parliament enacted the Right of Children to Free and Compulsory Education Act in 2009, which came into force from April 1, 2010. Even though the five-year recommendation period of the Act was over in April 2015, most of the provisions of the Act remained unimplemented. Besides, the Act suffers from a number of glaring deficiencies some of which are listed below:

(i) The Act excludes from its scope the education of children at the pre-primary and secondary levels.

(ii) It does not prescribe imparting education through the medium of the mother tongue without which it will never be possible to eliminate the inequality and discrimination characterizing the present school education system.

(iii) The Act does not provide for the creation of an autonomous mechanism for monitoring its implementation, suggesting improvement in the system, and functioning as the last Court of Appeal for grievances.

(iv) The norms prescribed in the Act are inadequate and skimpy.

(v) The Act does not include a financial memorandum, legally committing the government to provide all the resources required for implementing the Act within the prescribed time limit.

(v) Teacher Components

The Kothari Commission had made solid recommendations on various aspects of teacher status and teacher education. The concerns of teachers relating to their remuneration, retirement benefits and the conditions of work were covered in the Commission's recommendation. It recommended a national scale of pay for teachers and suggested that the principle of parity and uniformity across the government, local authority and private schools should be followed with respect to the salary of teachers and their recruitment and working conditions. An important recommendation of the Commission in this regard was that, "the practice of recruiting teachers with lower qualifications and recruiting qualified teachers with lower pay should be abandoned" (Government of India, 1966). Similarly, the Commission highlighted the significance of teacher education and stated that adequate financial provision should be made available for professional development of teachers. The recommendations of the Commission in this regard included such aspects as breaking the isolation in teacher education, improving the quality of training institutions and maintaining the standards of teacher education.

In the current context, though some of the concerns related to teachers have been addressed, many others still remain unattended. For instance, though the pay, remuneration and conditions of work of government school teachers are regulated, the working conditions of private school teachers are precarious. In an ongoing study by the Council for Social Development on the reach of private schools in India, the plight of teachers in the private schools of Tamil Nadu has been brought out wherein many of the female teachers remain unpaid, even during maternity. Hence, some teachers are forced to re-join the school in two or three weeks to protect their job. On the whole, as observed by Batra (2005), while teachers require a supportive environment and atmosphere to carry out their responsibilities, the reality is more complex, wherein most school teachers of India are under-trained, unqualified, under-compensated and highly demotivated.

(vi) Curriculum, Teaching Methods and Evaluation

Regarding curriculum and teaching methods, the Kothari Commission observed that rigid curricula and teaching methods were followed, making education boring. It recommended that such rigidity should be broken by introducing new educational practices. The report also expressed its concern on bookish knowledge and rote learning in the existing system, which left less scope for practical activities and experiences. The Report thus highlighted the need for an upgraded curriculum that focused on the development of useful skills and the inculcation of the right kind of interests, attitudes and values. The Commission further stated that teachers should be given the freedom to experiment with a new curriculum and try innovations and use sophisticated forms of newer techniques to impart education. On evaluation, the Commission recommended the process of continuous evaluation and also comprehensive internal assessment that evaluated the overall aspects of a student's growth.

Somewhat on the lines of these recommendations, the National Curriculum Framework of 2005 was designed which is child-centric and gives primacy to children's experiences, their voices, and their active participation (NCERT, 2005). Even the

Right to Education Act 2009 incorporated a number of child-friendly provisions, including dispensing with examinations up to Class 8 and replacing them with the continuous and comprehensive evaluations, doing away with corporal punishments, etc. While a lot has been said and done in terms of policies and programmes towards 'joy of learning' or 'child-centred learning', in terms of actual implementation in schools, there is a mismatch between the legal provisions and actual practice. It can be observed that the practices in most of the schools are largely centralized, examination-oriented, with inflexible daily schedule and rigid syllabi (Mehrotra, 2007). Similarly, in terms of teacher autonomy, though the Commission recommended providing space to the teachers to try out innovation, in practice, the autonomy of teachers is restricted and they are considered a taken-for-granted vehicle to implement the policies of the government, without having the right to create or initiate reforms on their own (Stacki, 2002). Similarly, as far as evaluation is concerned, the Right to Education Act, 2009 stipulated continuous and comprehensive evaluation (CCE) of the child's understanding of knowledge and his or her ability to apply the same (Government of India, 2009). As pointed out by Nawani (2013), such assessment measures should not be an isolated technique and the real essence will be diluted if it is not backed by concomitant changes in the classroom culture. Further, to implement it in the real sense, it is not sufficient if teachers are just trained, but empowering them in all aspects related to teaching, learning and assessing is critical (Nawani, 2013).

(vii) Three-Language Formula

The Commission stated that a language policy should be developed to promote national and social integration. The Commission was of the view that the mother tongue should have a claim as the medium of education at the school level. It also recommended a modified three-language formula, which should include the mother tongue or regional language, the official language of the Union so long as it exists and a modern Indian or European language (Government of India, 1966). The Commission also observed that Hindi alone, as a link language, can be the official language of the Union in the future. However, such a view, for a federal set-up like India, where different languages are spoken, requires deeper reflection and further consideration.

(viii) Financing of Education

With respect to financing of education, the Commission observed that meagre resources were spread thinly over a very large area, leading to considerable wastage. Hence the approach suggested by the Commission was to concentrate on a few crucial programmes. The major recommendation of the Commission was that the proportion of GDP allocated to education should be increased from 2.9 per cent in 1965-66 to 6 per cent in 1985-86. The Commission also recommended the allocation of two-thirds of the available resources for education to school education and one-third to higher education in the next two-three decades. It further stated that in the next ten years (1965-1975), incurring larger expenditure on upgradation of teachers' salaries, transferring pre-university courses from university to school stage, providing five years of effective education to all children and vocationalizing secondary education should be accorded priority (Government of India, 1966). For the decade from 1975-76, resource allocation should prioritize seven years of effective schooling and vocationalization of education. And after 1985, the Commission stated, the focus should be on the development of higher education.

In spite of the Commission's well-considered phased approach in dealing with the issue of financing education, the Indian education system continues to suffer largely due to underfunding of education, as can be noted from the budgetary allocation over the years. Though allocation of 6 per cent of GDP, as stipulated by the Commission, has been reiterated and promised in various policy documents and political party manifestos, we are yet to touch the proportion of 6 per cent and the allocation made so far has been roughly between 3 to 4 per cent of GDP. Even the RTE Act failed to include a Financial Memorandum, indicating the exact amount of resources required and committed by the government for giving effect to the Act (Dubey, 2010).

Tilak (2007) argues that attempts are made constantly to misinterpret the facts with respect to financing and quantitatively under-define the goals to cover up our dismal failure to allocate sufficient resources. He further states that the allocation to education is not determined by the level of economic development, but rather by the political will (ibid).

Reasons for the Gap Between the Vision and the Ground Reality

The vision of the Kothari Commission has not been translated into reality even after 50 years of the submission of the Report of the Commission. There is, thus, an immense gap between the vision and reality on the ground. The following are some of the factors which explain this:

- *Piecemeal Approach*: While the recommendations of the Commission and, for that matter the approach of the Right of Children to Free and Compulsory Education Act, 2009, are holistic, government has pursued them in a piecemeal fashion (Naik 1982 and Tilak 2007).
- *Major Shift in Government Policy*: The adoption by the Government of India in the early 1990s of a development strategy based on reliance on market forces and private participation has been a major factor behind the continuation and the widening of the gap between the vision and reality. The Commission had recommended that the state should assume full responsibility for providing education, while private players should have a minor role. It had further suggested that the government should oversee the management of private schools and those that are not managed in public interest should be eliminated or taken over by the government. The policy since the adoption of the neo-liberal approach to development has been just the opposite of this recommendation of the Commission. Today one has reached a point where the three-year action agenda recommended by the Niti Ayog prescribes the handing over of non-performing government schools to private players and exploring other avenues such as education vouchers and local government led purchasing of schooling services, in order to deal with "hollowing" of state-run schools (Government of India 2017).
- *Lack of Political Will*: The lack of political will in prioritizing education has undoubtedly been a major factor behind the deviation from the vision. This was highlighted by Naik as far back as in 1982 when he stated that the laid back approach of the leadership has contributed to the poor implementation of educational programmes. Amartya Sen and Jean Dreze (2003) pointed out that the main reason for the neglect of education in India has been that the children or their parents as a group do not constitute a political lobby. Even though in implementing the

recommendations of the Kothari Commission, the government did not follow a holistic approach of the Commission, it did formulate important programmes like the National Literacy Mission, *Sarva Shiksha Abhiyan*, etc. But these could not be implemented mainly because of lack of political will.

• *Gap Between the Vision and Strategies*: There is sufficient evidence to conclude that whereas the approach of the visionaries was holistic and long term and called for a change in paradigm, those who prepared the strategy for implementing the vision adopted an *ad hoc*, fragmentary, short-term and status quo approach. This is quite clear when one compares the Kothari Commission Report with the 1968 and 1986 National Education Policies.

ENDNOTES

1. The 12 task forces were on school education, higher education, technical education, agricultural education, adult education, science education and research, teacher training and teacher status, student welfare, new techniques and methods, manpower, educational administration and educational finance.

   The 7 working groups were on women's education, education of backward classes, school buildings, school community relations, statistics, pre-primary education and school curriculum.

REFERENCES

Batra, P. (2005). Voice and Agency of Teachers: Missing Link in National Curriculum Framework 2005. *Economic and Political Weekly, 40*(40), 4347-56.

Dreze, J. and Sen, A. (1996). *India: Economic Development and Social Opportunities.* New Delhi: Oxford University Press.

Dreze, J. and Sen, A. (2003). 'Basic Education as a Political Issue'. In Tilak, J.B.G , *Education, Society and Development: National and International Perspectives*, New Delhi: NIEPA & APH Publishing Corporation.

Dubey, M. (2007). Roadmap of a Common School System in Bihar. *Economic and Political Weekly, 42*(29), 2999-3005.

Dubey, M. (2010). The Right of Children to Free and Compulsory Education Act, 2009: The Story of a Missed Opportunity. *Social Change,* 40(1), 1-13.

Dubey, M. (2011). Universalizing School Education: A Missed Opportunity. In M. Mohanty, *India Social Development Report 2010: The Land Question and the Marginalized* (pp. 80-87). New Delhi: Oxford University Press.

Government of India. (1966). *Report of the Education Commission 1964-66: Education and National Development*. New Delhi: Government of India: Ministry of Education.

Government of India. (2009). *The Right of Children to Free and Compulsory Education Act 2009*. New Delhi: Ministry of Human Resources Development.

Government of India. (2017). *India: Three Year Action Agenda - 2017-18 to 2019-20*. New Delhi: NITI Aayog.

Mehrotra, D.P. (2007). Origins fo Alternative Education in India: A Continuing Journey. In K. Raj, S. Vittachi, and N. Raghavan, *Alternative Schooling in India* (pp. 25-44). New Delhi: Sage.

Naik, J. (1982). *The Education Commission and After*. New Delhi: Allied Publishers Private Limited.

Nawani, D. (2013). Continuously and Comprehensively Evaluating Children. *Economic and Political Weekly, 48*(2), 33-40.

NCERT (2005). *National Curriculum Framework, 2005*. New Delhi: NCERT.

Pankaj, A. and Poornima, M. (forthcoming). Unequal Access to Elementary Education in India: Government vs Private Schools. In T. Haque, and Reddy, Narasimha, *India Social Development Report 2018: Rising Inequalities in India*. New Delhi: Oxford University Press.

Schultz, T.W. (1971). *Investment in Human Capital: The Role of Education and of Research*. New York: Free Press.

Stacki, S. (2002). *Women Teachers Empowered in India: Teacher Training Through a Gender Lens*. New York: UNICEF.

Tilak, J.B. (2007). The Kothari Commission and Financing of Education. *Economic and Political Weekly*, 42(10), 874-882.

6

Historical Context of the Kothari Commission Report (1964-66)

Sadhna Saxena

The Kothari Commission Report, as it is popularly known after the name of its Physicist Chairperson, remains a subject of intense debates in educational circuits and universities even after 53 years. Major committees have been set up after the Kothari Commission to deliberate upon different aspects of education covered in the report and make further recommendations on them. On the whole, this remains one of the most comprehensive reports on education and almost a turning point in the history of Indian education. However, to discern the vision of the report, it is important to understand the historical, economic and cultural context of the report. In the popular perception, the report is known for some of its major recommendations such as allocation of 6 per cent of GDP to education, common school system, university autonomy, and proper recruitment and remuneration of teachers to attract talented people to this profession. The other issues generally discussed with regard to the report include the concept of school complexes, importance of university-school linkages, three-language formula, vocationalization of education, thrust on national and emotional integration and national development through science and technology. These constitute the popular perception of the Kothari Commission Report. However, at a deeper level, the Commission created a rigid binary of modern and traditional (or backward) where traditional citizens were assumed to be non-rational who hamper the national development. Commenting on this, Jain (2009) says that this perspective , "failed to see that ideological conflicts arise from different perspectives of social ordering and priorities and are shaped by interests and games of power" (244). Interestingly, the recommendations of the report are part of the curriculum of education courses in universities but rarely, there is formal engagement with the issues of the historical context and ideological underpinnings of the Commission's report.

Therefore, the popular discourse remains fragmented as focus on recommendations does not help in constructing a larger vision which underlies the Commission's work. This approach does not throw light on how the Commission perceived the problems of that period and how it sought their solutions through education. The following were some of the most important national issues of the 1960s in the context of which the Commission carried out its work:

Firstly, the English-speaking ruling elite was keen to propagate the US-inspired strategy of agricultural modernization based on modern technology. This became so important in the Kothari Commission Report that the concept like basic education got completely sidelined. The focus shifted from social sciences, village industries, handicrafts, etc. which were the constituents of basic education, to science and technology, modernization of agriculture and industrialization for which 'army' of scientists and engineers were required. The education system, therefore, was required to set up engineering and agricultural universities instead of devoting maximum resources to school education.

Secondly, the report's title is Education and National Development. And the model of development that unfolds as one reads through the report is the model of development as pursued at that point of time by the developed world. In fact, in the report there is an anxiety about lagging behind almost by 200 years, the developed world.

Thirdly, in the 1960s one of the big challenges in political life had to do with the ongoing resistance against the forces working against economic pressure from the World Bank and the United States on an already deeply indebted economy. Large landowners constituted a major component of social forces which had been working for some time to undermine the weak but significant moves made in the 1950s, towards making distribution of land more equitable. These moves had two main objectives—social transformation, and improvement of agricultural productivity. Of the more than 70 per cent of the population dependent on land at that time, one-third was landless, and half the people who owned land had less than an acre. The abolition of the *Zamindari* system and imposition of land ceilings were two major steps that had been taken at that time to change the distribution of land. However, the delay in implementation and in the process the legal loopholes brought out, actually worked in favour of the land owners. In this context, Kumar (1996) wrote, "While in the earlier period, technical solutions to the agrarian question and problems had to compete with the socio-political solutions of redistribution of land, by this time politics and economics of technology-based change in agriculture as a solution to food scarcity had taken precedence over options challenging dominance of rural landed gentry (2368)."

Fourthly, the problem of food insecurity was an important context, which is mentioned in the Kothari Commission Report, along with the American pressure to resolve this by following American agro-technologies. Food security was undoubtedly a major issue. How does a country resolve the issue was also one of the important issues discussed at that point of time and that was reflected in the Kothari Commission Report as well. The publication in 1962 of *Silent Spring*, by Rachel Carson in America, gave rise to unprecedented public debate in that country on the degradation of the environment due to the use of chemicals in agriculture. The adverse publicity and legislative action generated by the debate made American fertilizers and pesticides companies intensify their search for foreign markets. India offered a highly suitable place for the operation of the American agro-business, based largely on the use of chemical fertilizers and pesticides. Given the rising demand for food following the growing population, and the consequent apprehensions of famines, the Indian elite was looking for precisely these kinds of solutions. And even though there was a general shortage of skilled personnel, we had enough trained manpower that could, after some further training be deployed for implementing programmes for increasing food production based on the so-called new technology. Above all, India had a vast farming sector waiting to be penetrated by countless forms of modernization. Agricultural universities at that time were set up after the model of America's land-grant universities and they had actually started initiating the process of reshaping Indian agriculture under American guidance. So, in the context of food scarcity, the approach to modernization of agriculture in India, that the Kothari Commission Report talks about, got decided on the basis of the American agro-based industry's need for markets; completely overlooking the reasons why the industry needed to do that in the first place. This ushered in the era of the green revolution, completely foreclosing the possibility of any alternatives by discrediting the traditional wisdom of the farmers.

In addition to the food crisis, resistance to land re-distribution, population explosion (a terminology that was quite prolifically used by the Americans as well as the Indian elite), illiteracy and slow industrial growth, the 1960s was a period of general unrest among youth due to the failure of the government's policies for eliminating poverty and tackling unemployment. This was the period when the hope that independence generated had started waning. The Kothari Commission's work needs to be located in this context which is not generally done.

In the above context, it is not unexpected that the Commission put a distinctive emphasis on the articulation of the agenda of science and technology which is equated with the goal of modernization and enhanced productivity. As Kumar (1996) says, if one were to summarize the thousand-page report in one word, then that would surely be modernization. It is a recurrent theme in almost all sections of the report. Under this heading, it deals with the problems of self-sufficiency in food, economic growth and full employment and social and national integration and political development. Of these, the first and the most important is food. Education is considered as the main instrument of development, an instrument of change and revolution. The report emphasizes that the basis of the distinction between modern and traditional society is development and development means science-based technology which helps modernization and industrialization.

The theme of self-sufficiency in food finds a recurring mention throughout the first chapter of the report. It is emphasized repeatedly that self-sufficiency of food can only be achieved by applying principles of science and technology through agriculture. Science is being seen as synonymous with modernization. Science-based technology is defined as the basis for the difference between the traditional and the modern societies.

"In a traditional society, production is based largely on the empirical process, experiences and trials and errors. In modern society, it is basically rooted in science. Science is treated as an institution rather than a process to knowledge, else it would be difficult to see why empiricism of the so-called traditional society, based on trial and error, behaviour and experiences, does not qualify to be called science."

This is what unfolded in the whole process of the Green Revolution. We find the roots of this in the context of education, in the Kothari Commission Report. Given the context of severely unequal access to land and rural resources, institutions enabled the bigger land owners to enhance their material prosperity and consolidate their land holdings. This was the vision embedded in the new strategy of modernization which was named somewhat later as the Green Revolution, as we all know it today. A lot has been written about it, including its adverse impact on environment. Similarly a lot has been written by way of the critique of the model of industrialization which as it was followed, led to the exploitation of natural resources and massive displacement of the poor, especially the tribals. The question is whether the education model provided in the Kothari Commission Report, with its recurrent theme on modernization, and development, and productivity which has to be increased through science and technology, provided space for it. As stated above, the discussion on the recommendations of the report, as is generally done, obfuscates the larger vision. Perhaps, even now, the report needs to be critically discussed to understand the lasting impact it has had on the Indian school and higher education system.

REFERENCES

Jain, Manish (2009). 'Civics Curriculum and the Idea of Citizens since the Late Nineteenth Century'. Ph.D. Thesis (Unpublished). Delhi: Department of Education, University of Delhi.

Kumar, Krishna (1996). 'Agricultural Modernisation and Education—Contours of a Point of Departure'. *EPW*. Vol. 31: 35, 36, 37.

7

National Education Policies (1968 and 1986) and the Ramamurti Committee Report (1992)

Vinay Kantha

Education emerged as a terrain of open contestation[1] from the middle of the 19th century, or to put it differently, as a key factor in the history of modernization in India. The colonial rulers sought to introduce a new system of education, basically to serve their own interests, in the second quarter of the 19th century, which got comprehensively defined in structural and ideological terms some decades later. The Woods Dispatch came in 1954, three universities were founded in 1957, and the Crown rule commenced from 1958. The Indian renaissance started exploring possibilities of alternatives in education alongside a growing demand for Western education in the later part of the century, coinciding with the emergence of Indian nationalism. This, in turn, resulted in many interesting educational experiments during the 20th century. Gandhi and Tagore, among others, proposed alternative visions and approaches for the design of a new system of education, different from the very traditional and the colonial, different from the Western education which had nourished the Indian version of nationalism. With the attainment of independence, new promises were made by the state, by means of the Indian Constitution, accompanied or followed by reports of Committees and Commissions, and eventually by some policy enunciations. Ironically till 1968, there was no separate policy document on education, presumably because the Constitution itself laid down some guiding principles and an assurance of universal basic education. A second round of policy debate was witnessed between 1985 and 1992, which was accompanied by a detailed Plan of Action (POA). A third round of debate is more recent, and it has yielded constitutional amendment and legislative changes. One of the first questions that need to be asked is what kind of vision—explicit or implied—the authors of these policies had and secondly, what the education system actually achieved in the following years and decades.

Changing Policy Framework After Independence

The promise of the Constitution was simple, explicit and unexceptionable—universal education up to the age of fourteen within a period of ten years of its commencement. Meanwhile, there were commissions on higher and secondary education, presuming perhaps that the Constitution had taken ample care of elementary education. These reports envisaged a larger vision of education. But for want of preparation at the basic level on the one hand and genuine and sustained commitment to the recommendations of these reports, there was a decline in quality, with at best a modest expansion at the post-elementary level. The Education Commission headed by D.S. Kothari presented the first comprehensive report on education, which was followed by the National Education Policy of 1968. The Kothari Commission was a belated statement on education, outlining the Nehruvian vision of national development, which ironically was being challenged and had already run into trouble by the time the Education Policy was announced two years later. The unredeemed promise of the Constitution and unfulfilled tasks in terms of the Preamble of the Constitution, were so large and, of course, general, that one is apt to miss that the policy document failed to meet the contemporary expectations.

Interestingly, the second policy statement seems to have arrived a few years too soon. Five years after the New Education Policy of 1986 a new economic policy was ushered in with its reliance on market, private sector and linkages with the global economy. Indeed the new economic policy was on the anvil, and the educational policy was of a piece with the policy in the making except the lip service it was under compulsion to pay to the constitutional principles. While the Ramamurti Committee was constituted to review the policy and POA of 1986, it turned out to be a critique of both the economic and educational policies.

The government was in a quandary, and expectedly through another Committee, namely, the Janardan Reddy Committee, it had to undertake damage control exercise. Acharya Ramamurti was a diehard Gandhian, and he was bent upon making a strong pitch for the Gandhian system of education, buried long ago by the middle class, the policy planners, politicians in power and bureaucrats.

This second round of policy enunciation also reveals a break-down of the consensus noticeable in large measure in the years after independence, which had already surfaced in the body politic in many forms including the emergence of ultra left ideology or rejection of national parties in many states. The contradictions in the policy paradigm were more glaring, and the voices of criticism, and sometimes, cynicism, became increasingly shrill in the years to come.

In the meanwhile, the global context of educational debates was re-defined by several conventions, conferences and charters, say, for example, the Committee on the Rights of the Child (CRC), (1989), First World Conference on Education at Jomtein, Thailand (March 1990) and the Dakar Framework of Action (World Education Forum 2000), which influenced Indian policies with India soon joining the globalization bandwagon. As programmes like the District Primary Education Programme (DPEP) followed there were newer debates on policy framework as well as pedagogy, reflected in a large number of documents. Sarva Shiksha Abhiyan (SSA) constitutional amendment (2002) and Right to Education Act (2009) have to be understood in this context, which takes forward the debates of the earlier epochs of history.

In fact, contestation with regard to the ideologies, agenda, policies, programmes or their manner of execution has become more and more complex with the passage of time. Older debates persist, while new layers get added. The state has no doubt emerged as the key player in defining the policy framework, even as what it has succeeded in achieving is not very substantial. Broadly speaking, there are three sets of policy frameworks proposed or implied in the government documents. The first one has the focus on liberal democratic-modernization; the second is a neoliberal market-friendly, externally dominated policy framework; and the third one is the society-oriented Indian-quasi-official approach which finds place even in the official policies. If the 1968 Policy can be placed in the first category, the Ramamurti Report represents the third approach to educational policy.

Traditional systems generally remain outside the state system, represented by *madrasas*; or network of institutions claiming to promote traditional culture like Dayanand Anglo Vedic (DAV), Ramakrishna Mission (RKM), etc; or education in social institutions like *ghotuls* etc; or apprenticeship-based skill training in family or workplaces.

II

1968 Policy[2]: Cryptic Policy Statement on a Comprehensive Report

One of the ironies of educational policy in India is that actual policy (that is, the operational version) is apparently authored by bureaucracy, notwithstanding the plethora of reports prepared painstakingly by experts and educationists. The Kothari Report[3] was a comprehensive document touching upon almost all aspects of education in India, while the 1968 policy was less than an eight page long- simplistic, bland and seemingly unmindful of the complexities involved in the task of 'radical reconstruction' of education on the broad lines recommended by the Education Commission, which it found "essential for the economic and cultural development of the country, for national integration and realizing the ideal of a socialistic pattern of society". If the Policy of 1968 would have been interpreted, understood and operationalized in the light of the report, truly and essentially, it might have made some difference to the system of education, but the actual results were at best patchy, inadequate and indeed, different. In fact, even a cursory look at facts and figures reveal that not much effort was made to meet the basic commitments of the 1968 Policy, not to mention the recommendations of the Kothari Report. Three most glaring failures included a low level of outlay for education, much below the commitment of six per cent, reluctance to move towards the Common School System and default on the promise of free and compulsory education. Of the seventeen principles listed in the 1968 Policy, few were faithfully followed.

'Development' was the catch phrase till this phase. The Kothari Report chose to give itself the title 'Education for National Development'. The 1968 Policy recalls that leaders of the freedom struggle stressed the 'unique significance of education in national development'. Of course, the cultural aspect of development was added to economic development, stress on science and technology was balanced by references to moral and social values, yet there is a clear utilitarian approach to education, more anxious to develop human beings as a resource for the nation. Likewise, it states that the education system must produce young men and women of 'character and ability' committed to 'national service and development'. (para 3)

'Nation' is another dominant theme of both the Kothari Report and 1968 Policy. It was not merely an after-glow of the national movement, but a commitment to the idea of strengthening the 'nation-state'. Understandably, there was a conscious plea to create a 'sense of common citizenship' (para 3). The idea of 'national progress and security' too finds mention which needs to be fostered for which education is a vital factor. (para 2)

The ideal of the socialistic pattern of society and egalitarian concerns are reflected in the reiteration of the constitutional commitment of free and compulsory universal elementary education, or equalization of educational opportunity, though it turned out to be nothing more than lip service. Gandhi is reluctantly acknowledged by a simple mention of basic education scheme (para 1), and a new watered down version of work-centric education in the form of work-experience, which is clubbed with national service. The community linkage part is barely recognized, though the state is seen as the main provider of education.

Spanner in the Wheel: Ramamurti Committee Report

The year 1985-86 marks a transition, a watershed in the history of Indian education. A series of initiatives and documents bring out the major changes which were in the offing. The following documents are in a way inter-related and should have laid down a comprehensive policy-cum-plan of action for reconstructing the education system in India at this juncture:

1. Challenges of Education: A Policy Perspective (Ministry of Education, Government of India, New Delhi (1985)[4]

2. National Policy on Education 1986 (NPE 1986)[5] and Programme of Action POA, 1986[6] (Ministry of Education, Government of India, New Delhi (1986)
3. Towards an Enlightened and Human Society: Report of the Committee for Review of National Policy on Education 1986 (NPERC or Ramamurti Committee Report) 1990 (Ministry of Education, Government of India, New Delhi (1990)[7]
4. Report of the CABE Committee on Policy (Janardhan Reddy Committee Report, 1992), (Ministry of Education, Government of India, New Delhi (1992)[8]
5. National Policy on Education 1986 (as modified in 1992), 1992 (Ministry of Education, Government of India, New Delhi (1992)[9]
6. Programme of Action (POA), 1992 (Ministry of Education, Government of India, New Delhi (1992)[10]

Among these documents, the Ramamurti Committee Report stands apart, as it presented a critique of the new policy framework which was being proposed by the other policy papers since 1985-86. It called for a paradigm change harking back to the Gandhian ethos and scheme of education. Of course, given its limitations as merely a Review Committee it was perhaps not entirely free to write on a blank slate, yet in its own way the Report suggested corrections which were placed in a distinctively different paradigmatic frame. Predictably, it was unacceptable to the government at that juncture and the Reddy Committee Report took up the task of undoing the damage done. It is thus of immense value that the Ramamurti Report is examined at length for what it was. However, to put it in perspective, the tenor and approach of the 1986 Policy needs to be kept in view.

While the 1968 Policy was supposedly based on the Kothari Report, the 1986 Policy was preceded by an administrative appraisal of the prevailing educational situation in the country. It did not have a well thought out or properly articulated theoretical foundation. Education was thus seen largely as an administrative enterprise, rather than an instrument of social transformation, or an end in itself as Sen[11] and many others, including authors of the human development concept[12], would assert soon thereafter.

As for achievements, NPE 1986 noted the 'considerable expansion' of educational facilities measured in terms of coverage of habitations and augmentation of facilities. It further noted that "Perhaps the most notable development has been the acceptance of a common structure of education throughout the country and the introduction of the 10+2+3 system by most states. In the school curricula, in addition to laying down a common scheme of studies for boys and girls, science and mathematics were incorporated as compulsory subjects and work experience assigned a place of importance".

These observations were followed by the bureaucratic lament in the following words:

> While these achievements are impressive by themselves, the general formulations incorporated in the 1968 Policy did not, however, get translated into a detailed strategy of implementation, accompanied by the assignment of specific responsibilities and financial and organizational support. As a result, problems of access, quality, quantity, utility and financial outlay, accumulated over the years, have now assumed such massive proportions that they must be tackled with the utmost urgency.

NPE 1986 observed that education in India stands at the crossroads today and rightly pointed out that neither normal linear expansion nor the existing pace and nature of improvement can meet the needs of the situation. But after that it makes a debatable proposition that "In the Indian way of thinking, a human being is a positive asset and a precious national resource, which needs to be cherished, nurtured and developed with tenderness, and care, coupled with dynamism". To see a human being primarily as an asset and resource is at best a limited agenda of education, while goals of education have generally been defined both in the older literature and by the leading reformers and leaders of freedom struggle in more idealistic terms.

Yet NPE 86 was right in saying that "The catalytic action of education in this complex and dynamic growth process needs to be planned meticulously and executed with great sensitivity" and that "India's political and social life is passing through a phase which poses the danger of erosion of long-accepted values. The goals of secularism, socialism, democracy and professional ethics are coming under increasing strain."

As the Committee itself noted, its approach in reviewing the National Policy on Education, 1986, and its implementation, was guided by the following principal concerns:

* Equity and social justice.
* Decentralization of educational management at all levels.
* Establishment of a participative educational order.
* Inculcation of values indispensable for creation of an enlightened and humane society.
* Empowerment for work

The Committee averred that the above concerns have been built into the recommendations of the Committee as underlying all-pervasive perceptions so as to realize the constitutional and cultural goals of education. This averment was indeed to create a justification for the kind of critique and recommendations the Review Committee proposed, because in its thrust and overall approach NPE 1986 was generally removed from these concerns, even if here and there some of these terms and phrases could, of course, be located.

As for equity and social justice, which is the principal concern in the Ramamurti Report, in clear contrast in Part IV of NPE 1986 there is rather a limited formulation titled 'Education for Equality', which is largely described in programmatic terms, rather than as an act of faith (though ironically under the subtitle Education for Women's Equality, the phrase 'an act of faith' has been used explicitly). The concepts of equity and justice[13] have a wider and deeper connotation, implying a different order of commitment, which is difficult to find in any of the documents of the period. For want of large systemic changes (say, CSS within education system, or more egalitarian social order and economic policy framework, even outside), which have been strongly advocated by the Ramamurti Report, it is not possible to move towards greater justice.

Equity as defined in the dictionary means 'the quality of being fair and impartial'. Its meaning is different, and possibly more nuanced than equality. The idea of justice and fairness is added on to a rather flexible notion of equality, less mechanical and more contextualized. While the meaning given to equality is more dependent on 'sameness' or 'evenly balanced', fairness and due correction to the mechanical interpretation of equality are germane to the concept of equity[14]. That is why an understanding of the context and idea of social justice is important for its full appreciation. The Indian Constitution lays down the principle of affirmative action in respect of vulnerable sections of society, which implies extra facilities and protections, but NPE 1986 and POA prescribe the supplementary system of education for those who needed the maximum support. The introduction of non-formal education with low paid instructors without the infrastructural facilities that a school should have, was perhaps the most regressive step, which was made more painful by the introduction of the Navodaya Vidyalayas for a privileged few. Thus the mention of the common school system in NPE 1986 is a travesty of the ideas of equity and justice. The Ramamurti Committee rightly criticized this arrangement and called for a stop to its further expansion.

Decentralization and establishment of participative educational order provides a different framework of educational management than the one underlying NPE 1986 or POA. Further, in the formulation of Ramamurti's recommendations, this framework opens up to the larger society, or for that matter, to politics and economy as well. Although so far as recommendations of NPE are concerned, in Part X, phrases like decentralization, people's involvement, etc. are used but at the same time there is a stress on management perspective and accountability. In Part VII (Making the System Work), disciplining and accountability are not only emphasized but elaborated through a proposed strategy based on 'a system of performance appraisal' or 'insistence on observance of acceptable norms of behaviour'.

By laying down the guiding principle of 'inculcation of values indispensable for creation of an enlightened and humane society' the Ramamurti Committee Report brings back the normative social concerns of education as we come across in the earlier discourse on education in the renaissance period or the era of freedom struggle. The focus shifts away, as far as possible in a review exercise from programmatic framework around the state system to the very goal and purposes of education, particularly in the context of society at large. The idea of empowerment for work accordingly takes a new meaning.

Chapter 3 of the Ramamurti Report is given the title, 'Roles, Goals and Values in Education' and starts with a quote from Gandhji: "The goal of education is to establish a non-violent and non-exploiting social and economic order." Taking that as a long term basic purpose of education, the Report defines the role of education, more specifically and concretely, in terms of a process—as a lifelong process of **Learning to Be by Learning to Become**. The Report declares that the social dimension of education necessitates that education be essentially value-based. It refers back to the acculturating role of education mentioned in NPE 1986, but moves to the deeper levels of culture lying in the foundational values, world-views, mindsets, etc. It views re-establishment of links between education and life, and hence between the school and the community as a major task of reconstruction of the education system, and comes up with the concept of community school, which is organically linked with the community. (para 3.12.3 to 3.12.6).

Regarding the objective of vocationalization, the Committee makes it clear that its view is different from the one under the NPE. It reverts to the Gandhian scheme of basic education and asserts that "It is not merely to impart specific saleable manual skills but to relate hand with heart so that productive labour and socially useful work becomes a medium for developing creative intelligence and a knowledge base on which one could keep building throughout life" (para 8.2.2) Accordingly, there is a full length analysis and a detailed set of recommendations with regard to vocational education in Chapter 8, which is titled significantly, as 'Education and Right to Work'.

There are some areas of early education where NPE 1986 made a definite advance over the 1968 Policy. One such area is Early Child Care and Education (ECC&E). NPE 1968 had ignored the recommendation of the Kothari Commission on pre-primary education. After that the National Policy on Children was announced in 1974, and ICDS was introduced during the Fifth Plan. As Ramamurti's Review Committee approvingly remarked, "...NPE 1986 is a historic document in that it boldly recognises the importance of ECCE and lays down the 'holistic' principles on which the programme is to be developed". However, the NPE/POA approach to ECCE was found "fragmented with large implementation gaps and divided responsibility." The Ramamurti

Committee was strongly supportive of ECCE for two reasons: it will help in contributing to the universalisation of elementary education and ensuring equality of opportunity for women. Due to the latter, it should have a linkage with women's participation in work and education. The Committee recommended linkage with schools as well, under a decentralized, community-based, participatory strategy. Consequently in the context of diversities of situations, a child-centred plural approach would be desirable.

Education of teachers is another area which was emphasised in all the documents in the 1985-92 period. One of the significant institutional ideas put forward by the NPE 1986 was the proposal to establish well-equipped DIETs in all districts. While the proposal was favourably viewed by the Ramamurti Report, its recommendations seem to be more focused on the process aspect. Moreover, the internship model appears to be overemphasized as the issues relating to quality of teachers are far more complex, calling for a multi-pronged strategy. The education complex proposal is quite welcome, but there are multiplicity of factors which need to be addressed. One risk of laying great stress on tasks, accountability, professional competence and intangible rewards could be a neglect of material benefits, which has indeed become a reality today. Teachers are a harassed lot, and their cadre itself is under threat, while the latest Act, that is, the RTE Act 2009, saddles them with huge responsibilities while giving them almost no assurance of a respectable career.

The Ramamurti Committee Report is rather a detailed exercise, as it seeks to cover both philosophy and programme, theory and practice or implementation. While keeping the NPE and POA as the point of departure, it goes into other reports as well, examines the extent of implementation, analyses the possible causes of failures and makes recommendations on a variety of issues. It will be useful however to look into the core issues raised by the Ramamurti Committee Report, where it has something important to say, which may sometimes be different from the two Policy documents notified in 1968 and 1986.

III

Debates on Issues and Concerns

There are many issues which emerge as important or core issues of education in India as one starts examining the two national education policies on the one hand, and various educational reports on the other hand. We intend to analyse here the two policy documents of 1968 and 1986 and the Ramamurti Report.

i. Ideological Issues, or More Specifically, Education as an Agency of Modernization

History of modernization in India is intertwined with growth of a new kind of education in the colonial milieu, first in the period of the 19th century renaissance and then during the freedom struggle. Raja Rammohan Roy, the founder of the Brahmo Samaj, is often described as the father of modern India. Rather perceptively, Jones[15] has described the modernizing variety of socio-religious reform movement, of which Roy was the first major leader, as 'acculturative' as against 'transitional', the latter bearing similarity to the erstwhile social movements of the past. The spread of modern education was one of the major enterprises of the leaders of reform movements. It is widely believed, with considerable justification, that nationalism was constructed and the national movement was spearheaded by the Western educated intelligentsia during the last quarter of the 19th century. The rise and growth of a new nationalist ideology and culture on which a newer type of politics and political mobilization was built is crucially linked with debates on education in India, which was carried forward even after attainment of independence. After all, in independent India too, the state-sponsored education system inherited from the colonial masters was never radically reconstructed. Ideologically, the only notable change was an acceptance of the modern idea of the Indian nation-state which permeates the Constitution and the educational agenda. It was rather natural that 'national development' was described as the main goal of education by the Kothari Commission. The policies of 1968 and 1986 also endorsed the principles of modernization and development in their own terminology.

Whatever be the ideological alternatives offered by Gandhi or Tagore or even DAV institutions promoted by Arya Samajis, none of these could be described as non-modern. They promoted different versions of modernization, and even education in the madarsas or Sanskrit schools were not altogether immune to the modern influences. However, the major difference between government schools and Gandhian scheme of basic education related to the normative concerns and the social orientation. The Ramamurti Report makes an unsuccessful attempt to bring back Gandhi, drawing attention to the weaknesses of the contemporary education system by all standards. What should be the form of modernization remains a moot question in the debates on education and it is unlikely to fade away for a long time to come. In any case, the ideological agenda of education will remain a perennial dilemma—or preoccupation—for educationists and policy makers.

ii. Education and Economy, or Education in Development Discourse

The preference for English education on the part of the contemporary elite was largely due to a desire for a place in the emerging colonial system, in particular for getting government jobs or entry into the new professions, legal. medical, educational or others around the colonial regime. With development assuming a new overarching dominant preoccupation of governments and planners worldwide after the Second World War, education was viewed as the main vehicle for achieving development in independent India. The 1968 Policy declared, "The Government of India is convinced that a radical reconstruction of education on the broad lines recommended by the Education Commission is essential for economic and cultural development of the country..."

In 1986, education was described as ' a unique investment in the present and the future' and this was accepted as 'the cardinal principle' and the key to NPE (para 2.4). In fact the moralistic fervour of the earlier educational debate was rather muted, references to moral concerns were only ritualistic and the economic role of education was emphasized. Vocationalization was accordingly given considerable importance in the document (para 5.16 to 5.23). The need of skilled manpower was highlighted, technical and management education also came up as major concerns.

Unfortunately, even as the debate on development[16] was redefined in the early 1990s (recall design of the Human Development Index by UNDP, the sustainable development idea of the 1992 Earth Summit and development being highlighted as a human rights issue in the Geneva Declaration of 1993), it did not register in the contemporary educational discourse in India. Even later, it could influence the policy debate rather feebly. Thus in India while the liberalization-privatization debate was picked up with alacrity, the global discourse on people-oriented human development or human right concepts were largely ignored. Sen has extended the human development debate into many areas through his emphasis on 'expansion of human capabilities'[17] and highlighting 'the agency aspect' of human development, beyond just evaluative (and measurement)aspect.

The Ramamurti Committee Report called for 'an enlightened and humane society', which had a distinct moral flavour. But it seemed to be located in the past. This Report had criticized the principle of looking at man merely as a resource, and had objected to the Ministry of Education being re-named as the Ministry of Human Resource Development. Yet it neither took up the new ideas on development, nor picked up the rights agenda. It was still a moral plea in the Gandhian style.

iii. Education, State and Society

If the period 1985-92 is seen as a watershed in the history of the evolution of a new educational policy in India, the most fundamental change appears to be regarding the diminished role of the state. In the Indian Constitution or Kothari Report or 1968 Policy, there was no doubt about education being the responsibility of the state, but as many observers have pointed out, there has been a gradual retreat of the state from education in the post-liberalization era. While referring to the IMF-World Bank's structural adjustment programme and Ambani-Birla Report, Sadgopal[18] draws attention to the Jomtein Conference (1990) and Dakar Framework of Action (2000) to explain the increasing abdication of the state from the education sector. Sadgopal quotes the following significant observations by Tomasevski: "The language of the final document adopted by the Jomtein Conference merged human needs and market forces, moved education from governmental to social responsibility, made no reference to the international legal requirement that primary education be free of charge, introduced the term 'basic education' which confused conceptual and statistical categories."

Indeed while there was a growing trend of commercialization and privatization in the education sector, sometimes even in respect of elementary education, there was also a new discussion on the need of involving the community 'as an effective means of promoting primary education, both in quantitative and qualitative terms'[19]. However, as Govinda and Diwan (2003) rightly observe: "the move appears to have been prompted essentially by the utilitarian value of involving the community, which could possibly improve the deteriorating efficiency and effectiveness of the school system". NPE 1986 and POA recommended participation and even 'empowerment' of the local community which got a further fillip by the subsequent 72nd and 73rd constitutional amendments. However, this new concept of community visualized a role for the locals in a manner much different from what Gandhi or Tagore had envisioned in their schemes of education, or even what Acharya Ramamurti had in mind in his review report.

Whether it was Plato or Dewey among the educationists, or in India, Vivekanand or Gandhi or Tagore, education had a clear purpose for society, Dewey remarks in the opening paragraph of his book, *The School and the Society*, "We are apt to look at the school from an individualistic standpoint, as something between the teacher and the pupil, or between the teacher and the parent....... Yet the range of outlook needs to be enlarged. What the best and the wisest parent wants for his children, that community must want for all children. Any other ideal for our schools is narrow and unlovely; acted upon, it destroys our democracy." The policy framework of NPE 86 and POA based thereupon is largely guided by an individualistic agenda for education, governed by market forces, with the state hesitant about re-fashioning it to create an egalitarian social and economic order. The Ramamaurti Committee sought to reinstate the vision of social transformation through education though it was careful to point out the limitations of education as a sub-system. It is most emphatically articulated in the Preface written by Ramamurti on his own. He ruefully observes that 'we have pursued a model of economic development that has led to the creation of two Indias—one of the rich, the other for the poor' and asserts that 'for the poor, development, democracy and education should mean emancipation'. Like Gandhi he would like the 'village itself as a unit for an integrated programme of education, democracy and development'. 'Participatory education, participatory development and participatory democracy will be possible only when we decide upon a policy of planned decentralization'. He makes it clear that this decentralization will involve a clear shift of power from the state to the civil society. Ramamurti, like Gandhi, takes a holistic view of education and puts forward ideas like 'village as school' and 'community school' along with a decentralized participatory framework to give it an operational shape.

Undoubtedly, many ideas and prescriptions of Ramamurti appear to be utopian and can be attacked on the same ground on which the basic education system has been criticized from time to time[20]. J.B. Kripalani, a close associate of Gandhi found the original proposal of Gandhi, among other things, 'reactionary, anti-revolutionary, medieval, unpractical, faddist [and] spiritual'. Regarding its impracticality, N.R. Malkani had remarked that India lacked 'teachers who were also artisans and artisans who were also teachers' and to try 'to create a new pedigree teacher unknown in India' would be an extraordinarily difficult undertaking'. The idea of education being made self-supporting was found repugnant by those insisting on basic education being a definite state responsibility. To the rights-activists, it denied a basic right of the child, now a full-fledged fundamental right. The scheme of sale of produce to support education was then also criticized on the ground that it reduced a learning child into child labour. Often people have tended to dismiss basic education as a failed idea. Recommendations of the Ramamurti Committee Report occasionally, and personal views of Acharya Ramamurti in large measure, come close to the scheme of basic education, but unfortunately there is no convincing defence put up in the document, nor well thought out modifications proposed.

iv. Some Systemic Issues in Indian Education

The Kothari Report had recommended a radical reconstruction of national system of public education based on the idea of the Common School System with a network of neighbourhood schools which was capable of ensuring quality education to all children at least up to the age of fourteen years. It had prescribed a uniform 10+2+3 structure for the full range of educational institutions from elementary to tertiary, with supplementary ones for technical and professional education. The commitment to create properly equipped institutions had not materialized even after nearly four decades after independence, necessitating a review of the strategy. Unfortunately among the modifications thought of, the most disappointing was a retreat from the basic commitment of creating credible institutions of schools and colleges, and preference for alternative arrangements like Non-Formal Education (NFE) or open schools or distance learning courses, etc.

School vs NFE Centres: Arguably the most debilitating systemic innovation in the Indian education system was the introduction of Non-Formal Education (NFE) during the Sixth Plan period which was implemented after NPE 1986 as a major Centrally Sponsored Scheme. The flawed logic and internal contradictions in the 1986 Policy and POA relating to NFE were noticed and debated at length by the Ramamurti Committee, which observed: "The above listed highly desirable features of NFE are indeed relevant to formal schools as well and they are also the essence of the child-centred approach mentioned by NPE. The criteria mentioned by POA for selection of NFE instructors—being local, being already motivated, acceptable to the community, being preferably from the weaker sections in the society, having given some evidence of work in the community—are the criteria relevant to the formal school teachers also. Therefore, it is unclear why the policy has advocated NFE, in effect as a parallel system." (Section 6.4.6)

Based on this logic the Ramamurti Committee recommended that the formal system be itself 'non-formalized' to include all the desirable features of NFE instead of setting up two parallel systems, one for the children from better off sections of society and the other for poor girls and working children. (ibid 151-53)

Multiple System of Education: The system of Navodaya schools, on the other hand, was introduced at the other end of the spectrum within the public system of education, which obviously went against the principle of equalization of educational opportunity. And outside the public system there was a multilayered private system of schools and colleges which have tended to proliferate in the post-1986 period and, then in the post-liberalization era. Today in place of a common school system, multiple systems of education functions within the overall system, each competing with the other. For example, there are systems rooted in the British-born Indian educational system which are themselves bifurcated into sub-systems. This duality within the British-born educational system is reflected in the state and privately controlled systems of convent education. Further, there are systems which are based on taking a re-look at earlier indigenous learning traditions, like the ashram education system, the madrasas, Sanskrit Vidyalayas, Saraswati mandirs, etc. The Ramamurti Report generally took a position against such a multi-layered system of education, but rather weakly.

Decline in the Status of Teachers and the Scheme of Para-Teachers: Another major systemic distortion which has contributed to the decline in the quality of education in India is the gradual replacement of regular teachers with ill-paid and under-qualified para-teachers. While this phenomenon is mainly driven by financial consideration, that is, saving money on teachers' salaries, and may be on training as well, there are indirect justifications created by several things stressed by NPE 86 and even, the Ramamurti Report. NPE laid emphasis on the principle of accountability and 'code of professional ethics' (of course to be prepared, and operated by teachers' associations only), in addition to creating conditions for the teachers to be competent, creative and innovative. The Ramamurti Report, on the other hand, expressed its preference for realistic, experiential, practice-oriented internship model of training as against institution-based, theory-oriented training. Further, laying equal stress on professional competence as on material conditions, almost as independent principles, may have serious implications. While all these are welcome ideas, but equally, these can be manipulated, and have unfortunately been successfully manipulated, to lower the status of teachers.

v. Contents and Processes of Education

There is an increasing concern regarding content and process of education with qualitative decline in school education becoming more and more noticeable. Debates on curriculum and pedagogy is a relatively new phenomenon in the policy documents or in the institutional context, as challenges before education, or for that matter, in the society, polity and economy become more complex. The 1968 Policy did not take up these issues explicitly, but in the

1986 Policy this finds mention in Part VIII. However, right from the beginning, there was a felt need for examination reform, which continues to be a common concern of policy documents as well as curricular debates. Teacher training has also been a major area as well as the range of subjects to be taught at various levels. In both these areas, the 1986 Policy and Ramamurti Committee had a lot to recommend. Indeed it is quite noticeable that from this phase of policy making in education, quality issues have gradually come into sharper focus. It may be due to several reasons, of which continuous decline in quality is perhaps the most obvious. J.P. Naik had famously remarked on the growth of education post-independence that it is caught up in the elusive triangle of 'equality, quality and quantity'. Of course, decline in quality has something to do with expansion of education, but it will need to be examined whether it is by simple default or a definite design, whether the resource constraint for education is a policy choice or just unavoidable. While systemic issues cannot be brushed aside, the pedagogic side is of equal importance, and the two sides are again interlinked.

Debates on contents and processes, quality aspects, curricular reforms, etc have become keener and sharper in the recent decades for many reasons, genuine as well as obfuscatory. If the 1986 Policy was apparently more concerned about these compared to the 1968 document, the Ramamurti Report devoted a full chapter to contents and process. Meanwhile, we had curriculum frameworks being prepared by NCERT, the latest one being a much talked about exercise.

The Ramamurti Committee sums up that "the intervention programme, according to POA, are to be implemented in areas of content reorientation, process reorientation, development of technical support system and mobilization and motivation by effective use of communication technology and monitoring mechanism." However, the Committee has a different take on almost everything that was suggested by NPE 1986 and POA. While approving of the national core curriculum recommended by NPE, the Committee called for 'full scope being provided in addition to the core curriculum, for diversity in content and pedagogy according to the socio-cultural milieu of the school, college and university'. Decentralization was stressed by the Ramamurti Report in all interventions, a word of caution added to the simple extension or imposition of technology including computers, or recourse to greater broad basing and subtleness suggested in giving value education. The phrase 'hidden curriculum' has been used at several places in the report.

Among the subjects to be covered by school syllabi, language is arguably the most important, which also has a place as the medium of instruction. In the 1968 Education Policy, the following principles are laid down: energetic development of regional languages and literature, implementation of three language formula, development of Hindi as envisaged in Article 351 of the Constitution, provision of facilities for the teaching of Sanskrit and strengthening of study of English as an international language. NPE 1986 simply endorses the 1968 Policy, which is reiterated by the Ramamurti Report as well. However, this report devotes a full chapter to Languages in Education, discusses status and problems and suggests guidelines. One principle which it highlights is the need of introducing the mother tongue as the medium of instruction at the primary level.

Examination reform has been an important subject discussed by various committees and commissions in the pre-independence and post-independence period. According to the 1968 Policy, there were two major goals of reforms: first, to improve reliability and validity, and second, to make evaluation a continuous process aimed at helping students to improve level of achievement, rather than at 'certifying' the quality of performance at a given point of time. The 1986 Policy spelt out the reforms more elaborately in functional terms (para 8.24), which was extended further by the Ramamurti Report after making an appraisal of status of implementation of reforms. If NPE 1986 recommended preparation of a National Examination Reform Framework, the Review Report felt the need of a permanent Examination Reforms Commission. In all these reforms, greater stress is laid on teacher-dependent, institution-based internal evaluation on a continuous basis.

Fuller debate on comprehensive curricular reforms was gradually emerging as an important concern of NCERT and like institutions, which gathered momentum after NCF 2000.

IV

Implications for Future

It is naive to think that India can ever have a singular vision of education, even among the policy makers or the middle class. Yet there was a fair degree of agreement in the middle class Western-educated intelligentsia about the need of nationalism and its correlate in education. Ironically, however, two of the foremost educational thinkers of modern India, Gandhi and Tagore, differed from the generally agreed position on nationalism as well as education. As Nandy perceptively notes, "In both, Tagore and Gandhi, the fear of nationalism grew out of their experiences of the record of anti-imperialism in India, and their attempt to link their concepts of Indianness with their understanding of a world where the language of progress had already established a complete dominance." Further, he remarks, "They did not want their society to be caught in a situation *where the idea of the Indian nation would supersede that of the Indian civilization, and where the actual ways of life of Indians would be assessed solely in terms of the needs of an imaginary nation-state called India*" (italics mine)[22].

It is interesting to note how quickly the whole idea of nation, especially in terms of national consciousness, was relegated to the background in the educational discourse. The Policy of 1968 highlighted the 'unique significance' of education for 'national development', though it has also referred to the role of education for 'cultural and economic development'. As noted earlier, the NPE 1986 viewed education as a 'unique investment in the present and the future' and laid emphasis on 'human resource development', a terminology which was objected to by the Ramamurti Committee for its bland utilitarian tone. However, apart from manpower requirement to be fulfilled by education, the 1986 Policy underlined its acculturating role, though it was conceptually removed from the idea of culture that Gandhi or Tagore had in mind. If at all 'nation' occurs in the NPE 1986, it is either for the state (that is, nation-state), plain and simple, or to emphasize commonness or uniformity. The 1986 document was happy about the introduction of a common 10+2+3 structure, recommended a common scheme of studies with core curriculum, but seems to be rather indifferent about the idea of the common school system. For the individuals also, if the citizenship idea was found important in the early years after independence, the human resource idea dominated from the 1980s.

The Ramamurti Committee Report also hardly mentions 'nation', but the five principles mentioned there (and discussed above) shift the focus towards 'a humane and enlightened society'. While the creation of an egalitarian society was hardly there on the agenda of the exercise to formulate the two policy documents, notwithstanding the Preamble of the Indian Constitution, the Ramamurti Committee seeks to bring into focus 'equity and social justice', a modern terminology. However, strategies proposed by the Committee, were by and large Gandhian, making a strong pitch for decentralization and community involvement.

If plural strategies, situated in specific socio-cultural milieus, are found desirable in a country as vast and diverse as India, plurality of approaches and visions may be unavoidable. This should necessitate rethink on the role of the state, rather than expecting the state to withdraw and leave the field open for market forces. As Tagore remarked once: The Raj or State has a regulatory role, while only Samaj or society is capable of promoting creativity and innovation. The state has to play the provider role in terms of the clear constitutional mandate, while it should not abdicate its second role as the regulator, because in the absence of such a role by the state, larger social interests are likely to suffer due to crass commercialization in the market. From national development and human resource development, we can move to the agenda of human development. But that too does not settle the basic issues relating to education. Even if not all problems can be solved in the domain of education, and conceding that education at best is a sub-system of the larger system as emphasized by Acharya Ramamurti, the task of regeneration of society and redesign of economic and political order cannot be ignored in debates on education.

It is widely being felt today that the Indian education system faces a deep crisis and the crisis is deepening every day. The disease is very severe in nature and there appears to be no possibility of curing it in any way through even well-thought out reforms. The crisis is manifest through several symptoms, which include the rank devaluation of certificates and degrees, the low quality of teaching and research, the absence of creativity in scientific research and education due to the system's negative approach to creativity. These have led to an absolute decline in the number of artists, dancers, singers, and musicians, which has resulted in an impoverishment of Indian society as a whole and the degeneration of the status of teachers and scientists into contract labour.

While being infected with the grave difficulties purveyed above, the Indian educational system has at the same time become a fertile ground for commercial and profit-oriented interests who see in the desperate need among young people for being certified for employment, a new avenue for ruthless business opportunities. This necessitates a thorough revision of the existing policy framework and implementation strategies. There are enough clues for it in the various reports.

REFERENCES

1. Bhattacharya, Sabyasachi (ed), *The Contested Terrain, Perspectives on Education in India,* Orient Longman Ltd., New Delhi (1998).
2. Ministry of Education, *National Policy on Education 1968,* Government of India (1968).
3. Ministry of Education and Culture, *Education and National Development: Report of the Education Commission (1964-66),* Government of India, New Delhi (1966).
4. Ministry of Education, *Challenges of Education: a Policy Perspective,* Government of India, New Delhi (1985).
5. Ministry of Education, *National Policy on Education 1986 (NPE 1986),* Government of India, New Delhi (1986).
6. Ministry of Education, *Programme of Action POA,* 1986 Government of India, New Delhi (1986).
7. Ministry of Education, *Towards an Enlightened and Human Society: Report of the Committee for Review of National Policy on Education 1986* (NPERC or Ramamurti Committee Report) 1990 Government of India, New Delhi (1990).
8. Ministry of Education, *Report of the CABE Committee on Policy* (Janardhan Reddy Committee Report 1992) Government of India, New Delhi (1992).
9. Ministry of Education, *National Policy on Education 1986 (as modified in 1992),* Government of India, New Delhi (1992).

10. Ministry of Education, *Programme of Action (POA),* 1992 Government of India, New Delhi (1992).
11. Dreze, J. and Sen, A. *India: Economic Development and Social Opportunity,* Oxford University Press, New Delhi (1995)
12. Fukuda-Parr, S. and Kumar, A.S. (eds), *Readings in Human Development: Concepts Measures and Policies for a Development Paradigm,* Oxford University Press, USA, 2003.
13. Sen, A.K., *The Idea of Justice,* Allen Lane, an imprint of Penguin Books, London (2009).
14. Sachs, Wolfang (ed), *The Development Dictionary,* Orient Longman, New Delhi (1997).
15. Jones Kenneth W., *Socio-Religious Reform Movements in British India,* Cambridge University Press in association with Orient Longman, Cambridge (1989).
16. Fukuda-Parr, S. and Shiva Kumar, A K. (eds), *Readings in Human Development,* Oxford University Press, New Delhi (2003).
17. Ibid.
18. Sadgopal, Anil, *A Post-Jomtein Reflection on the Education Policy,* in Ravi Kumar (ed), *The Crisis of Elementary Education in India,* Sage Publications, New Delhi (2006).
19. Govinda, R. and Diwan, Rashmi (eds), *Community Participation and Empowerment in Primary Education,* Sage Publications, New Delhi (2003).
20. Fagg, Henry, *Back to the Sources: A Study of Gandhi's Basic Education,* NBT, New Delhi (2002), (Chapter 6, pp. 62-70).
21. Naik, J.P., Tagore Memorial Lectures, *Equality, Quality and Quantity: The Elusive Triangle in Indian Education,* Allied Publishers, New Delhi (1975).
22. Nandy, Ashis, *The Illegitimacy of Nationalism,* Oxford University Press, Delhi (1994).

8

Report of the Common School System Commission, Bihar (2007)

Muchkund Dubey

On July 22, 2006, the Chief Minister of Bihar, Mr. Nitish Kumar, in his valedictory address in a seminar on the Common School System (CSS) held in Patna, declared his government's intention to establish a CSS in Bihar and to set up a Commission to prepare a plan of action for this purpose. Soon thereafter, the Government of Bihar constituted the Common School System Commission Bihar, under the Chairmanship of Prof. Muchkund Dubey, former Foreign Secretary to the Government of India, and former Professor Jawaharlal Nehru University. The two other members of this Commission were Prof. Anil Sadgopal, former Professor of Education and Dean, Faculty of Education, University of Delhi, and Dr. Madan Mohan Jha, at that time Commissioner and Secretary, Department of Human Resource Development, Government of Bihar. The Commission commenced its work from September 10, 2006 and submitted its Report to the Chief Minister on June 8, 2007.

The Commission's task was not to make recommendations on how to improve and expand the existing school education system in Bihar but to prepare a plan for an alternative system of education, i.e. a Common School System for the state. This was the only example in the annals of education in India when a detailed study was undertaken and recommendations made, with a year-wise plan and cost estimation, for establishing a CSS in one of the states of India.

The terms of reference given to the Commission were, among others:

(i) To carry out a comprehensive study of the present school system in the state.

(ii) To recommend norms and standards and other necessary provisions for ensuring education of an equitable quality for all children in the state, and to make an assessment of its financial implications.

(iii) To recommend a framework for the Common School System from the standpoint of ensuring children's Fundamental Right to Free and Compulsory Education under Article 21-A of the Constitution.

(iv) To formulate a plan of action for implementing the Common School System in the state.

(v) To examine, within the context of building the Common School System, the pace-setting role of Gandhi's Basic School (*Buniyadi Vidyalaya*) and recommend a plan of action accordingly.

(vi) To study the teacher education institutions available and functioning within the state and their curricula and make recommendations in order to mould them according to the requirements of the Common School System.

Apart from fulfilling its basic mandate of preparing a plan of action for the establishment of a CSS in Bihar, the Commission's report traces the historical evolution of school education in Bihar; deals with the theory and practice of the concepts of right to education and equal opportunity, elaborates the concept, content, rationale and scope of CSS; presents a status report on the school education in Bihar; and deals with some of the issues relating to CSS in Bihar, particularly types of schools, pre-elementary education, time frame for the establishment of CSS, components of free and compulsory education, education of children with disabilities and medium of education and the teaching of languages.

Since the establishment of a common school system in Bihar was the central objective underlying the work of the Commission, it will be useful at the very outset, to summarize in brief its views on the concept, content, rationale and scope of CSS. The Commission defined CSS as a system of schools providing education of an equitable quality to all children, irrespective of their caste, creed, community, language, gender, economic condition, social status and physical or mental ability. According to the Commission, the commonness of the CSS derives from the application of common minimum norms and standards for quality education by all schools in the system. These norms and standards ensure both the quality and equality of the system.

The most fundamental among the norms is the adherence by all schools in the CSS to the values which hold together the society in which the system operates. In the Indian context, these are the principles of equality and social justice enshrined in the Indian Constitution. In addition, the system must provide the following:

(a) Minimum infrastructure consisting of land and building; minimum number, size and furnishing of classrooms; provision of drinking water and toilets; playgrounds and sports facilities; libraries, laboratories, and teaching aids; and easy access and other required facilities for the children suffering from disabilities.

(b) Well-qualified trained teachers and optimal pupil-teacher ratios.

(c) A common curriculum framework with a core component and with comparable syllabi applicable to all schools, but adequate flexibility in relation to textbooks, teaching aids, teaching-learning process, evaluation parameters, etc.

(d) A pedagogy which is holistic and child-friendly and which has a liberating influence.

(e) A decentralized school management with adequate autonomy and representation of parents, particularly mothers.

(f) A common language policy.

Moreover, the CSS is based on the concept of neighbourhood schools according to which a school must admit all the children living in the neighbourhood, which is to be specified and delineated for each school.

The basic rationale of a CSS is that it promotes equality and social justice, helps in nation-building and the creation of social capital and is most conducive to providing good education.

The Commission has asserted that no developed or developing country has achieved universalization of school education without a state-funded and state-regulated common school system. This is true among others, of all the Scandinavian countries, the United States, Canada, most of the European countries, and China, South Korea and Cuba among developing countries.

It is recalled in the Commission's Report that in India, the adoption of a CSS was first recommended by the Kothari Commission, subsequently endorsed by a number of other commissions and committees, and twice approved unanimously by the Indian Parliament. However, the support for the CSS remained confined to the realm of rhetoric. In practice, it was never taken up seriously. This has been mainly because of the dominance of the elite in educational policy making. Parents belonging to this class send their children to exclusive schools with better infrastructure, teachers and teaching standards and have, therefore, no stake in a CSS. The two formidable obstacles today identified by the Commission, for establishing CSS are:

(i) Its far-reaching financial implications due in no small measure to the cumulative neglect of the past.

(ii) The emergence in the country of a whole hierarchy of schools catering to the needs of different groups of children.

The report, however, proceeds on the assumption that there is no reason why a CSS cannot be established in India as a whole or in an Indian state even now, if there is a political will to do so.

In carrying out its basic mandate, i.e. preparing a plan of action, the Commission set before it the following overall objectives:

(i) The goal of free and compulsory education for all children in the age group 5-14 years will be reached in five years starting from April 2008, and ending with the financial year, 2012-2013.

(ii) The goal of universalizing secondary education, i.e. class IX and X will be reached in eight years commencing from the base year of 2008-09 and ending with the year 2015-16.

(iii) The goal of providing facilities according to the norms established in the report for senior secondary level education, to 70 per cent of the children completing secondary education, by 2016-17.

The CSS recommended in the report covered the age group of 5-6 years even though it has been excluded from Article 21-A and subsequently from the Right of Children to Free and Compulsory Education (RTE) Act, 2009, enacted to give effect to this article. This limited provision for compulsory pre-primary school was made because the foundations for elementary and secondary education is laid at the pre-elementary stage, and because if the children in the age group 6 to 14 years are provided free and compulsory education, it will be arbitrary and discriminatory to deprive the children at the pre-primary level from enjoying the same right. Besides, the inclusion of at least one year of pre-primary education was considered necessary also because of India's commitment to this goal under the UN Convention on the Rights of the Child.

The universalization of secondary education (Classes IX and X) as part of the CSS was recommended because there would be an inevitable pressure for entry into secondary education once elementary education was universalized. The CSS was extended to the senior secondary level (i.e. Classes XI and XII) and 70 per cent transition to this level was provided because this is a legitimate part of school education, because the completion of senior secondary education has now become a pre-condition for access to higher education and the world of work, and because the age group 17-18 years is included in the standard UN definition of childhood.

There was a built in provision in the Report for implementing Article 21-A of the Constitution. Free education was stipulated to be free, not only for tuition fees but for all other expenses, whatsoever, including the supply free of cost, of textbooks, essential stationery items, school uniforms and midday meals.

When the Commission started its work, it found that Bihar had 13 school types, in terms of the grades taught. In order to facilitate the application of the common norms and standards, the Commission recommended the reduction of these 13 school types to only three types, i.e.

(a) Primary Schools (*Prathmik Vidyalayas*) consisting of one year of pre-primary and 1-5 years of primary.

(b) Middle Schools (*Madhya Vidyalayas*) consisting of one year of pre-primary and 8 years of elementary (Classes I-VIII).

(c) Secondary and Senior Secondary Schools (*Madhyamik Vidyalayas*) consisting of secondary and senior secondary schools (Classes IX-XII).

A critical component of the Commission's mandate was to recommend a set of norms and standards for ensuring both equity and quality in school education. The norms and standards recommended by the Commission are the most extensive included in any of the plans and programmes of school education in India. Besides, separate sets of norms and standards are recommended for children at the pre-primary level, elementary level and the secondary level. The norms and standards relate to access to schools, school land, physical infrastructure, school furniture and equipment, number of teachers required and their qualifications, teachers education requirements and elements of free and compulsory education. Besides, norms for curriculum, pedagogy and teaching of languages were also established. Among the norms and standards, the following may be highlighted:

(i) A primary school will be provided within 1 kilometre from habitation; a middle school within 3 kilometres and a secondary/senior secondary school within 5 kilometres.

(ii) A primary school will have a capacity of 210 students; a middle school, 440 students; and a secondary/senior secondary school, 420 students.

(iii) Each class or section in a primary and middle school will have 40 students; at the secondary level, 40 students; and at the senior secondary level, 30 students.

(iv) Norms relating to school land and total floor area calculated on the basis of square metres per child, were prescribed for each of the three categories of schools.

(v) In each primary and middle school, there would be a hall for pre-elementary children measuring 50 square metres.

(vi) Norms were laid down for school furniture, including desks, benches, computers, library equipment and books, utensils for midday meals, equipment for games and sports, instruments for teaching art and music, school equipment, teaching-learning equipment, etc.

(vii) It was recommended that each primary school should have eight teachers; a middle school, 17 teachers; and a secondary/senior secondary school, 20 teachers. The derived pupil-teacher ratios in these schools would be 35:1, 30:1, and 22:1 respectively.

(viii) All teachers would be trained and otherwise qualified according to the norms of the National Council for Teachers' Education (NCTE).

After establishing the norms and standards, the Commission went about estimating the total number of children at different levels of schooling, i.e. primary, middle, and secondary and senior secondary, to be brought to school and provided with education of equitable quality. The size of school-going children in the population in each of the age groups was estimated year-wise up to the end of the implementation period, i.e. 2016-17, taking the base year data from the 2001 Census and applying an assumed population growth from that date till the date of implementation. This rate of growth was assumed to be moderately lower than the decadal population growth rate.

By applying this methodology, the child population in all the age groups taken together came to slightly over 3 crores in 2007-08, gradually rising to 3.72 crores in 2016-17. Going by the available information on the capacity of existing schools, it was estimated that at most only 1.5 crore students were in schools in 2007-08. Thus, in order to achieve the goals set for the CSS, the state had to bring to school the backlog of 1.5 crore children plus 72 lakh more who will be reaching the school-going age during the nine-year implementation period. This added up to a total of 2.2 crore additional children to be brought to school, calling for nearly two-and-a- half times increase in the capacity of schools in Bihar existing in 2007-08.

The next step was to calculate the number of schools to be built and teaching as well as non-teaching staff required for each school at different levels. For calculating the number of schools, the norm regarding the optimum capacity of schools at the three levels were used. Norms for the number of teaching as well as non-teaching staff required for each school at the three levels, were used for estimating the total strength of the required teaching and non-teaching staff.

Before moving to estimate the total cost of establishing the CSS, the Commission determined the unit costs of building and equipping schools, of the salary of teaching and non-teaching staff and the non-salary items of recurring expenditure. To determine these unit costs, the Commission took into account the practices followed by institutions and programmes, particularly the Central Board of Secondary Education (CBSE), *Sarva Shiksha Abhiyan*, 2007, Bihar Education Programme, 2007, those established in the reports of the two committees on right to education set up by the Government of India under the chairpersonship of Tapas Majumdar in 1999 and 2005, and the policy norms of the National Education Policy, 1986. In addition, the Commission made its own judgement for determining unit costs of several items based on the knowledge of its members and enquiries made by them.

By applying the unit cost, the Commission calculated the cost of building a new school in each category. The cost of repairing or upgrading an existing school was assumed to be half of that for building a new school. A major problem that the Commission faced was the determination of the unit cost relating to the salaries of teachers. It encountered a bewildering variety of practices of providing salaries and emoluments followed by the bewildering variety of schools operated in Bihar by different departments, agencies and entities. The Commission adopted "the state level average teacher salary" applied by CABE in its report on the Right to Education Bill 2004. This figure was adjusted against inflation since 2004. Since this figure was only for teachers of primary and middle schools, the Commission increased it by Rs. 2000/- and Rs. 3500/- respectively for secondary school teachers in the trained graduate and postgraduate categories. The Commission did not encounter much of a problem in recommending the non-salary component of the recurring expenditure which was accounted for almost entirely by measures necessary for providing free school education, i.e. provision free of cost, of books, stationery, school uniforms, midday meals, etc.

A very important component of the non-recurring expenditure calculated in the report is the cost to be incurred for renovating existing teacher education institutions and building new institutions in this category. This part of the report entitled "Teachers' Education in the Common School System" (Chapter 9) contains one of the most exhaustive sets of recommendation ever made in the country in recent years, for revamping teachers education institutions in a state of India. The recommendations include transforming the existing Cluster Resource Centres, Block Resource Centres, District Institutes of Educational Training (DIETs), Primary Teacher Education Colleges (PTECs), and State Council of Educational Research and Training (SCERT), instituting Gandhian pedagogy in the Bihar school system, expanding and revamping teachers' education for secondary education through B.Ed. degrees and the role of universities in teachers' education and education planning and research.

The Commission found that teachers' education institutions in Bihar suffered more than in any other state of India from the cumulative neglect over decades. The institutions which were supposed to have been built, like DIET, were either never built or remained partially built. The existing institutions like SCERT, Training Colleges, Primary Teacher Education Colleges (PTECs), Block Resource Centres, etc., had been allowed to decay to the point of becoming almost non-functional. The Commission in its recommendations put forward a three-year plan of structural and process-oriented transformation of the entire system of teachers education in order to respond to the challenges of moving towards the CSS. To this end, suggestions were made for total revamping of courses taught by these institutions, and the recruitment of additional faculty starting from the level of researchers to professors for expanding and upgrading the institutions in each of the above categories.

Among the measures recommended by the Commission in this chapter, the one deserving particular mention is transforming Cluster Resource Centres into Cluster Teacher Forum or *Sankul Shikshak Manch* (SSM) which will bring together teachers belonging to all schools in a specified area on a common platform for sharing experience and fostering peer group interaction and learning. A major innovation proposed was to make the teachers, through the SSM responsible for school inspection, thus replacing the present almost defunct system of school inspection by officials of the Education Department of the state. The Commission also recommended the strengthening and expansion of B.Ed.

Training Colleges and University Department to take care, both qualitatively and quantitatively the enhanced requirement of teachers' education to man posts at the secondary level of schooling.

In compliance with one of its terms of reference relating to the then existing 391 *Buniyadi Vidyalayas* (basic education schools), the Commission came out with a major innovation whereby the curriculum of all the primary and middle schools of the state would be transformed within the five-year period starting from 2008, on the basis of the Gandhian pedagogic principle of acquiring knowledge, building values, and developing skills through productive work. It was recommended that 150 of these *Buniyadi Vidyalayas* would be converted into Buniyadi Education Curriculum Development Centres. These centres would be responsible for developing work-centred curriculum for the elementary stage of education. The remaining *Buniyadi Vidyalayas* would be merged with the CSS.

The Commission calculated the non-recurring costs of building and renovating teachers' education institutions and the recurring cost of running them on a restructured basis. It included in this estimate the recurring cost of providing in-service, on-service and induction training of teachers and of Buniyadi Education Curriculum Development Centres.

In a separate chapter, the Commission recommended restructuring the departmental and field level administration of school education, the basic intention behind which was to entrust such administration to experts in the field of education and create a special service for this purpose.

The Commission also made recommendations for reconstituting school management committees based on the principles of democracy, decentralization and predominant role of parents, particularly mothers, in these committees. Two almost identical draft legislations for the management of schools, one for primary and middle schools and the other for secondary schools, were proposed.

A distinguishing feature of the report of the CSS Commission was its elaborate recommendations on medium of education and teaching of languages. These recommendations form a part of Chapter 5, on issues relating to the CSS and are also included in the draft Bill recommended by the Commission to be enacted for giving effect to the CSS. This was perhaps for the first time since the early 1990s that the three-language formula originally recommended by the University Education Commission (1948-49) and later adopted by the Indian Parliament in 1968, was revisited with such meticulous care and attention. Without going into all the details contained in the recommendations on the subject, the main elements of the language policy recommended by the Commission can be summarized as follows:

(i) The first three years of school education consisting of one year of pre-primary and the first two years of primary stage, will be imparted through the medium of the child's mother tongue.

(ii) The children from the Hindi-speaking region will also be familiarized with Hindi mainly through spoken words and visuals at this stage. The mother tongue will be replaced by Hindi as the medium of instruction from Class III and this will continue up to Class X.

(iii) For children coming from the non-Hindi speaking region, familiarization with Urdu or the regional language will start from the pre-primary stage till Class II and Urdu or the regional language will replace the mother tongue as a medium of instruction from Class III. This will continue up to Class X.

(iv) Given the importance of the English language in modern times, familiarization with English will also start for children coming from both Hindi and non-Hindi speaking regions during the first three years of school education. English as a language (and not as a medium of instruction) will be introduced from Class III and will continue up to Class X.

(v) Children coming from the Hindi-speaking region will be required to offer a third language from Class VI. This will be one of the modern Indian languages other than Hindi and will include Sanskrit and Urdu. Children coming from the non-Hindi-speaking region will be required to learn Hindi as the third language starting from Class VI.

(vi) At the Higher Secondary level, Hindi and English will be taught as compulsory languages for students coming from the Hindi-speaking region; and Urdu or the regional language as well as English will be taught as compulsory subjects to students coming from the non-Hindi-speaking region.

(vii) Hindi will be used as the medium of instruction for students in the Hindi-speaking region, and Urdu or the regional language will be used as the medium of instruction for students coming from the non-Hindi-speaking region, up to Class XII, unless 10 students or more in either category opt for being taught through the medium of another language of their choice. In that case, special arrangements for teaching these students through the medium of their preferred language will be made.

In addition to the above, the Commission recommended giving priority to recruiting local teachers for teaching through the medium of the mother tongue and giving them on-service training for teaching through the mother tongue during the first three years of school education. The Commission also recommended arrangements for conducting research in local folklore, legends, festivals, etc. in order to make teaching at this level interesting and enjoyable.

The CSS report contains a separate chapter under the title "Legal Framework for Common School System". After a brief introductory section which traces the origins of the basic principles and values of school education, this chapter contains the text of a legislation recommended to be adopted by the Bihar legislature for giving effect to the CSS. The title of this legislation is: 'The Bihar Right to Education and Common School System (Equality, Excellence and Social Justice), Bill, 2007'. It needs to be underlined that this was recommended two years before the RTE Act, 2009, was adopted by the Indian Parliament.

A distinguishing feature of the proposed legislation was its provision for the constitution of a State Commission for School Education, entrusted with the responsibility to monitor all aspects of the functioning of the CSS in Bihar; to act as the Court of Last Appeal in relation to any grievances regarding non-implementation of any provision of the Act; to tender policy advice to the State Government and Local Bodies regarding effective implementation of the Act; and to commission surveys, studies and research, as necessary, for the discharge of its functions. One of the major problems with the RTE Act has been that instead of establishing a similar Commission at the central level, it entrusted the task of monitoring the implementation of the Act to the National Commission for Protection of Child Rights which is under-staffed, non-existent in most states and saddled with the additional task of protecting the rights of the child in areas other than education. Besides, the task entrusted to the Commission on Child Rights is confined to monitoring of implementation of the RTE Act, whereas the mandate of the proposed Commission in the Bihar CSS Act is much more extensive.

Apart from the issue of medium of education and teaching of languages, the Commission dealt with a number of other important issues relating to the establishment of CSS in Bihar. These included pre-elementary education, education of children with disabilities, midday meals and incentives for bringing to school children in the street and those employed as labour. The Commission considered these issues very carefully and seriously. The implications and pros and cons of possible actions on each of these issues were succinctly brought out and definitive recommendation made. The sections devoted to these issues are short and precise, but they are complete in themselves without being comprehensive. These sections are likely to be a very useful source of reference for those who want to have an understanding of these issues and are looking for ideas and suggestions on how to deal with them.

Chapter 13 of the report is by far its most important part. It is in this chapter that the cost of establishing a CSS in Bihar within the stipulated time frame is calculated and a detailed year-wise plan is drawn up for building schools, recruiting teachers', training teachers, and strengthening and expanding teachers education institutions. This chapter provides a complete year-wise phased programme for implementing the CSS. The aggregate expenditure required for building the CSS has been obtained by adding up the different components of the non-recurring and recurring items of expenditure. The total estimated expenditure for implementing the CSS came to Rs. 2,04,650.7 crores or an average of Rs. 22,739 crores per annum at 2007-08 prices. In order to calculate the additional resources required, the amounts that the state government would be spending on school education during the nine-year period on a year-to-year basis were deducted. This amount was projected to be Rs. 6,555.3 crores for the base year 2008-09. As the required expenditure for that year for implementing the CSS was estimated to be Rs. 17,254.9 crores, the additional expenditure required to be made in the first year of the implementation period, i.e. 2008-09 was estimated at Rs. 10,699.6 crores. This additional expenditure called for a 61 per cent increase in the total expenditure estimated to be made by the state government on education that year.

This figure may appear daunting. Taking into account the tight budgetary position of the state government, a 61 per cent increase under the heading of school education in its budget could be regarded as going beyond the financial capacity of the state government. On the other hand, given the great significance and the magnitude of the task of replacing the present school education system by a common school system and given the cumulative neglect of school education all over the country, and on a much larger scale in the state of Bihar, mobilization of resources on this scale was absolutely essential.

Besides, Rs. 10,699.6 crores is not such a huge amount when we consider that there have been hundreds of projects under implementation of the central and state government, each of which stipulate expenditure exceeding this amount. Can't the establishment of a CSS in one of the most populous states of the country, deserve investment on the scale of one of these hundreds of projects?

Moreover, it should be remembered that only a part of the expenditure of this amount was estimated to be of a recurring nature. The bulk of the expenditure estimated, was non-recurring which would not have been required to be incurred after the CSS would have come fully into operation by the end of 2016-17.

The report makes calculations to demonstrate that if 6 per cent of India's GDP had been devoted to education, of which according to the observed trend, 75 per cent would have been incurred for school education and if Bihar had got 8.3 per cent of this expenditure, which is proportionate to its share of the country's population, the total amount available to Bihar would have fallen short of the total expenditure estimated by the Commission for the year 2008-09, by only Rs. 1,748 crores, an amount which would not have been difficult to mobilize. The Commission made a number of suggestions for mobilizing the additional resources estimated by it to be required for implementing CSS in Bihar. These included:

(i) All central contributions for Bihar under Sarva Shiksha Abhiyan to be channelled for implementing the CSS.

(ii) All projects and programmes in the state not consistent with the approach of CSS to be discontinued forthwith and the resources thus released to be used for financing the CSS.

(iii) The rural and urban community to be mobilized for helping to build schools and equipping them mainly through donations of land and by way of providing various components of infrastructure.

(iv) The state government increasing the share of school education in the total budget from the then existing level of 13 per cent of the budget to 20 per cent.

(v) And finally, if necessary, approaching national financial institutions, particularly banks, to provide loans to the state government as their contribution under the corporate social responsibility under the Companies Act.

It can be asserted with some confidence in retrospect that if all these suggestions for mobilizing resources had been pursued, financing would not have come in the way of the implementation of CSS in Bihar, and the state would have set an example the emulation of which country-wide would have revolutionized the school education system in India, without which it will not be possible to attain inclusive and sustainable development of the country.

Part III
Inequality in Education

9

Inequality and Imbalances in the Education System of India: Insights from NSSO 71st Round

Susmita Mitra

This statistical essay highlights one of the important and disconcerting features of the Indian education system, i.e. its inherent inegalitarian character. Equality in education matters at every level, from individual students, who deserve to be treated fairly and have the opportunity to fulfil their potential and achieve their aspirations, up to the society at large because only a society having an egalitarian education system can be sustainable as it can draw on the talents of all, not remain divided and blurred by discrimination.

Unfortunately, in India, educational facilities are unequally distributed among regional, socio-economic, gender, religion, caste and occupational groups of population. This paper documents the extent of inequality of educational opportunity in the country through statistics largely drawn from the latest, 71st round (2014), of the National Sample Survey Organization (NSSO) data.

Section I: Universalization of Education

The NSSO defines a literate person as one who can read and write a simple message in any language with understanding. As per the 71st round of NSS for the year 2014, about 25 per cent, i.e. one in every four persons of the age of 7 years and above is still illiterate (Table 1). The percentage of illiterate population is more in rural areas (29.2 per cent) compared to urban areas (14.1 per cent). Similarly, the percentage of illiterate population is more for females (32.9 per cent) compared to males (16.8 per cent).

Although this picture is more or less true for all the individual states/UTs, there are also regional disparities. For example, there is a difference of more than 20 per cent between rural and urban literacy rates in many states/UTs, like Andhra Pradesh (60 per cent rural literacy rate and 81.1 per cent urban literacy rate), Arunachal Pradesh (72.9 per cent rural literacy rate and 92.9 per cent urban literacy rate), Madhya Pradesh (66.2 per cent rural literacy rate and 86.0 per cent urban literacy rate), Telangana (58.0 per cent rural literacy rate and 83.4 per cent urban literacy rate), and Dadra & Nagar Haveli (68.2 per cent rural literacy rate and 91.1 per cent urban literacy rate). The rural female literacy rate is less than 60 per cent in many states/UTs, like Andhra Pradesh (50.5 per cent), Bihar (54.2 per cent), Jharkhand (55.2 per cent), Madhya Pradesh (54.3 per cent), Rajasthan (49.4 per cent), Uttar Pradesh (56.5 per cent), and Dadra & Nagar Haveli (57.2 per cent).

To have a clear picture of rural-urban and gender gap, Table 2 presents state-wise ratios of female to male and rural to urban data. By definition, a lower fraction implies higher rural-urban and gender gap. The gender gap is prominent in Rajasthan both in rural as well as urban areas with female to male literacy ratio as low as 0.64 and 0.77 respectively. On the other hand, female to male ratios are higher in the north-eastern states like Arunachal Pradesh (rural ratio 0.92 and urban ratio 0.94), Assam (rural ratio 0.91 and urban ratio 0.95), Meghalaya (rural ratio 0.99 and urban ratio 0.95), Mizoram (rural ratio 0.95 and urban ratio 1.00), Nagaland (rural ratio 0.96 and urban ratio 0.97), Sikkim (rural ratio 0.97 and urban ratio 0.99), and Tripura (rural ratio 0.92 and urban ratio 0.93).

The rural-urban gap is prominent in Telangana for both males and females, with rural to urban literacy ratio being as low as 0.77 and 0.61 for males and females respectively. However, in many states/UTs the rural-urban gap, measured in terms of rural to urban literacy ratio, is much higher for females compared to their male counterparts, e.g. Andhra Pradesh (male ratio 0.80 and

Table 1: Literacy Rates (%) for Persons (Age 7 Years and Above) for Each State/UT

State/UT	Literacy Rate (%)								
	Rural			Urban			Rural + Urban		
	Male	Female	Total	Male	Female	Total	Male	Female	Total
Andhra Pradesh	69.6	50.5	60.0	87.3	75.1	81.1	75.4	58.2	66.8
Arunachal Pradesh	75.8	70.0	72.9	95.1	89.4	92.2	78.9	73.2	76.3
Assam	88.7	81.1	85.1	93.8	89.1	91.6	89.4	82.1	85.9
Bihar	75.7	54.2	65.5	86.2	72.2	79.5	76.9	56.2	67.0
Chhattisgarh	80.3	60.0	70.4	91.6	76.2	84.3	82.7	63.1	73.1
Delhi	95.8	79.1	88.9	93.3	86.5	90.2	93.5	86.1	90.3
Goa	96.9	88.2	92.2	94.3	86.1	90.4	95.1	87.1	91.1
Gujarat	84.1	63.4	74.0	94.0	82.2	88.5	88.4	70.8	79.9
Haryana	83.2	62.0	72.9	90.9	76.6	84.4	85.7	66.8	76.6
Himachal Pradesh	92.0	76.2	84.1	98.7	87.2	93.2	92.8	77.4	85.1
Jammu & Kashmir	83.1	62.5	73.3	85.4	70.6	78.3	83.5	64.2	74.4
Jharkhand	77.0	55.2	66.4	89.5	77.5	83.7	79.6	59.9	70.3
Karnataka	76.3	60.7	68.5	91.7	81.5	86.8	82.5	68.6	75.5
Kerala	97.1	91.9	94.4	97.6	94.8	96.1	97.4	93.2	95.2
Madhya Pradesh	77.4	54.3	66.2	92.4	78.6	86.0	81.4	60.7	71.3
Maharashtra	87.2	70.3	78.8	93.9	86.0	90.2	90.2	77.0	83.8
Manipur	92.1	81.4	87.0	96.5	87.5	92.0	93.5	83.5	88.6
Meghalaya	93.2	92.5	92.9	99.6	94.6	96.9	94.3	93.0	93.6

Contd...

State/UT	Literacy Rate (%)								
	Rural			Urban			Rural + Urban		
	Male	Female	Total	Male	Female	Total	Male	Female	Total
Mizoram	95.5	91.1	93.2	99.6	99.4	99.6	97.4	94.8	96.2
Nagaland	97.5	93.3	95.4	98.4	95.0	96.7	97.6	93.7	95.7
Odisha	81.3	65.8	73.6	91.2	77.2	84.1	83.2	67.8	75.5
Punjab	79.9	66.8	73.6	91.2	85.0	88.3	84.0	73.4	79.0
Rajasthan	77.7	49.4	63.7	88.2	68.0	78.6	80.7	54.1	67.6
Sikkim	90.0	87.6	88.8	94.3	92.9	93.5	90.7	88.5	89.7
Tamil Nadu	81.9	64.7	73.0	92.1	82.7	87.4	86.9	73.7	80.2
Telangana	68.8	47.0	58.0	89.8	76.8	83.4	76.8	58.3	67.7
Tripura	91.0	83.6	87.5	93.8	87.0	90.5	91.7	84.4	88.2
Uttar Pradesh	77.8	56.5	67.6	84.4	72.5	78.8	79.2	60.1	70.1
Uttarakhand	91.5	74.6	83.7	94.3	85.4	90.1	92.1	77.2	85.1
West Bengal	78.7	68.3	73.6	91.4	85.0	88.4	82.7	73.3	78.3
A&N Islands	82.9	78.9	81.0	93.8	89.1	91.5	87.2	82.9	85.0
Chandigarh	91.5	66.1	80.2	96.6	93.7	95.4	96.4	92.6	94.7
Dadra & Nagar Haveli	79.4	57.2	68.2	94.3	86.4	91.1	87.0	69.6	79.0
Daman & Diu	89.0	73.2	81.1	86.1	95.9	89.4	86.4	90.0	87.8
Lakshadweep	98.7	92.4	95.7	95.4	87.9	91.7	96.1	88.7	92.7
Puducherry	93.4	77.8	85.9	94.7	84.2	89.4	94.4	82.0	88.4
All-India	**79.8**	**61.3**	**70.8**	**91.1**	**80.8**	**85.9**	**83.2**	**67.1**	**75.4**

female ratio 0.67), Bihar (male ratio 0.88 and female ratio 0.75), Gujarat (male ratio 0.89 and female ratio 0.77), Uttar Pradesh (male ratio 0.92 and female ratio 0.78), Chandigarh (male ratio 0.95 and female ratio 0.71), and Dadra & Nagar Haveli (male ratio 0.84 and female ratio 0.66).

Table 2: Female to Male and Rural to Urban Literacy Ratio: Reflection on Disparity

State/UT	Female/Male Literacy Ratio		Rural/Urban Literacy Ratio	
	Rural	Urban	Male	Female
Andhra Pradesh	0.73	0.86	0.80	0.67
Arunachal Pradesh	0.92	0.94	0.80	0.78
Assam	0.91	0.95	0.95	0.91
Bihar	0.72	0.84	0.88	0.75
Chhattisgarh	0.75	0.83	0.88	0.79
Delhi	0.83	0.93	1.03	0.91
Goa	0.91	0.91	1.03	1.02
Gujarat	0.75	0.87	0.89	0.77
Haryana	0.75	0.84	0.92	0.81
Himachal Pradesh	0.83	0.88	0.93	0.87
Jammu & Kashmir	0.75	0.83	0.97	0.89
Jharkhand	0.72	0.87	0.86	0.71
Karnataka	0.80	0.89	0.83	0.74
Kerala	0.95	0.97	0.99	0.97
Madhya Pradesh	0.70	0.85	0.84	0.69
Maharashtra	0.81	0.92	0.93	0.82
Manipur	0.88	0.91	0.95	0.93
Meghalaya	0.99	0.95	0.94	0.98
Mizoram	0.95	1.00	0.96	0.92
Nagaland	0.96	0.97	0.99	0.98
Odisha	0.81	0.85	0.89	0.85
Punjab	0.84	0.93	0.88	0.79
Rajasthan	0.64	0.77	0.88	0.73
Sikkim	0.97	0.99	0.95	0.94
Tamil Nadu	0.79	0.90	0.89	0.78
Telangana	0.68	0.86	0.77	0.61
Tripura	0.92	0.93	0.97	0.96

Contd...

State/UT	Female/Male Literacy Ratio		Rural/Urban Literacy Ratio	
	Rural	Urban	Male	Female
Uttar Pradesh	0.73	0.86	0.92	0.78
Uttarakhand	0.82	0.91	0.97	0.87
West Bengal	0.87	0.93	0.86	0.80
A&N Islands	0.95	0.95	0.88	0.89
Chandigarh	0.72	0.97	0.95	0.71
Dadra & Nagar Haveli	0.72	0.92	0.84	0.66
Daman & Diu	0.82	1.11	1.03	0.76
Lakshadweep	0.94	0.92	1.03	1.05
Puducherry	0.83	0.89	0.99	0.92
All-India	**0.77**	**0.89**	**0.88**	**0.76**

While the gender gap in the literacy rate is a result of the country's patriarchal nature (which is clearer from the sharp contrast of statistics in the north-eastern states, since many of those are matriarchal), the rural-urban gap in the literacy rate is a result of unbalanced urbanization and development pattern. If the rural people are deprived of education, which is a necessary condition of any development process, then what kind of spillover effect of urbanization-led growth we are planning and implementing is going to be?

Even after completing 70 years of independence, there still exists caste-wise inequality in India, which is reflected in the literacy rate as well. The literacy scenario for different social groups is presented in Table 3. Compared to Scheduled Tribes (STs) and Scheduled Castes (SCs), the situation is relatively better for the Other Backward Classes (OBCs). There are a number of states where the literacy rate is even less than 60 per cent for SC population, e.g. Andhra Pradesh (58 per cent) and Bihar (57 per cent), as well as for ST population, e.g. Andhra Pradesh (51 per cent), Haryana (52 per cent), Rajasthan (55 per cent), and Telangana (57 per cent). The situation is worse for the SC and ST female population. There are states where the literacy rate of SC females is even less than 50 per cent, e.g. Bihar (46 per cent) and Rajasthan (47 per cent), and there are even more number of states where the literacy rate of ST females is less than 50 per cent,

Table 3: Literary Rates (%) for Persons (Age 7 Years and Above) for Each State/UT by Social Group

State/UT	ST			SC			OBC		
	Males	Females	Persons	Males	Females	Persons	Males	Females	Persons
Andhra Pradesh	59	43	51	65	51	58	74	55	64
Arunachal Pradesh	79	73	76	87	85	74	--	97	99
Assam	92	85	89	91	84	88	88	81	85
Bihar	78	46	60	66	46	57	77	55	67
Chhattisgarh	78	57	68	80	64	72	87	66	77
Delhi	--	91	95	91	77	85	87	77	83
Goa	92	74	83	98	83	91	99	90	94
Gujarat	78	56	67	90	72	81	87	66	77
Haryana	67	39	52	80	55	69	85	64	75
Himachal Pradesh	85	71	78	91	73	82	96	76	85
Jammu & Kashmir	78	53	66	86	68	77	84	61	73
Jharkhand	74	56	65	75	58	67	82	60	72
Karnataka	71	56	64	74	57	65	85	72	78
Kerala	90	88	89	94	84	89	98	93	95
Madhya Pradesh	69	50	60	78	59	69	84	61	73
Maharashtra	76	59	68	88	72	80	92	80	86
Manipur	92	83	88	89	73	81	95	84	90
Meghalaya	94	93	94	84	90	88	--	48	87
Mizoram	97	95	96	--	--	--	--	--	--

Contd...

State/UT	ST			SC			OBC		
	Males	Females	Persons	Males	Females	Persons	Males	Females	Persons
Nagaland	98	95	96	--	72	86	97	90	94
Odisha	73	52	62	79	64	72	88	73	80
Punjab	69	61	65	76	63	70	89	76	83
Rajasthan	68	40	55	78	47	63	82	55	69
Sikkim	87	86	86	93	89	91	94	92	93
Tamil Nadu	73	62	68	82	67	75	89	76	82
Telangana	68	44	57	69	56	62	77	58	68
Tripura	90	81	86	91	84	88	92	86	89
Uttar Pradesh	79	62	71	74	52	63	78	58	69
Uttarakhand	--	62	77	90	70	81	88	78	83
West Bengal	71	54	63	79	69	74	84	75	80
A&N Islands	74	68	71	--	--	--	85	94	92
Chandigarh	--	--	--	94	85	90	95	99	97
Dadra & Nagar Haveli	81	58	69	66	58	62	84	70	79
Daman & Diu	--	82	96	--	93	97	95	88	91
Lakshadweep	96	89	93	--	--	--	--	--	--
Puducherry	69	--	78	97	74	86	95	83	89
All-India	**75**	**57**	**67**	**78**	**60**	**69**	**84**	**66**	**75**

e.g. Andhra Pradesh (43 per cent), Bihar (46 per cent), Haryana (39 per cent), Rajasthan (40 per cent), and Telangana (44 per cent).

Apart from inequality among the rural-urban population, gender and different social groups, there is economic inequality as well. Among the 75 per cent of people who are literate, Table 4 presents the national picture of percentage distribution of these people by completed level of education for each quintile class of usual monthly per capita consumer expenditure (UMPCE). People in the first quintile are the poorest and in the fifth quintile are the richest. About 39.3 per cent of the poorest people in the rural areas and 31.9 per cent poorest people in the urban areas are only literate and have not even completed the primary level of education.

Table 4: Percentage Distribution of Literates (For All Age) by Completed Level of Education for Each Quintile Class of UMPCE#

Completed Level of Education	Quintile Class of UMPCE					
	1	2	3	4	5	all
		Rural				
literate but Below Primary	39.3	33.6	29.2	25.7	19.1	28.6
Primary	25.9	25.3	24.2	22.8	18.1	23.0
Upper Primary	19.9	21.7	21.6	21.3	20.1	20.9
Secondary and Higher Secondary	13.1	16.6	20.8	24.2	30.7	21.6
Diploma/Certificate	0.2	0.5	0.8	1.2	2.8	1.2
Graduation and Above	1.6	2.3	3.4	4.8	9.3	4.6
All	100.0	100.0	100.0	100.0	100.0	100.0
		Urban				
Literate but Below Primary	31.9	24.4	18.3	13.6	8.0	18.2
Primary	24.0	20.3	18.1	13.2	7.9	16.1
Upper Primary	20.3	22.2	19.1	16.3	10.3	17.2
Secondary and Higher Secondary	18.8	25.2	30.4	34.3	31.5	28.7
Diploma/Certificate	0.8	1.2	2.2	3.4	4.5	2.6
Graduation and Above	4.2	6.5	11.8	19.2	37.8	17.1
All	100.0	100.0	100.0	100.0	100.0	100.0

#Usual Monthly Per Capita Consumer Expenditure (UMPCE)

Table 4 can be read in both the causal directions. On one hand, it can be interpreted as less accessibility of the poor people to higher education and on the other hand it can also be inferred as a direct relation between education level and income. For example, share of people in the richest group who have completed graduation and above (9.3 per cent) is almost 6 times of those who are in the poorest group (1.6 per cent) in the rural areas, whereas in the urban areas the jump is 9 times (with 37.8 per cent in the richest group compared to 4.2 per cent in the poorest group. In urban areas this larger gap might be due to larger income options with higher level of education.

Thus, in terms of universalization of education, data reveal that even today on an average one person per four is illiterate. This is simply the average picture, whereas the country has rural-urban gaps, gaps between general and Scheduled Castes, and that between people of different income levels. On top of these, the education status of females is worse than its male counterparts in all the cases. While discussing the formal education system, enrolment and dropout rates are better indicators of educational status of population, compared to literacy rates. Therefore the enrolment and dropout rates are discussed in the following section.

Section II: Enrolments and Dropouts

Table 5 presents the population of never enrolled persons vis-à-vis the percentages of people who are currently enrolled and attending the classes, in the age group of 5 to 29 years in different regions. The table shows that on an average, 8.1 per cent of males and 14 per cent females in the rural areas have never enrolled for education. The percentages are relatively less for the urban areas (4.6 per cent males and 6.7 per cent females). However, there are large regional disparities. The percentages of never enrolled males in rural areas are higher than the national average in states/UTs like Bihar (15.1 per cent), Uttar Pradesh (11.2 per cent), Chandigarh (10.2 per cent), and Dadra & Nagar Haveli (21 per cent). On the other hand, percentage of never enrolled females are higher than the national average in many states/UTs like Bihar (24 per cent), Jharkhand (18.6 per cent), Madhya Pradesh (18.9 per cent), Rajasthan (22.1 per cent), Uttar Pradesh (18.9 per cent), and Dadra & Nagar Haveli (20.2 per cent).

Table 5: Enrolment Status of Persons Aged 5-29 Years for Each State/UT

State/UT	Rural				Urban			
	Males		Females		Males		Females	
	Never Enrolled	Enrolled and Attending	Never Enrolled	Enrolled and Attending	Never Enrolled	Enrolled and Attending	Never Enrolled	Enrolled and Attending
Andhra Pradesh	7.3	53.6	12.0	47.8	2.8	58.0	4.9	53.6
Arunachal Pradesh	7.1	70.7	13.0	64.9	3.3	75.0	3.9	62.7
Assam	4.0	60.0	8.4	52.0	5.7	57.9	6.4	56.3
Bihar	15.1	61.8	24.2	55.2	7.2	65.9	12.6	63.5
Chhattisgarh	6.3	56.8	9.1	56.3	4.6	59.4	7.2	59.5
Delhi	5.4	47.1	8.3	36.6	3.9	54.9	6.7	53.6
Goa	8.4	37.2	3.7	60.2	0.0	61.5	6.2	66.7
Gujarat	5.8	54.6	10.0	47.9	2.4	52.5	5.8	49.9
Haryana	4.9	59.0	7.5	53.9	6.6	57.7	9.9	52.8
Himachal Pradesh	1.3	69.1	1.9	65.3	0.0	55.2	2.4	59.2
Jammu & Kashmir	3.9	68.0	8.1	67.3	4.1	59.8	3.9	62.5
Jharkhand	8.6	62.1	18.6	54.9	2.2	56.3	5.9	60.1
Karnataka	6.3	53.3	8.3	48.1	2.5	52.2	4.6	49.6
Kerala	0.3	66.8	0.8	64.5	0.0	63.7	0.1	61.7
Madhya Pradesh	7.6	54.4	18.9	49.6	3.2	57.3	6.1	57.5
Maharashtra	3.9	58.2	5.1	50.7	3.2	55.8	2.4	49.9

Contd...

State/UT	Rural				Urban			
	Males		Females		Males		Females	
	Never Enrolled	Enrolled and Attending	Never Enrolled	Enrolled and Attending	Never Enrolled	Enrolled and Attending	Never Enrolled	Enrolled and Attending
Manipur	2.8	70.6	6.4	54.2	2.5	76.5	3.2	66.7
Meghalaya	3.9	59.3	3.9	56.5	0.1	68.0	7.0	65.4
Mizoram	4.1	62.6	7.3	58.8	1.3	70.5	1.4	60.9
Nagaland	3.1	68.6	3.3	60.3	0.1	64.3	2.0	60.3
Odisha	5.8	51.8	9.9	47.7	7.3	52.1	12.2	51.0
Punjab	4.2	55.8	5.7	55.5	2.0	57.3	6.2	56.2
Rajasthan	9.3	62.9	22.1	50.5	7.5	61.4	15.3	54.3
Sikkim	1.0	67.5	1.3	65.9	0.5	43.7	2.5	63.8
Tamil Nadu	1.2	61.0	3.1	54.9	1.0	56.6	1.5	56.4
Telangana	4.8	61.6	12.4	52.1	2.3	65.4	3.1	51.2
Tripura	4.9	66.7	5.2	47.1	1.9	58.9	4.7	48.9
Uttar Pradesh	11.2	59.9	18.9	54.7	11.9	55.3	14.7	56.8
Uttarakhand	1.4	70.3	3.0	58.5	3.4	65.4	5.2	60.3
West Bengal	7.9	53.0	9.8	53.7	3.7	55.5	5.2	51.8
A&N Islands	1.4	45.2	5.2	57.9	2.6	61.5	1.2	67.5
Chandigarh	10.2	43.6	13.5	45.0	1.6	55.8	9.6	55.4
Dadra & Nagar Haveli	21.0	37.7	20.2	47.0	0.5	45.8	0.0	55.6

Contd...

State/UT	Rural				Urban			
	Males		Females		Males		Females	
	Never Enrolled	Enrolled and Attending	Never Enrolled	Enrolled and Attending	Never Enrolled	Enrolled and Attending	Never Enrolled	Enrolled and Attending
Daman & Diu	1.8	51.8	6.6	49.9	20.3	20.1	0.2	41.5
Lakshadweep	0.0	55.9	0.0	55.1	1.1	46.3	0.0	50.9
Puducherry	2.4	50.6	0.0	50.2	4.1	52.8	5.0	49.5
All-India	**8.1**	**58.7**	**14.0**	**53.0**	**4.6**	**57.0**	**6.7**	**54.6**

Data show some interesting trends about never enrolled persons. In states like Haryana and Odisha, the percentages of never enrolled persons are higher in urban areas compared to rural areas for both genders (in Haryana 4.9 per cent males and 7.5 per cent females in rural areas and 6.6 per cent males and 9.9 per cent females in the urban areas have never enrolled, whereas in Odisha the rural percentages for male and female are 5.8 per cent and 9.9 per cent in contrast to 7.3 per cent and 12.2 per cent respectively in the urban areas). On the other hand, in Dadra & Nagar Haveli, there is significant difference between rural and urban areas, with 21 per cent males and 20.2 per cent females in rural areas and only 0.5 per cent males and 0 per cent females in the urban areas having never enrolled.

Regional data for caste, religion and income-wise population of never enrolled persons is not available. However, gender, caste, religion and income-wise national scenario of never enrolled persons is presented in Table 6 with rural and urban disparity, which shows that across all categories, the rural situation is worse than the urban situation. Caste-wise, the percentage of non-enrolment is higher among STs, followed by SCs and OBCs. Among various religious groups, Muslims have the highest percentage on non-enrolment, both in rural and urban areas. However, when it comes to income-wise disparity, the situation is more or less the same for the poorest people (UMPCE quintile 1) in both rural and urban areas. Approximately the situation is two times worse in quintile 2, three times worse in quintile 3, four times worse in quintile 4 and five times worse in quintile 5 in the rural areas compared to the urban areas. The data reveal that currently income inequality is more prominent than other inequalities.

The main reasons for never-enrolling are cited as parents' lack of interest in their children's education (29.2 per cent), followed by financial constraints (20.5 per cent) and their engagement in domestic activities (15 per cent). The last column of reasons as 'other' is simply a mathematical manipulation done for rounding up the percentage of reasons to 100, by the NSS data source. For example, in the cases of Kerala and Lakshadweep the percentage of never enrolled students are negligible. Thus the reasons for never-enrolling are also zero, and to round it up, the last column of reasons as 'other' is coming to 100. It should not be read as if there are other very prominent reasons for not enrolling in these two states.

Table 6: National Scenario of Percentage of Never Enrolled Persons, Gender, Caste Religion and Income-wise

	Gender		Caste			Religion					UMPCE		
	Males	Females	ST	SC	OBC	Hindus	Muslims	Christians	Sikhs	Others*	1	2	3
Rural	8.1	14.0	14.8	12.9	10.8	10.4	15.4	4.9	5.3	7.1	15.5	12.1	11.6
Urban	4.6	6.7	8.1	7.6	6.3	4.7	10.0	2.0	3.4	2.1	12.4	6.9	4.4

* Includes Jains, Buddhists, Zoroastrians and Others

Apart from the above mentioned main reasons (which are predominant in most of the states), in some states, about 10 per cent of persons never enrolled because they were required to earn for their families by engaging in different economic activities, e.g. Arunachal Pradesh (9.7 per cent), Jharkhand (11 per cent), Karnataka (10 per cent), Tamil Nadu (15.7 per cent), Telangana (11.8 per cent), and Puducherry (25.4 per cent). Also in some states/UTs, the reasons for never-enrolling is due to the fact that there is no tradition of education in the community, e.g. Gujarat (21.8 per cent), Haryana (16.6 per cent), Madhya Pradesh (10.8 per cent), Manipur (20.9 per cent), Rajasthan (11.8 per cent), Telangana (12.7 per cent), Uttarakhand (33 per cent), and very surprisingly, even in Delhi (11.7 per cent).

Table 8 presents the national scenario of these reasons for non-enrolling, gender, caste, religion and income-wise. Here also, we see prominently the main reasons for never-enrolling to be parents' lack of interest in their children's education, followed by financial constraints and their engagement in domestic activities. However, the reason of engagement in domestic activities is mainly predominant for females compared to their male counterparts, both in rural and urban areas. Among different castes, religion and people at different income levels, this reason is mainly a rural phenomenon, with the only exception of Christians where non-enrolment due to engagement in domestic activity is more prominent in urban areas compared to rural areas. Financial constraints is a major reason behind not enrolling in education in every quintile of UMPCE in the urban areas, except the richest people, where the reason was simply the other side of the coin, i.e. engagement in economic activities. Similarly, for urban Christians, the predominant reason of non-enrolling is engagement in economic activities.

Previously, Table 5 provided the population of never enrolled persons vis-à-vis the percentages of people who are currently enrolled and attending classes. Now, as per the NSSO definition, the remaining people {i.e.100 – (percentage of never enrolled + percentage of currently enrolled and attending)} are the ones who have ever enrolled but not attending currently, either because they have achieved the desired level of education, discontinuing without achieving the desired level but at least completed the last enrolment level, or dropouts without completing the last

Table 7: Percentage of Never Enrolled Persons (Age 5-29 Years) by Reason for Never-Enrolling for Each State/UT

State/UT	Not Interested in Education	Financial Constraints	Engaged in Domestic Activities	Engaged in Economic Activities	School is Far	Timings Not Suitable	Medium of Instruction Unfamiliar	No Tradition in the Community	Non-Availability of Female Teachers	Marriage	Others
Andhra Pradesh	46.5	12.3	8.0	6.9	8.9	0.0	0.0	2.6	0.0	2.5	12.2
Arunachal Pradesh	30.2	12.8	20.1	9.7	5.5	0.0	0.0	0.6	0.0	0.0	21.2
Assam	24.2	26.6	19.2	3.5	0.5	0.0	0.0	1.3	0.0	1.6	23.2
Bihar	29.3	19.2	21.5	4.8	1.6	0.1	0.3	4.6	0.0	0.0	18.6
Chhattisgarh	45.2	23.7	5.5	3.3	1.2	0.0	0.0	3.2	0.0	0.0	17.9
Delhi	11.3	31.8	19.4	3.0	0.0	0.7	0.0	11.7	0.0	0.0	22.1
Goa	0.0	48.6	0.0	0.0	0.0	0.0	0.0	0.0	0.0	0.0	51.4
Gujarat	31.3	17.0	7.9	0.2	0.1	0.0	0.0	21.8	0.0	0.0	21.6
Haryana	43.3	9.9	9.4	1.0	0.4	0.0	0.0	16.6	0.4	0.0	18.9
Himachal Pradesh	21.6	0.0	36.5	1.3	11.0	0.0	0.0	4.8	0.0	0.0	24.8
Jammu & Kashmir	21.4	30.6	124	3.3	1.4	0.0	0.0	3.4	0.0	0.1	27.5
Jharkhand	25.2	8.4	30.1	11.0	3.1	0.0	0.0	7.5	0.0	0.0	14.6
Karnataka	26.1	19.3	7.9	10.0	1.8	0.0	0.0	4.1	0.0	1.0	29.7
Kerala	0.0	0.0	0.0	0.0	0.0	0.0	0.0	0.0	0.0	0.0	100.0
Madhya Pradesh	28.9	16.9	18.7	3.4	3.1	0.0	0.0	10.8	0.0	0.7	17.5
Maharashtra	30.2	20.4	7.3	6.5	1.2	0.2	0.0	4.8	0.0	1.0	28.4
Manipur	13.9	14.9	19.2	8.6	0.0	0.6	0.0	20.9	0.0	0.4	21.5
Meghalaya	33.4	8.5	5.0	6.0	0.0	0.0	0.0	3.3	0.0	0.0	43.8
Mizoram	50.7	0.0	6.0	4.6	0.1	0.0	0.0	0.0	0.0	0.0	38.6

Contd...

State/UT	Not Interested in Education	Financial Constraints	Engaged in Domestic Activities	Engaged in Economic Activities	School is Far	Timings Not Suitable	Medium of Instruction Unfamiliar	No Tradition in the Community	Non-Availability of Female Teachers	Marriage	Others
Nagaland	7.9	8.5	4.4	4.7	0.0	0.0	0.0	0.0	0.0	0.0	74.4
Odisha	34.5	26.5	14.6	1.6	1.9	0.0	0.0	1.5	0.0	0.7	18.7
Punjab	30.1	37.5	3.0	2.1	0.0	0.0	0.0	9.7	0.0	0.0	17.6
Rajasthan	26.7	10.6	22.1	5.0	5.5	0.0	0.0	11.8	0.3	0.7	17.3
Sikkim	48.0	0.0	31.2	0.7	2.2	0.0	0.0	0.0	0.0	0.0	17.8
Tamil Nadu	38.6	14.1	7.2	15.7	3.9	0.0	0.0	0.6	0.0	1.6	28.4
Telangana	22.7	16.3	22.0	11.8	2.3	0.0	0.0	12.7	0.0	0.0	12.1
Tripura	6.8	27.1	5.5	0.7	0.0	0.0	0.0	3.9	0.0	0.0	56.0
Uttar Pradesh	26.8	24.4	11.8	3.1	1.6	0.0	0.2	0.3	0.1	0.1	31.7
Uttarakhand	15.9	4.1	12.8	0.0	0.0	0.0	0.0	33.0	0.0	0.0	34.2
West Bengal	33.5	36.7	5.4	3.2	0.7	0.0	0.1	1.3	0.0	0.0	19.2
A&N Islands	56.0	8.2	1.0	0.0	0.7	0.0	0.0	0.0	0.0	0.0	34.1
Chandigarh	0.4	28.7	4.4	0.0	0.0	0.0	0.0	1.1	0.0	0.0	65.4
Dadra&Nagar Haveli	0.0	25.1	3.7	0.0	0.0	0.0	0.0	0.0	0.0	0.0	71.2
Daman & Diu	1.5	95.3	0.0	0.0	0.0	0.0	0.0	0.0	0.0	0.0	3.1
Lakshadweep	0.0	0.0	0.0	0.0	0.0	0.0	0.0	0.0	0.0	0.0	100.0
Puducherry	0.8	0.0	7.2	25.4	7.2	14.9	0.0	0.0	0.0	0.0	44.4
All-India	**29.2**	**20.5**	**15.0**	**4.4**	**2.3**	**0.0**	**0.1**	**5.1**	**0.1**	**0.3**	**23.0**

Table 8: Percentage Distribution of Sex, Caste, Religion and Income-wise Persons by Reasons for Not Enrolment

			Not Interested in Education	Financial Constraints	Engaged in Domestic Activities	Engaged in Economic Activities	School is Far	Timings Not Suitable	Unfamiliar Medium of Instruction	Inadequate Teachers	Quality of Teachers Not Satisfactory	No Tradition in the Community	Non-Availability of Female Teachers	Non-Availability of Girls' Toilet	Marriage	Others
Gender	Rural	Males	33.2	21.5	4.8	8.9	1.8	0.0	0.2	0.0	0.1	2.9				26.5
		Females	27.0	16.3	23.4	1.7	2.9	0.0	0.1	0.0	0.0	6.7	0.1	0.0	0.6	21.1
	Urban	Males	29.5	32.8	3.8	6.9	0.4	0.0	0.0	0.0	0.0	2.2				24.3
		Females	27.1	30.0	13.4	1.1	1.7	0.0	0.0	0.0	0.0	6.3	0.0	0.0	0.4	20.0
Caste	Rural	ST	31.3	13.2	18.5	6.5	4.0	0.0	0.0	0.0	0.0	8.1	0.0	0.0	0.4	17.9
		SC	30.0	21.6	12.9	4.1	1.1	0.0	0.2	0.0	0.1	5.5	0.0	0.0	0.2	24.4
		OBC	29.6	17.3	19.0	3.9	2.8	0.1	0.1	0.0	0.0	4.0	0.1	0.0	0.4	22.7
	Urban	ST	32.9	40.2	4.1	0.6	0.0	0.0	0.0	0.0	0.0	4.0	0.0	0.0	0.1	18.1
		SC	24.3	33.4	9.3	4.0	0.1	0.0	0.0	0.0	0.0	5.1	0.0	0.0	0.3	23.4
		OBC	28.4	29.9	10.0	4.2	1.7	0.0	0.0	0.0	0.0	4.6	0.0	0.0	0.2	21.0
Religion	Rural	Hinduism	29.2	18.1	16.7	4.6	2.8	0.0	0.1	0.0	0.0	5.6	0.0	0.0	0.4	22.3
		Islam	30.5	19.3	14.3	4.2	1.5	0.0	0.1	0.0	0.0	4.1	0.2	0.0	0.1	25.7
		Christianity	29.6	12.8	7.1	6.1	1.9	0.0	0.0	0.0	0.0	0.6	0.0	0.0	0.0	41.9
		Sikhism	26.4	25.5	10.6	3.2	0.2	0.0	0.0	0.0	0.0	8.3	0.0	0.0	0.0	25.7
		Others	23.5	18.6	20.8	1.9	2.4	0.0	0.0	0.0	0.0	0.4	0.0	0.0	0.0	32.4
	Urban	Hinduism	28.8	28.7	9.2	3.0	1.6	0.0	0.0	0.0	0.0	4.8	0.0	0.0	0.3	23.6

Contd...

			Not Interested in Education	Financial Constraints	Engaged in Domestic Activities	Engaged in Economic Activities	School is Far	Timings Not Suitable	Unfamiliar Medium of Instruction	Inadequate Teachers	Quality of Teachers Not Satisfactory	No Tradition in the Community	Non-Availability of Female Teachers	Non-Availability of Girls' Toilet	Marriage	Others
		Islam	27.1	36.4	9.2	4.2	0.3	0.0	0.1	0.0	0.0	4.2	0.0	0.0	0.1	18.5
		Christianity	18.8	8.8	17.2	21.7	0.0	0.0	0.0	0.0	0.0	5.0	0.0	0.0	0.3	28.2
		Sikhism	18.3	49.0	9.0	2.1	0.0	0.0	0.0	0.0	0.0	0.0	0.0	0.0	0.0	21.7
		Others	53.9	3.6	0.8	13.3	0.0	0.0	0.0	0.0	0.0	0.0	0.0	0.0	0.7	27.8
UMPCE	Rural	1	29.8	22.5	13.5	3.5	2.1	0.0	0.1	0.0	0.0	5.6	0.0	0.0	0.5	22.4
		2	28.1	17.6	17.9	4.5	1.5	0.1	0.0	0.0	0.0	5.6	0.2	0.0	0.2	24.3
		3	30.3	16.7	15.1	5.0	4.2	0.1	0.2	0.0	0.0	5.0	0.0	0.0	0.6	22.9
		4	29.7	14.2	15.9	6.0	2.4	0.0	0.0	0.0	0.2	6.8	0.1	0.0	0.3	24.4
		5	29.3	17.5	22.5	4.2	2.2	0.0	0.4	0.0	0.0	1.8	0.0	0.0	0.0	22.1
	Urban	1	33.6	33.1	9.7	3.1	0.3	0.0	0.0	0.0	0.0	3.6	0.0	0.0	0.2	16.4
		2	25.3	33.2	8.4	3.5	1.3	0.0	0.0	0.0	0.0	5.4	0.0	0.0	0.4	22.5
		3	18.7	29.0	12.8	2.6	2.9	0.0	0.1	0.0	0.0	5.7	0.0	0.0	0.2	28.0
		4	27.5	22.5	4.4	1.4	1.2	0.0	0.0	0.0	0.0	3.8	0.0	0.0	0.1	39.1
		5	14.5	15.1	1.7	25.1	4.7	0.0	0.0	0.0	0.0	7.8	0.0	0.0	0.1	31.0

Table 9: Gender and Caste-Wise Percentage of Dropouts (Classes I-X)

States/UTs	All Categories			Scheduled Castes			Scheduled Tribes		
	Boys	Girls	Total	Boys	Girls	Total	Boys	Girls	Total
Andhra Pradesh	45.5	46.3	45.9	49.1	48.4	48.7	69.9	73.5	71.7
Arunachal Pradesh	62.4	60.3	61.4	100.0	100.0	100.0	65.1	60.6	63.1
Assam	74.1	70.7	72.4	70.4	65.8	68.2	70.5	69.0	69.8
Bihar	70.8	71.9	71.3	80.5	81.1	80.7	65.8	63.7	65.0
Chhattisgarh	50.2	51.4	50.8	55.4	56.4	55.9	53.5	53.7	53.6
Goa	15.8	17.4	16.6	49.3	52.7	51.0	--	--	--
Gujarat	49.5	59.3	54.1	39.1	52.6	45.5	65.3	68.0	66.6
Haryana	23.6	18.5	21.3	32.1	31.3	31.8	100.0	100.0	100.0
Himachal Pradesh	7.3	7.0	7.1	24.6	24.1	24.3	--	--	--
Jammu & Kashmir	45.5	42.6	44.2	60.2	59.2	59.7	79.5	84.6	81.7
Jharkhand	70.9	70.6	70.7	76.7	76.3	76.5	79.3	77.0	78.3
Karnataka	37.9	36.6	37.3	48.6	50.3	49.4	45.6	48.1	46.8
Kerala	--	--	--	6.0	2.2	4.1	34.3	25.3	30.0
Madhya Pradesh	32.0	53.7	42.3	33.5	49.4	41.0	55.4	71.7	63.0
Maharashtra	35.9	38.8	37.3	33.2	39.3	36.1	52.1	55.1	53.5
Manipur	72.0	70.3	71.1	63.1	63.7	63.4	80.2	78.2	79.2
Meghalaya	76.6	72.4	74.5	66.3	70.2	68.2	77.7	73.5	75.6
Mizoram	48.4	40.2	44.5	77.5	81.0	78.9	48.7	40.5	44.8
Nagaland	55.5	51.6	53.6	100.0	100.0	100.0	67.1	64.6	65.9

Contd...

States/UTs	All Categories			Scheduled Castes			Scheduled Tribes		
	Boys	Girls	Total	Boys	Girls	Total	Boys	Girls	Total
Odisha	62.3	61.6	61.9	69.9	69.3	69.6	77.0	77.0	77.0
Punjab	--	2.2	--	42.2	40.2	41.2	--	--	--
Rajasthan	54.3	69.4	61.7	65.1	78.1	71.6	57.5	70.0	63.7
Sikkim	61.5	53.1	57.4	72.8	70.5	71.7	39.9	22.1	31.2
Tamil Nadu	41.0	35.0	38.1	42.8	36.3	39.7	68.4	64.4	66.6
Tripura	50.9	48.3	49.6	35.8	34.0	35.0	66.9	67.7	67.3
Uttar Pradesh	44.2	50.7	47.2	53.8	51.1	52.5	36.3	24.4	31.0
Uttarakhand	35.1	37.4	36.2	43.0	48.1	45.5	34.3	35.4	34.8
West Bengal	62.6	58.5	60.6	64.9	65.1	65.0	73.3	74.4	73.8
A&N Islands	17.5	21.4	19.4	--	--	--	32.3	27.1	29.9
Chandigarh	--	--	--	--	--	--	--	--	--
D&N Haveli	44.3	59.4	51.7	30.0	16.3	23.7	51.0	67.0	59.2
Daman & Diu	26.4	23.3	25.0	--	--	--	24.8	24.2	24.5
Delhi	--	--	--	--	--	--	17.8	42.6	31.7
Lakshadweep	7.6	4.7	6.3	100.0	--	100.0	6.9	4.5	5.8
Puducherry	1.1	--	--	--	--	--	--	--	--
All-India	**48.6**	**52.2**	**50.3**	**55.0**	**55.6**	**55.3**	**64.4**	**67.6**	**65.9**

Source: Statistics of School Education 2011-12, Ministry of Human Resource Development
Note: Total dropouts by end of Class X as percentage of intake at the beginning of Class I

enrolment level. The third case being the worst, we analyse percentages of dropouts among those who have ever enrolled, in details.

Table 9 documents gender-wise and caste-wise percentages of dropouts during Classes I-X, defined as total dropouts by the end of Class X as percentage of intake at the beginning of Class I. The table shows that in almost all the states/UTs, percentages of dropouts are higher among SCs and STs compared to general categories (leading to higher than the average values of all categories). However, although on an average in India the dropout rate is higher for girls than boys, this cannot be generalized at state levels, because in most of the states/UTs the percentages are more or less the same, with the exception of Madhya Pradesh and Rajasthan where female dropout rates are higher than their male counterparts.

Table 10 shows percentage distribution of dropouts or discontinued persons (age 5-29 years) by type of household. In rural areas, on an average 40.9 per cent dropouts/discontinued persons belong to the household of self-employed in agriculture. Share of dropouts belonging to other household types are much less compared to self-employed in agriculture, and the distribution is more or less similar, e.g. self-employed in non-agriculture (14.1 per cent), regular wage/ salary earnings (11.5 per cent), casual labour in agriculture (16 per cent), and casual labour in non-agriculture (15.2 per cent). However, there are regional disparities. In some states/UTs there are high proportions (more than 50 per cent) of dropouts in regular wage/salary earnings households, e.g. Delhi (56 per cent), Goa (62 per cent), Chandigarh (74.6 per cent), Dadra & Nagar Haveli (71 per cent), and Daman & Diu (79 per cent). On the other hand, in urban areas, maximum dropouts are in the households of regular wage/salary earners (41.4 per cent), followed by self-employed households (37.2 per cent).

In the backdrop of the poor status of universalization of education, many persons who have never enrolled themselves in the formal education system, on an average 50 per cent of those dropping out from schools before completing Class X, it is a big question mark as to whether the government is really committed to the goal of Education for All.

Table 10: Percentage Distribution of Dropouts/Discontinued Persons (Age 5-29 Years) by Household Type for Each State/UT

States/UTs	Rural						Urban			
	Self Employed in Agri-culture	Self-Employed in Non-Agriculture	Regular Wage/ Salary Earnings	Casual Labour in Agri-culture	Casual Labour in Non-Agriculture	Others	Self-Employed	Regular Wage/ Salary Earnings	Casual Labour	Others
Andhra Pradesh	30.2	13.1	14.5	28.7	13.5	0.2	34.8	42.3	19.4	3.5
Arunachal Pradesh	60.1	9.9	24.8	3.9	1.3	0.0	28.2	58.2	9.5	4.1
Assam	39.2	22.0	16.0	9.0	12.3	1.4	46.3	31.9	16.3	5.5
Bihar	36.6	16.1	8.8	13.4	19.4	5.7	49.2	26.4	17.5	6.9
Chhattisgarh	51.6	6.4	5.6	22.1	13.4	0.9	22.8	40.7	28.7	7.8
Delhi	12.9	24.8	56.1	2.1	4.2	0.0	30.8	57.7	9.2	2.3
Goa	3.4	14.2	62.5	16.0	3.9	0.0	6.9	69.0	13.4	10.7
Gujarat	55.8	8.6	9.4	20.3	6.0	0.0	40.8	48.3	9.7	1.3
Haryana	35.0	10.3	22.0	9.0	20.0	3.7	38.6	46.8	12.1	2.5
Himachal Pradesh	38.8	15.1	24.4	0.5	19.2	2.0	15.7	61.6	21.3	1.4
Jammu & Kashmir	27.2	20.3	18.5	2.0	27.4	4.6	46.9	26.8	20.2	6.1
Jharkhand	37.9	12.0	11.1	4.0	30.4	4.6	23.7	36.9	28.0	11.4
Karnataka	47.5	9.1	12.8	17.0	11.9	1.7	33.8	39.7	24.1	2.5
Kerala	13.1	16.9	17.1	14.9	33.7	4.4	25.3	30.8	33.3	10.6
Madhya Pradesh	45.7	9.8	8.7	18.7	15.9	1.2	37.2	36.1	22.6	4.1
Maharashtra	44.1	14.2	11.4	22.3	7.2	0.7	35.4	48.4	14.3	1.9
Manipur	57.4	24.5	13.1	4.0	0.3	0.7	61.5	28.0	5.5	5.0

Contd...

States/UTs	Rural						Urban			
	Self Employed in Agri-culture	Self-Employed in Non-Agriculture	Regular Wage/ Salary Earnings	Casual Labour in Agri-culture	Casual Labour in Non-Agriculture	Others	Self-Employed	Regular Wage/ Salary Earnings	Casual Labour	Others
Meghalaya	52.6	13.6	14.4	8.3	10.5	0.6	36.7	39.9	17.5	5.9
Mizoram	69.6	15.6	10.8	0.0	3.2	0.7	41.6	45.5	9.9	3.0
Nagaland	51.0	10.9	35.5	0.0	0.7	1.8	30.2	57.8	7.2	4.8
Odisha	44.1	15.9	9.3	15.9	12.1	2.7	39.8	44.4	11.5	4.4
Punjab	33.5	13.7	17.5	10.0	20.7	4.6	47.1	43.4	7.7	1.8
Rajasthan	47.8	16.0	13.6	4.5	15.2	2.9	44.5	35.5	15.3	4.7
Sikkim	45.0	9.5	44.7	0.0	0.8	0.0	21.8	68.4	9.2	0.5
Tamil Nadu	17.0	14.3	20.6	22.8	22.7	2.6	30.0	45.9	20.0	4.1
Telangana	40.2	12.3	13.1	27.0	7.0	0.4	31.1	50.4	15.5	3.0
Tripura	32.7	26.6	8.8	2.2	25.0	4.8	40.0	32.6	24.3	3.1
Uttar Pradesh	52.2	13.1	6.7	8.9	16.4	2.7	46.2	33.4	15.7	4.6
Uttarakhand	50.0	18.1	10.6	8.0	7.2	6.0	27.9	42.8	20.5	8.8
West Bengal	23.2	21.1	9.9	29.0	14.4	2.4	43.7	32.2	20.7	3.4
A&N Islands	35.1	13.3	39.1	0.0	10.9	1.6	24.1	60.0	13.8	2.1
Chandigarh	0.0	0.0	74.6	0.0	13.4	11.9	39.4	54.7	3.3	2.6
Dadra & Nagar Haveli	1.0	7.6	71.1	0.0	19.4	1.0	5.1	91.1	3.8	0.0
Daman & Diu	1.0	18.8	79.2	0.0	1.0	0.0	6.1	93.7	0.1	0.0
Lakshadweep	50.0	14.3	17.9	17.9	0.0	0.0	37.5	41.4	19.5	1.6
Puducherry	1.3	10.3	35.6	18.9	34.0	0.0	31.1	43.6	21.3	4.0
All-India	**40.9**	**14.1**	**11.5**	**16.0**	**15.2**	**2.4**	**37.2**	**41.4**	**17.6**	**3.8**

Also, financial resources are the prerequisite for provisioning education, in terms of coverage as well as quality. Here also, available data do not show any serious commitment to universalizing quality education. The data on public expenditure on education vis-à-vis the dependency of students on the government education system are presented in the following section.

Section III: Attitude of Government Towards Education for All

The Kothari Commission's recommendation for spending at least 6 per cent of the national income on education was among a few of the Commission's proposals accepted by the Parliament and incorporated in the National Right for National Educational Policy, 1968. However, Table 11 shows that the government spent only about 1/3rd of that in 1970-71. Moreover, at no time during the period 1970-71 to 2012-14 did the percentage reach anywhere near 6 per cent. In most of the financial years during this period, it remained between 4 per cent.

Table 11: Public Expenditure on Education as Percentage of GDP

Year	Expenditure on Education by Education and Other Departments as Percentage of GDP
1951-52	0.64
1960-61	1.48
1970-71	2.11
1980-81	2.98
1990-91	3.84
2000-01	4.14
2001-02	3.68
2002-03	3.66
2003-04	3.40
2004-05	3.26
2005-06	3.34
2006-07	3.48
2007-08	3.40
2008-09	3.56

Contd...

2009-10	3.95
2010-11	4.05
2011-12	3.98
2012-13 (RE)	4.10
2013-14 (BE)	4.13

Source: Analysis of Budgeted Expenditure (2015) and various earlier issues
RE: Revised Estimate , BE: Budget Estimate

Low public expenditure on education is all the more unjustifiable when we take into account the fact that even now the majority of the students go to government schools (Table 12). The share of students going to government schools is higher in the rural areas compared to urban areas.

Table 12 shows that in rural areas, at every level of education till date, a majority of students go to government schools. However in Goa and Daman & Diu the share of private aided schools are higher consistently for primary, upper primary, secondary and higher secondary levels. On the other hand, in Delhi, particularly at the primary level, the mushrooming of private unaided schools is reflected very clearly in the data. In the urban areas, the trend of the mushrooming of private unaided schools are common in a number of states, like Andhra Pradesh, Haryana, Himachal Pradesh, Jammu and Kashmir, Jharkhand, Karnataka, Madhya Pradesh, Manipur, Punjab, Rajasthan, Tamil Nadu, and Telangana. On the other hand, in states/UTs like Tripura, West Bengal and Lakshadweep, the dominance of government schools is witnessed both in rural and urban areas, at all levels of school education.

Many people argue in favour of privatization of education. They often question: what is the harm if it is reducing the load on the government? These people view education as private good, where demand and supply brings market equilibrium. However, contrary to their belief, education is a public good and there is indeed significant harm in leaving it in the hands of the market. The economic logic behind the latter proposition is presented in the following paragraphs.

In a market, a good is produced up to the point where net private benefit (i.e. private benefit—private cost) is ≥ zero. The

Table 12: Percentage Share of Students in Different Types of Schools at Different Levels of Education in Rural and Urban Areas

State/UT	Rural									Urban								
	Primary			Upper Primary			Secondary & Higher Sec.			Primary			Upper Primary			Secondary & Higher Sec.		
	Govt.	Pvt. Aided	Pvt. Unaided	Govt.	Pvt. Aided	Pvt. Unaided	Govt.	Pvt. Aided	Pvt. Unaided	Govt.	Pvt. Aided	Pvt. Unaided	Govt.	Pvt. Aided	Pvt. Unaided	Govt.	Pvt. Aided	Pvt. Unaided
Andhra Pradesh	28.7	0.3	10.7	20.7	0.2	3.4	13.9	1.2	9.3	8.6	2.6	22.9	6.9	1.6	10.3	5.7	2.8	15.0
Arunachal Pradesh	27.8	1.0	1.5	22.0	0.0	1.0	31.1	1.7	0.4	22.1	3.8	3.3	14.5	2.0	2.1	23.5	3.4	2.0
Assam	41.9	1.1	2.5	2.7	0.7	1.0	20.6	1.5	0.9	17.5	4.2	9.8	14.1	2.5	6.9	10.0	5.8	7.5
Bihar	44.9	0.4	5.3	20.0	0.1	1.7	19.3	0.9	1.2	20.6	0.7	21.2	11.4	0.4	7.9	15.7	0.3	6.1
Chhattisgarh	38.3	1.1	4.1	18.9	1.1	1.9	26.4	0.1	1.4	21.6	3.2	18.8	8.3	1.9	8.7	9.7	3.4	7.6
Delhi	13.8	4.9	31.3	2.2	0.0	9.1	11.6	0.1	9.4	18.1	6.1	11.2	10.8	3.6	5.3	16.6	2.8	3.9
Goa	7.8	15.6	2.2	4.2	20.8	0.0	7.9	26.9	0.0	7.7	11.9	0.9	7.8	16.1	0.3	9.3	32.7	0.0
Gujarat	40.1	3.1	2.3	21.4	1.9	0.7	12.9	6.1	2.4	11.4	17.3	10.3	6.3	7.6	5.7	6.0	12.2	5.0
Haryana	21.6	2.4	15.0	14.8	1.2	5.1	15.8	1.8	9.3	6.0	4.6	31.4	4.7	2.4	11.8	4.5	1.6	13.6
Himachal Pradesh	18.7	1.2	11.4	1.5	0.2	4.7	23.2	0.4	5.1	8.4	2.3	26.3	5.3	0.3	7.9	13.2	2.1	9.5
Jammu & Kashmir	22.9	1.0	17.8	13.7	0.1	6.7	22.5	0.1	5.3	7.1	2.5	29.2	3.9	1.3	10.3	12.6	0.3	9.9
Jharkhand	40.2	1.7	6.0	18.6	1.7	2.8	18.9	1.7	2.0	18.2	5.2	19.0	7.4	2.1	8.9	6.8	5.3	12.4
Karnataka	30.2	5.1	6.1	17.5	2.4	1.5	17.0	6.0	3.3	10.5	11.4	15.5	6.5	7.1	7.0	6.1	10.2	7.5

Contd...

State/UT	Rural									Urban								
	Primary			Upper Primary			Secondary & Higher Sec.			Primary			Upper Primary			Secondary & Higher Sec.		
	Govt.	Pvt. Aided	Pvt. Unaided	Govt.	Pvt. Aided	Pvt. Unaided	Govt.	Pvt. Aided	Pvt. Unaided	Govt.	Pvt. Aided	Pvt. Unaided	Govt.	Pvt. Aided	Pvt. Unaided	Govt.	Pvt. Aided	Pvt. Unaided
Kerala	13.8	6.0	9.9	9.1	6.5	4.9	16.7	8.8	6.0	10.5	7.3	13.9	7.4	5.8	5.6	13.6	7.5	7.5
Madhya Pradesh	33.8	2.1	7.9	22.4	1.7	3.8	17.4	1.9	3.4	11.0	4.3	20.2	6.8	3.2	9.0	7.9	5.1	14.9
Maharashtra	31.0	4.5	3.5	15.0	7.4	0.7	9.6	13.9	1.8	10.3	13.3	9.0	6.5	10.1	3.4	5.3	16.1	4.0
Manipur	26.9	1.8	12.7	10.0	1.8	4.7	13.2	2.7	11.0	12.2	0.9	24.6	6.3	0.8	10.5	8.7	1.5	14.7
Meghalaya	30.5	7.1	7.0	9.9	11.3	2.4	10.6	15.1	1.8	6.0	16.9	7.1	2.0	11.5	5.4	6.2	18.6	5.8
Mizoram	32.4	1.0	9.5	17.1	0.6	5.7	20.3	2.6	3.5	13.9	7.3	13.1	9.6	4.9	7.9	17.7	6.4	4.6
Nagaland	17.7	13.5	3.9	9.5	5.9	2.4	10.7	9.3	10.8	3.6	8.8	18.4	2.1	5.0	9.1	2.7	12.2	20.0
Odisha	39.0	0.4	3.7	21.3	0.2	0.6	23.5	3.2	1.5	16.7	3.2	12.4	11.8	1.1	5.0	14.7	6.0	7.3
Punjab	24.5	1.7	15.9	13.0	0.9	5.6	15.4	2.2	7.5	7.6	4.8	21.0	2.9	2.5	10.6	9.9	8.7	13.6
Rajasthan	28.3	0.2	17.4	13.1	0.1	7.1	12.1	0.1	1.9	7.1	0.8	27.4	5.6	0.7	14.6	8.3	0.6	15.8
Sikkim	32.6	0.3	10.3	21.8	0.0	1.0	29.7	0.2	0.5	13.4	2.1	14.4	10.5	0.0	9.0	21.8	3.0	11.4
Tamil Nadu	19.5	3.5	10.6	16.5	2.8	3.4	20.7	4.8	2.7	9.7	5.4	18.8	7.9	3.1	9.1	11.9	5.3	7.6
Telangana	19.2	0.9	14.7	13.2	0.3	5.8	16.9	0.2	12.3	7.4	1.6	30.9	4.3	1.2	14.7	3.8	0.4	17.9
Tripura	41.6	1.1	1.3	24.3	0.0	0.1	25.4	0.3	0.8	28.9	1.3	3.9	20.4	0.2	0.6	27.9	1.5	1.3
Uttar Pradesh	26.4	3.6	19.1	10.3	2.1	6.8	5.2	6.0	9.4	6.9	4.8	29.5	4.1	2.6	11.1	6.0	5.7	11.4

Contd...

State/UT	Rural									Urban								
	Primary			Upper Primary			Secondary & Higher Sec.			Primary			Upper Primary			Secondary & Higher Sec.		
	Govt.	Pvt. Aided	Pvt. Unaided	Govt.	Pvt. Aided	Pvt. Unaided	Govt.	Pvt. Aided	Pvt. Unaided	Govt.	Pvt. Aided	Pvt. Unaided	Govt.	Pvt. Aided	Pvt. Unaided	Govt.	Pvt. Aided	Pvt. Unaided
Uttarakhand	35.4	0.0	7.6	20.5	0.4	2.6	19.7	1.3	1.7	4.7	6.0	24.9	3.9	4.4	10.3	11.9	1.7	7.0
West Bengal	38.2	0.7	2.4	25.7	0.6	0.5	23.2	0.8	0.4	19.6	3.5	7.3	18.7	2.2	2.9	21.6	2.5	3.1
A&N Islands	21.0	4.6	5.0	18.2	0.0	0.0	30.2	0.0	0.0	16.9	1.2	3.7	17.5	4.1	2.6	29.7	3.2	3.1
Chandigarh	27.7	7.1	5.3	17.1	6.8	2.7	21.7	2.3	0.0	16.0	4.1	4.5	11.4	2.6	3.1	28.2	4.9	6.8
Dadra&Nagar Haveli	54.6	10.4	0.0	20.5	0.7	0.0	8.7	0.5	0.0	18.8	1.6	11.5	13.8	0.0	6.0	22.7	1.2	6.6
Daman & Diu	7.7	11.8	5.0	9.9	11.1	0.0	28.3	14.1	0.0	26.7	21.3	10.8	3.0	5.9	2.9	13.4	4.4	0.6
Lakshadweep	20.1	0.0	0.0	30.3	0.0	0.0	41.3	0.0	0.0	33.8	0.0	0.0	21.6	0.0	0.0	29.6	0.0	1.6
Puducherry	23.3	0.2	14.5	11.9	0.4	6.6	18.2	0.6	2.5	18.3	4.9	17.4	6.9	2.8	6.1	10.8	3.1	8.3
All-India	**32.0**	**2.2**	**10.0**	**16.8**	**1.7**	**3.6**	**15.1**	**3.7**	**5.0**	**11.2**	**6.3**	**18.7**	**7.5**	**4.0**	**8.1**	**9.4**	**6.4**	**9.1**

market does not take into consideration the social benefit. Thus, markets can be problematic where the net private benefit does not equal the net social benefit, which is the social benefit (the sum of private benefits of all individuals in a society) minus the social cost (the sum of private costs of all individuals in a society). The market will fail to transact if it is socially beneficial although privately costly (net social benefit > 0 but net private benefit < 0). In these cases government intervention is necessary. Education as a merit good possesses the characteristic, where net social benefit is higher than net private benefit. This phenomenon is also known as positive externality. When a person gets education he gets a private benefit. But there are also benefits to the rest of society, e.g. he is now able to educate other people as well as his next generation and this is how the entire society is benefited as a result of his education. The market failure process of education is explained in the following diagram:

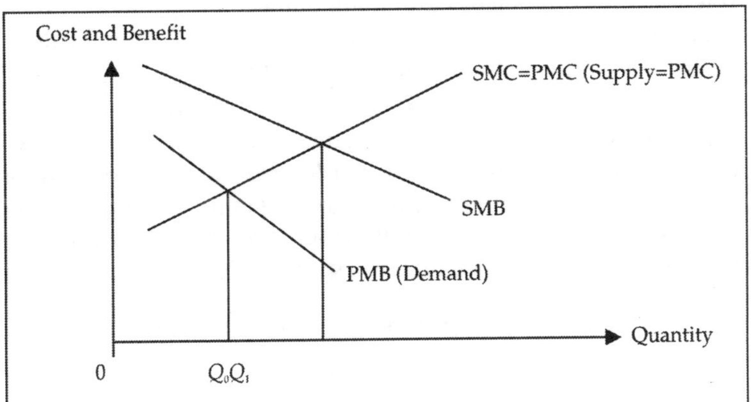

Source: Prepared by Author

Figure 1: Market Allocation vs. Socially Optimal Allocation of Education

In the above diagram cost and benefit of producing/ providing education is measured in the vertical axis and quantity is measured in the horizontal axis. The upward sloping curve is the supply curve which is equal to private marginal cost (PMC) of providing education. Since there is no difference between private marginal cost and social marginal cost (SMC) in providing education, we have PMC = SMC. However, because of the positive externality of education discussed above the social marginal benefit (SMB) of education is much higher than the demand curve which is given by private marginal benefit (PMB). Thus, in case of education, $0Q_0$ will be the market allocation of education, whereas $0Q_1$ is the socially efficient allocation of education. Thus, the above analysis based on the public finance theory clearly calls for government intervention and predominantly government financing in the domain of education.

In fact that is why in most of the advanced countries primary education is a state subject and it is provided free to all. In India, in the post-independence period this was the idea behind keeping education a state subject. The private schools that existed in the 1960s and 1970s were more in philanthropic form. However, the belief system of neoclassical economists who believe that education or expenditure decision on education is essentially an optimization problem faced by an individual with minimal or no role played by the state, gradually gained the ground. Thus in India setting up of a private school began as a viable business option, leading to commoditization of education.

There is a fundamental distinction between looking for a job in the market after being educated, and education itself becoming a commodity. The harmful effects of commoditization of education include compromising equality of opportunity, increase in expenditure on education, and compulsory private tuitions. These issues are analysed statistically in the next section.

Section IV: Commoditization of Education

The increasing expenditure on education is one of the most serious contemporary concerns in the Indian education system. Table 13 shows comparison of average expenditure per student in the two most recent NSS Rounds on education, and the calculated percentage increase (between 2007-08 and 2014), both in rural and urban areas. It can be seen from the table that there has been a sizeable percentage increase in the average expenditure, particularly at the primary level (226.3 per cent). In the rural areas the increase is from Rs. 826 to Rs. 2811 (240.3 per cent) and in the urban areas the increase is from Rs. 3626 to as high as Rs. 10083. The contemporary rural urban inequality is also revealed from the table. In urban areas, expenditure per student at primary level

Table 13: Comparison of Average Expenditure Per Student at Different Levels in NSS 71st Round (2014) and 64th Round (2007-08)

Level of Attendance	Rural			Urban			Rural + Urban		
	71st Round	64th Round	% Increase	71st Round	64th Round	% Increase	71st Round	64th Round	% Increase
Primary	2811	826	**240.3**	10083	3626	**178.1**	4610	1413	**226.3**
Upper Primary	3242	1370	**136.6**	11446	4264	**168.4**	5386	2088	**158.0**
Secondary	5100	3019	**68.9**	13547	7212	**87.8**	7459	4351	**71.4**
Higher Secondary	9820	6327	**55.2**	20179	8466	**138.4**	12619	7360	**71.5**

(Rs. 10083) is nearly four times that in rural areas (Rs. 2811). The following two tables (Table 14 and Table 15) bring out average expenditure on education in more details, e.g. who spends how much, and on what type of school?

Table 14 documents average expenditure per student vis-à-vis lower and upper limits of each quintile class of UMPCE to give a clear picture that on an average expenditure on education is significantly higher compared to the usual monthly expenditure on consumption. For example, in rural areas, the average expenditure per student even at the primary level (Rs. 1027) is more than the upper limit of quintile 1 (Rs. 786); at upper primary level, expenditure on education is more than 1.5 times, at secondary level, it is more than 3.5 times, at higher secondary level, it is approximately 6.5 times. The proportion increases with higher level of quintile class, and for quintile 5, average expenditure at higher secondary level (Rs. 13353) is beyond comparison with the lower limit of that quintile (Rs. 1667).

In urban areas, the situation is even more problematic. The average expenditure per student even at the primary level (Rs. 3465) is nearly 3 times that of the upper limit of quintile 1 (Rs. 1200). Any household spending slightly more than Rs. 3333 as consumption expenditure per month will be considered in quintile 5 in urban areas, whereas average expenditure at higher secondary level for this quintile is Rs. 38663. This shows the extent of commoditization of education.

Table 15 shows average expenditure for different types of schools, namely, government, private aided and private unaided schools. From the two calculated ratios (between expenditure on private aided and government schools, and expenditure on private unaided and government schools), it is clear that even at primary level, in rural areas, average expenditure in private aided schools is 6.7 times more than that of government school, and average expenditure in private unaided schools is 8.2 times more than that of government schools. Average expenditure increases with levels of education in all types of schools, e.g. in government school, expenditure in higher secondary (Rs. 6056) is more than 6 times of that in primary level (Rs. 965). Further, expenditure in private aided schools for higher secondary is nearly 2 times of that in government schools and in private unaided schools it is more than double.

Table 14: Average Expenditure Per Student vis-à-vis Lower and Upper Limits of Each Quintile Class of UMPCE

	Rural					Urban				
Level of Attendance	**1**	**2**	**3**	**4**	**5**	**1**	**2**	**3**	**4**	**5**
Primary	1027	1667	2462	3375	7595	3465	6213	9095	14936	28658
Upper Primary	1281	1950	2793	3241	8044	3677	6436	8754	15659	30211
Secondary	2801	3573	4260	4675	9618	5417	8010	9829	15759	30815
Higher Secondary	5095	6596	7681	8205	13353	7472	9869	13548	20588	38663
Lower Limit	0	786	1000	1287	1667	0	1200	1667	2250	3333
Upper Limit	786	1000	1287	1667	--	1200	1667	2250	3333	--

Table 15: Average Expenditure Per Student at Different Levels of Education for Different Types of Schools

Level of Attendance	Rural					Urban				
	govt.	Pvt. Aided	Pvt. Unaided	Pvt. Aided/ Govt	Pvt. Unaided/ Govt.	Govt.	Pvt. Aided	Pvt. Unaided	Pvt. Aided/ Govt	Pvt. Unaided/ Govt.
Primary	965	6452	7907	**6.7**	**8.2**	2149	11881	14242	**5.5**	**6.6**
Upper Primary	1605	6013	9514	**3.7**	**5.9**	3358	12074	18553	**3.6**	**5.5**
Secondary	3328	5896	11222	**1.8**	**3.4**	5540	14096	21565	**2.5**	**3.9**
Higher Secondary	6056	10803	13988	**1.8**	**2.3**	9668	20066	30810	**2.1**	3.2

In urban areas also, this trend of average expenditure being significantly higher in private aided schools than its government counterparts; and even higher for private unaided schools prevails. Moreover, there is a huge rural-urban expenditure gap. For example, in government schools, at primary and upper primary level, urban expenditures are more than double than their rural counterparts. The stark nature of inequality becomes evident from a simple fact that to receive primary level of education, parents sending their children to private unaided schools in the urban areas spend nearly 15 times more than parents sending their children to government schools in the rural areas.

Table 16 shows different components of expenditure for each state/UT, with course fees being the major component of the total cost, followed by books-stationery-uniforms, and private coaching. However, there are regional disparities. In Delhi and Chandigarh, the total expenditure is nearly double of the national average, and more than 6 times of that in Chhattisgarh. In Tripura and West Bengal, the component of course fees is much less, and the major share of cost component is private coaching. However, the total expenditure in these two states is less than the national average. Course fees in Delhi is more than 15 times of that in Tripura.

Tuitions have become a must for Indian students. Table 17 shows percentage of students taking private coaching at different levels of education. It can be seen from the table that on an average 23.1 per cent boys and 20.1 per cent girls at primary level, 28 per cent boys and 24.6 per cent girls at upper primary level, and 37.8 per cent boys and 34.7 per cent girls at secondary and higher secondary level take private coaching.

Moreover, there are a number of states/UTs where the share is much higher than the national average, e.g. Bihar, Delhi, Jammu and Kashmir, Jharkhand, Manipur, Odisha, Tripura, West Bengal, and Daman and Diu. Percentages are significantly high for states like Tripura and West Bengal, e.g. in Tripura as many as 87 per cent male students and 91.4 per cent female students and in West Bengal 89 per cent male students and 92 per cent female students rely on private coaching for their education at secondary and higher secondary level.

Table 16: Average Expenditure (Rs.) Per Student During Current Academic Session Pursuing General Course by Items of Expenditure for Each State/UT

States/UTs	Item of Expenditure					
	Course Fee*	Books, Stationery and Uniform	Transport	Private Coaching	Other Expenditure	Total
Andhra Pradesh	4499	1570	776	179	334	7358
Arunachal Pradesh	2446	1773	221	238	1239	5917
Assam	1544	1034	403	695	476	4152
Bihar	1283	1047	250	1383	288	4251
Chhattisgarh	1322	876	338	195	262	2993
Delhi	9386	3151	2605	2984	1366	19491
Goa	2975	2202	1775	1272	241	8465
Gujarat	2952	1816	928	1234	513	7442
Haryana	8353	2315	1415	1177	646	13905
Himachal Pradesh	4039	2440	1121	371	396	8367
Jammu & Kashmir	3330	1772	914	901	394	7311
Jharkhand	1630	1217	454	889	354	4543
Karnataka	4417	1667	754	471	555	7863
Kerala	3881	2241	1586	1081	538	9326
Madhya Pradesh	2266	1205	615	640	168	4894
Maharashtra	3955	1715	1233	1898	490	9292
Manipur	4352	2685	1074	1200	702	10012
Meghalaya	3351	1552	938	238	958	7037
Mizoram	4817	2739	611	62	1812	10041
Nagaland	6199	2405	406	180	2310	11501
Odisha	1309	1012	345	1679	240	4584
Punjab	6869	2568	1748	962	453	12600
Rajasthan	3792	1583	804	426	198	6804
Sikkim	2598	1957	388	588	321	5853
Tamil Nadu	5661	1854	1233	425	601	9773
Telangana	5992	2037	1106	115	349	9600
Tripura	622	1409	364	3413	364	6174
Uttar Pradesh	2416	1368	501	615	175	5074
Uttarakhand	2643	1429	686	662	473	5893
West Bengal	1504	1369	528	3082	209	6692
A&N Islands	1778	2811	1311	2124	168	8191
Chandigarh	8118	2898	2181	4218	1011	18426
Dadra&Nagar Haveli	2533	1933	1249	905	472	7092
Daman & Diu	4978	2339	1334	2178	1097	11926
Lakshadweep	431	663	85	234	1090	2504
Puducherry	6677	1868	1911	460	520	11436
All-India	**3133**	**1518**	**749**	**1040**	**349**	**6788**

* Includes Tution Fee, Examination Fee, Development Fee and Other Compulsory Payments

Table 17: Percentage of Students Taking Private Coaching for Levels of School Education for Each State/UT (Rural + Urban)

	Primary		Upper Primary		Secondary and Higher Secondary	
	Males	Females	Males	Females	Males	Females
Andhra Pradesh	13.5	7.1	13.7	12.8	12.6	6.8
Arunachal Pradesh	9.9	4.9	2.8	2.5	12.2	9.3
Assam	9.1	8.1	16.4	16.9	41.1	38.2
Bihar	46.8	39.7	55.7	42.9	67.2	63.1
Chhattisgarh	5.7	6.4	7.6	3.5	15.5	10.1
Delhi	32.2	36.6	40.6	42.1	42.5	48.8
Goa	13.6	15.5	27.4	20.0	32.4	36.7
Gujarat	19.2	15.2	18.0	12.1	32.4	29.3
Haryana	11.7	8.8	18.6	12.0	24.2	20.0
Himachal Pradesh	3.8	2.7	8.9	4.8	15.1	11.9
Jammu & Kashmir	31.5	28.3	27.5	28.6	36.7	38.5
Jharkhand	29.3	27.7	36.3	33.7	54.2	42.9
Karnataka	11.6	16.6	14.7	8.6	13.9	14.7
Kerala	22.7	20.6	29.9	26.9	41.1	42.2
Madhya Pradesh	13.2	9.2	17.9	10.5	37.7	34.0
Maharashtra	21.6	19.2	24.4	19.4	34.2	35.6
Manipur	34.4	28.7	33.5	39.6	54.7	50.8
Meghalaya	5.2	1.9	4.8	5.8	7.5	14.7
Mizoram	1.7	1.7	2.5	0.9	4.4	1.4
Nagaland	3.4	1.4	1.4	5.1	8.7	7.3
Odisha	45.0	42.4	43.6	47.2	63.4	59.4
Punjab	21.6	18.2	22.1	23.3	28.8	23.3
Rajasthan	5.4	3.5	6.6	6.4	19.4	20.0
Sikkim	5.6	7.5	9.2	6.6	36.5	17.3
Tamil Nadu	22.8	21.1	18.7	19.2	20.4	20.5
Telangana	6.8	3.1	9.3	3.2	6.7	2.1
Tripura	78.3	76.5	89.1	76.8	87.0	91.4
Uttar Pradesh	12.2	9.0	13.7	10.9	34.6	18.3
Uttarakhand	18.6	14.4	20.7	3.9	25.3	12.7
West Bengal	71.1	62.5	89.0	84.6	89.0	92.0
A&N Islands	18.6	31.8	34.9	21.7	40.5	28.6
Chandigarh	49.4	45.6	48.3	43.3	69.1	69.6
Dadra & Nagar Haveli	12.4	23.4	15.7	27.6	3.6	31.7
Daman & Diu	58.8	76.9	47.6	55.8	26.5	45.9
Lakshadweep	0.0	5.0	9.6	23.0	1.1	27.3
Puducherry	36.2	24.7	28.1	23.0	26.9	15.7
All-India	**23.1**	**20.1**	**28.0**	**24.6**	**37.8**	**34.7**

Summary and Conclusions

Educational facilities in India are unequally distributed among regional, socio-economic, gender, religion, caste and occupational groups of population as revealed by the latest NSSO data of the 71st round (2014). Even after prioritizing universalization of education just after independence, data shows that even today on an average one person out of four is illiterate. Moreover, there are rural-urban gaps in education, gaps between general and Scheduled Castes, and between people of different income levels. Further, the education status of females is worse than that of its male counterparts in all the cases.

In India, in the age group of 5 to 29 years, 8.1 per cent of males and 14 per cent females in rural areas, and 4.6 per cent males and 6.7 per cent females in the urban areas have never enrolled for education. There are large regional disparities and percentages of never enrolled females are higher than the national average in a number of states/UTs, like Bihar, Jharkhand, Madhya Pradesh, Rajasthan, Uttar Pradesh, and Dadra & Nagar Haveli. Interestingly, data show that in states like Haryana and Odisha, the percentages of never enrolled persons are higher in urban areas compared to rural areas for both the genders.

Across all categories, the rural situation is worse than the urban situation. Caste-wise, the percentage of non-enrolment is higher for STs, followed by SCs and OBCs. Among various religious groups, Muslims have the highest percentage of non-enrolment, both in rural and urban areas. However, when it comes to income-wise disparity, the situation is more or less the same for the poorest people (UMPCE quintile 1) in both rural and urban areas, but the rural-urban inequality increases sharply in quintile 2, 3, 4 and 5 revealing that income inequality is more prominent than other inequalities in contemporary times.

The main reasons for never-enrolling are cited as parents' lack of interest in their children's education, followed by financial constraints and their engagement in domestic activities. However, in some states/UTs people have never enrolled because they were required to earn for their families by engaging in different economic activities, or due to the fact that there is no tradition of education in the community. The reason of engagement in domestic activities is mainly predominant for females compared to their male counterparts, both in rural and urban areas.

Even among enrolled persons, there is a significant rate of dropouts or discontinuity. Dropout rates are more or less similar for girls and boys (with an exception in Madhya Pradesh and Rajasthan where female dropout rates are higher than their male counterpart), but, in almost all the states/UT, percentages of dropouts among SCs and STs are higher than general categories.

The poor status of education obviously raises a big question mark on the government's attitude towards education. Financial resources being a prerequisite for provisioning education, in terms of coverage as well as quality, the low public expenditure on education is not justifiable on any ground when till date the bulk of the students go to government schools. In rural areas, at every level of education, the majority of students attend government schools. However, in the urban areas, mushrooming of private unaided schools (particularly at the primary level) is common in a number of states/UTs like Andhra Pradesh, Delhi, Haryana, Himachal Pradesh, Jammu and Kashmir, Jharkhand, Karnataka, Madhya Pradesh, Manipur, Punjab, Rajasthan, Tamil Nadu, and Telangana. On the other hand, in Tripura, West Bengal and Lakshadweep, the dominance of government schools is witnessed both in rural and urban areas, at all levels of school education.

Education being a merit good/public good with positive externalities, there is significant economic loss in leaving it in the hands of the market. That is why in most of the advanced countries primary education is provided free to all. However, in India, setting up of a private school has today become a business option, leading to commoditization of education, restraining equality of opportunity, increasing expenditure on education and compulsory private tuitions.

The increasing expenditure on education is one of the significant current trends in the Indian education system as revealed in the two most recent NSS Rounds on education (2007-08 and 2014). There has been a huge percentage increase in the average expenditure per student, particularly at the primary level (226.3 per cent). In the rural areas, the increase is from Rs. 826 to Rs. 2811 (240.3 per cent) and in the urban areas the increase is from Rs. 3626 to as high as Rs. 10083. Moreover, in urban areas, expenditure per student at primary level is nearly four times than that in rural areas. On an average, expenditure on education is many times more compared to the usual monthly expenditure on consumption. Expenditure is significantly higher in private aided schools than their government counterparts and is even higher than that for private unaided schools.

Among different components of expenditure on education, course fees is the major component of the total cost, followed by books-stationery-uniforms, and private coaching. In spite of this, reliability on classroom teaching is low and a large proportion of students depend on private coaching for their education.

Thus, there are several policy and governance issues which need to be resolved in order to bridge the socio-economic and regional disparities in education. This can only happen if the governments—both central and state assume their responsibilities and make the necessary financial investment in this sector. Even after 70 years of independence, if we cannot educate every child of the country, it only shows the myopic vision of our policymakers. As Confucius observed many years ago: "If your plan is for one year plant rice; if your plan is for ten years plant trees; if your plan is for one hundred years educate children."

REFERENCES

Analysis of Budgeted Expenditure (2015) and various earlier issues, Ministry of Human Resource Development (MHRD).

Report No. 575 (71/25.2/1) (2014), "Education in India", NSS 71st Round, Ministry of Statistics and Programme Implementation, Government of India.

10

Perspectives on Education and Exclusion

Annie Namala

Marginalization Through the Present Form of Education

Education in India has maintained the social structure of the society instead of contesting it. This is really a problematic situation. Education has not only maintained marginalization but has also aggravated it.

Traditionally in India, there were many technologies possessed exclusively by some marginalized sections. For example, the leather technology was mainly with the *Dalits*. However, it is unfortunate to see that the major share of the profit from the leather industry at present is going to people of other classes, not the *Dalits*. This is just one example. In India, education has often taken away the cream of these skills and knowledge and handed it over to others, depriving the people of the communities who had the traditional knowledge.

Back in 1950, the Constitution of India clearly stated that India should universalize elementary education (upto 14 years of age) within a period of 10 years. We have not been able to do it even in 60 years. On the other hand, within the matter of 20-30 years we have reached Silicon Valley and currently most of Silicon Valley employees come from India. How come we achieve this and how could we not achieve minimum education for all our children? The answer is very simple. The whole system that we have created as far as education is concerned, is of maintaining and expanding the privileges of certain sections of the society at the cost of other sections.

The fact that the education system has neither taken a stand in favour of the marginalized nor questioned their exploitation makes the marginalized section sceptical about it. Primarily the education system that we have has accepted the social system we have, and has never really questioned the kind of exploitation or the oppression that this system has perpetrated for ages. This has alienated the marginalized community from the present system of education. The fact that it has not taken a stand for the marginalized nor questioned their exploitation makes it very suspect. Thus, there has been a marked difference between the kind of expectations we had from the free country and what it has actually delivered. It has, in fact, created a kind of a dilemma for the *Dalits* and other such communities. For, currently they do not have the kind of system that they have been used to, and have benefited from. Instead, they are coping with another system where they are ashamed of the skill and professional knowledge they have. This has resulted in a lack of self-confidence.

Education: A Ray of Hope Also

One thing that can be said to the credit of the present system is that it has given us a taste of education. Today all the *Dalits* have put their children in schools, at least in the 1st Standard. Thus we have 100 per cent enrolment. The education system has created a desire for knowledge, and a kind of hope and confidence among the *dalits* that their getting educated or acquiring knowledge would lead them somewhere. That is where the whole confusion lies; the confusion of desiring private education, desiring English education, and some skills.

It is really disturbing to see that nowadays we are so preoccupied with moving forward economically and socially that we have started looking at education as an investment. If we are investing something then we want a return from it. The certificate or the degree gives meaning to the investment that we have made. A certificate makes a meaning for the future and knowledge becomes subservient to that.

We talk about liberty, equality and fraternity, and then also about social justice. But what we do not realize is that all these values need to be integrated with social justice for the latter to be really practical.

The positive point that we have today is a desire for education among the tribal or *Dalit* community. There is a belief that education and learning will provide better options, and opportunities and thus there is a willingness to invest in education. These families do invest considerably in education. There are families where investment is done in the education of one particular child and the rest of the family contributes to it. So it is not justified to say that "these people" are not interested in learning but come to school only for the midday meal.

Personally, I have talked to the slum children and I have seen the kind of struggle they would wage to pass the 10th Standard and then go for a job while taking up simultaneously a correspondence course or distance learning. Later on they would enter another job (which may be in unorganized sector) and then they might at the same time opt for technical education. The kind of struggle that they willingly undertake to access education is a massive capital that they really invest to take the educational system forward.

The Challenges Ahead

Education is so connected to every other aspect of society be it politics or any other such aspect, that it is really a challenge to build an education system that can be a meaningful intervention in the people lives.

The first barrier I feel, is the availability of schools, particularly for the marginalized community. If we really want to build an education system that has some meaning for the communities which are at the margin, the communities that are finding it hard to access education, we need to look at the kind of access they have. We often talk about physical access or the infrastructure. However, there are also issues of social access. To have social accessibility of education, we need to have a socially inclusive system, a system which is non-discriminatory, and gives a sense of identity and dignity to all children. We really need to define what social access of education is. Only then, we can put in place a system which can ensure social access.

A simple calculation of economic access reveals the reality. Till a few years ago, the amount of a pre-matric scholarship used to be Rs. 15 to 20 per month. However, today students easily spend Rs. 3000 to 4000 on education besides school textbooks and tuition fees. If we add tuition fees to this then the cost may go up anywhere between Rs. 8000 to 10,000. The government rarely revises its economic norms of education.

To sum up, at the policy level we need to define social access. We also need to revise norms of economic access at regular intervals so that we are able to provide really meaningful education. Next is financing of education in general. There is a huge gap between what is needed and what is available. There are a few funds that the government has created specifically to meet the needs of marginalized groups. These are SC and tribal sub-plans, earmarked funds for minorities, etc. There is also a need to build an agency of the community in accessing meaningful education. The agency of the community has to be both among the providers of education and among its beneficiaries.

Part IV

Role of People's Movement

11

School Education in India and the Role of Deliberative Activism: The Pratichi Experience

Kumar Rana

I. About a Beginning: 2013

Legislation of the Right of Children to Free and Compulsory Education (RTE) Act, 2009, is somewhat ironical in the sense that the largest democracy in the world required a coercive law for guaranteeing her children of 6-14 years age free and compulsory education, a right that should have been guaranteed through moral bindings. Given the centrality of universal education and a tremendous demand for the same among all sections of the Indian people on one hand and the failure of the state and society to make sufficient, let alone equitable, room for all children on the other, the enactment of the law can be seen as a much required public intervention. At the same time, given the tentative record of our respecting legal commitments, it is difficult to imagine the RTE Act to take an automatically active form.

The very lack of moral commitment that has kept our children deprived of this moral right has already shown some of its ugliness in various forms including governmental and societal reluctance towards the implementation of the Act. The wider public deliberation—debate, discussion and agitation, which has had their role in giving birth to the law, has to continue to be instrumental in reinforcing social morality by making sensible use of the legal provisions.

It has been recognized for decades that the state of school education in India in general is far less than satisfactory. But this did not result in much improvement. And public policy has been meditatively indifferent to the cause. Even, as we can see from the Programme for International Student Assessment (PISA) Report, the quality of education delivered in the schools—both public and much glorified private ones—is nowhere near the standard that is internationally acknowledged as respectable. However, one needs to be careful lest the very diagnosis adds to the disease. There have undoubtedly been clear signs of some serious efforts to overcome existing problems. This has been made possible by the explicit impatience among large sections of the Indian public—organizations as well as individuals. The impatience resulted in reformed implementation of policies pertaining to the delivery of school education in some of the states including Kerala, Tamil Nadu, Mizoram, Tripura, Himachal Pradesh and some others. This has contributed further to spread such impatience among other states.

The enactment of the RTE is nothing but a cumulative result of the country-wide movements concerning the demand for universal opportunity for school education. It is true that the educational guarantee provided through the RTE is confined to the elementary level; but there are optimistic signals, including the constitution of the Rashtriya Madhyamaik Siksha Abhiyan (RMSA), that secondary school education would also be brought under the purview of univerzalisation.

We must take note of the fact that one of the vital problems of school education, that is, access to schools, has largely been overcome; other infrastructural issues including paucity of teachers, classrooms and so on are on the way to being taken care of. Then we have the core concern of the quality of education. Universal access in itself is not the guarantee of equal opportunity of learning for all. The divisiveness based on social identity, economic class and gender that has restricted so many children from attending schools has to a large extent been removed through expansion of school infrastructure, launching of the Midday Meal scheme, etc. All these are certainly an achievement.

While these achievements give some solace, they add substantially to many challenges that lie ahead. The principal challenge is the universalization of learning achievement in order to eliminate exclusion of many children owing to their historically constructed disadvantaged background—being poor and low caste; belonging to minority religious, linguistic and cultural groups; and being girls. There is a plethora of evidences to show that poor and inequitable standard of school functioning is not only owing to the much maligned teachers' irregularity and discriminatory treatment of children in the classroom but also, in many cases, due to pedagogical issues, including neglect of teachers' education. These have led to children helplessly quitting their studies midway.

Public deliberation and efforts, based on various sets of collaborations including between parents and teachers, professionals belonging to higher education and primary education, social activists and public officials, political bodies such as teachers' unions and social outfits, media, intellectuals and so on, are central to translate the good of equitable education into reality.

I would like to elaborate this with some of our experiences. Modest as they are, they might be useful for educational practitioners across the country. While establishing the Pratichi Trust to make some meaningful contribution to the causes of education, health and gender equality, the organization chaired by Amartya Sen, had underlined empirical research and dissemination of the research findings among the wider public as the primary mode of intervention. And, ever since the constitution of a research team in 2001, elevated later to the Pratichi Institute, the trust has been following this line humbly but very loyally, and we have some satisfaction in that the interventions made have contributed to bringing in some changes in the functional aspects of school education in West Bengal, particularly at primary level.

Public dissemination of the findings of our researches on the primary school system, thankfully, created a much required noise on the issue. Helped immensely by media reports, the issue of functionality of schools became a focal point of societal churning, which played a major role in at least making the schools regularly functional. This had a subsequent impact on children's attendance and learning achievement. While in 2001-02, the rate of children's attendance veered around 54 per cent, it went up to 64 per cent in 2008-09. Of course, the Midday Meal programme which was launched in the state in 2003-04, made considerable difference, and public debate and discussion played a vital role in fighting the initial resistance to the implementation of the cooked meal scheme in the schools. With ensured regularity of the functioning of the schools and higher degree of children attendance, the level of unsatisfactory performance of the children also decreased. While 30 per cent of the surveyed children of Grades III and IV in 2001-02 could not even read and write, the figure came down in 2008-09 to 4 per cent. That a child of Grade III or IV could not even read and write is a shame in itself, but, the decrease in the degree of this basic inability clearly shows the possibility of success.

Angry social deliberations on the issue exerted their impact not only on public policy implementation but also on the teachers and their unions (who at a later stage played a vitally positive role) and also on the political parties then in power. The Communist Party of India (Marxist) (CPIM) sent letters to its party members advising them to take the issue seriously. Also, intellectuals who had so far been more inclined to debating on issues of 'higher subjects' started showing an interest in the 'lesser topic', namely primary education. And, although the teachers' unions faced the harshest criticism from different quarters, including the political parties they had affiliations with, the unions, particularly the All Bengal Primary Teachers' Association (ABPTA), the largest teachers' union in the country with a membership of 120,000, came forward to take up the challenge of making the schools regularly functional.

The Pratichi Trust played here a crucial coordinating role by organizing a series of consultancy meetings and larger public discussions, involving parents, teachers and others. Subsequently, other unions also joined the meetings. How remarkable the achievement is can be imagined from the fact that all the primary teachers' unions, irrespective of their ideological belief and political affinity, came together in a single platform in order to find ways and means for the implementation of the RTE in the state. The ABPTA undertook some specific programmes, namely, School Improvement Programme and a survey of the state's readiness to the implementation of the RTE. The unions also played a very crucial role to add sustainability to the launching of the Midday Meal programme. Indeed, when the state government found itself clueless as to how to launch the scheme in the schools of Kolkata city, it was the ice-breaking effort of the unions that showed a broad avenue by initiating the programme in some selected schools.

Surely, collaboration with the unions is not the only answer to myriad questions pertaining to the delivery of education. There are many issues, including teachers training and orientation which in their present shape are seemingly designed to be fruitless. This along with issues like mechanical and routine provisions for participation of the larger public in the delivery of education, and most importantly, closed planning processes without any room for the teachers and others for experience-based reflections on the issues, need to be resolved at various policy levels. But, the collaboration with the unions that occurred through public deliberation offers valuable lessons for all involved in the practice of education.

To cite another example of the potential of public deliberation: in the initial phase of the implementation of the RTE, teachers were found not indifferent but hostile to the Act. They were made to believe through various channels that it was meant for privatizing the education system entirely, and that it was an instrument of oppression against the teachers. Such beliefs were constructed through hearsay, as most of the teachers did not have any real knowledge about the Act. Only a fortunate few had access to the original document, and even if others could find it from different sources, they could hardly comprehend the substance of the legislative directions. For, the document was in English—legal English. Perplexing as the situation was, it required some immediate works to be done. We prepared a Bangla translation of the document, which the state government committed to multiply and circulate among all teachers, but alas, that did not occur even after three years of enactment of the law. Thanks to the support of the United Nations Children's Fund (UNICEF), Kolkata, we organized a series of workshops on the issue and circulated limited copies of the translation of the Act. This small intervention made quite a difference: teachers appeared to be ready to discuss over the issue, and as mentioned above, one of the teachers' unions took the initiative to carry out a survey of the preparedness to implement the Act.

A major problem that our educational planning suffers from is the hierarchical structure of the system where scope of practising democracy at various levels is very limited. But, as has been found from researches and practices, horizontality in the planning process could play a very fruitful role here as many of the problems that emerge due to faulty planning could be resolved at the very level of planning by using meaningfully the real life experiences of the grass root level practitioners.

Lessons learnt from an exercise carried out by us could be useful to illustrate the point. We organized a series of teachers' writing workshops where altogether 400 teachers recorded in writing their day-to-day experience of school functioning. The write-ups are vastly illuminating. For, they do not just speak about the problems, but tell us about myriad ways of solutions to specific problems related to teaching and learning, parent-teacher collaboration, operation of the Midday Meal programme, improving school infrastructure and environment through local participation, and so on. Some of the write-ups are so brilliant that they could easily walk into post-editorial pages of vernacular newspapers. An analysis of the writings and a selection of them have been compiled by us into a volume with the title *Kalomchari – Penwalk.*

If deliberative participation at all levels of policy formulation and implementation has a huge advantage, the lack of the same can be irretrievably counterproductive. For example, the RTE provisions of 'no detention', 'continuous and comprehensive evaluation (CCE)' and 'no corporal punishment' have been taken from scientifically developed notions across the globe. But, given the practices of detention, annual examination and corporal punishment in the Indian school system for generations, the notions came to the teachers and parents as a shock: unpreparedness for accepting the newer concepts has made them so resistant as to taking these concepts absolutely mechanically and in a negative way. Many of the teachers told us that they feel discouraged to teach for they find no reason for teaching—'children will automatically be promoted to higher grades, then what is worth teaching?'

On the other hand, many of the children seem to have developed such a negative feeling about the new system that they have become indifferent to studies. Now, as we find, some teachers have enviable clarity on the scientific basis of these issues. They could have been involved as highly productive resource persons to motivate their colleagues. Had their views been accommodated during the planning process, incorporation of these essential issues could have been much easier and thus much more acceptable to the teachers' community in general. Also, had these teachers been involved in teachers' training and orientation and had there been room for listening to the dissenting voices, implementation of the RTE in its essence would have been much more perfect.

While coercive law has its own power of exacting loyalty, it suffers from its inherent inability to stir people's moral sentiments and voluntary commitments. And, morality is very closely—inseparably—connected with pluralistic deliberations, which are not only based on mutual respect, consideration and appreciation of freedom but also contribute to inculcate these values and take them forward. Education being a freedom enhancing achievement, the process of education cannot be separated from freedom, based upon deliberative interactions.

II. Five Years Later: 2018

In the past five years, the deliberative interactions initiated by Pratichi have made very substantial advancement to organize teachers into a platform to expand primary education through transforming the primary schools. The platform, called Siksha Alochana (literally meaning Discussing Education), is an initiative of a number of primary school teachers, Pratichi Institute, and some of the academics and activists of West Bengal. It aims to enhance primary education in West Bengal through interactions among primary school teachers of various schools at one level and between the concerned teachers and the larger public of West Bengal at another. With plausibility of change being the main driving force behind the organization of the platform, *Siksha Alochana* has been active in emboldening the examples of positive changes initiated by some of the teachers in alliance with the local communities and is engaged in expanding the experiences. To illustrate, the initiative that began in only about a score of schools across mainly two districts, namely North 24 Parganas and South Dinajpur, has now rooted itself in about 200 schools across 20 districts of the state. Contrasting sharply with the popular belief of absenteeism being a congenital characteristic of primary school teachers, many teachers have proactively come in contact with *Siksha Alochana* to join the course of transforming the so-called poorly functioning primary schools into institutions of effective delivery of education. What is more encouraging is that many of the teachers have found very positive response to their invitation to the poor and disadvantaged communities to participate in the process of transformation.

While recognizing the outstanding dedication and commitment of the organizers of *Siksha Alochana*, it is important to point out that the formation of the platform cannot be seen as simply a result of good intentions. Rather, the social commitment involved in the process of organization reflects a deep undercurrent of social demand for resisting the current of immorality awfully manifested in the delivery of school education in recent times. With the growing repudiation of the meaning and content of education, the publicly delivered school education that should have played a role of the protector of the ideal of education—freedom, equality, and justice—has tended to be on retreat, allowing the powerful to turn a virtue, that is education, into a mere commodity, and leaving the helpless in the hands of destiny. Socially meaningful researches by Pratichi Trust and Pratichi Institute and other organizations and individual researchers have played a crucial role not only in bringing into light the paradox of the state education system but also underscoring the social demand for reinstating the meaning and content of education. That some of the teachers, no matter how small the number is, have come up with extraordinary empathy and courage to transform the schools into fruitful social institutions by ensuring fuller participation of children, parents, and teachers, strikingly exemplifies this social demand for positive change. It is the existence and recognition of the social demand that have resulted in bringing the teachers and researchers into a jointly conceived platform of social action.

Of course, it did not happen overnight. It took more than a decade to develop, through many discussions informed by findings of research and experiences of action, an understanding to build up an effective platform for discussion, action, and further research, and enhance individual and social capabilities—teaching and learning, research and documentation, and public engagement.

The decision to build up the platform was taken at a meeting of teachers, researchers, and other activists in 2015. The focus of discussion veered mainly around how to improve the quality of teaching and learning. In 2016, *Siksha Alochana* held its first annual general meeting. By this time, practices and interactions encouraged the members of *Siksha Alochana* to further incorporate elements of overall school functioning. Also, it decided to prepare a report on primary education in West Bengal by using the experiences of the teachers who have already accomplished significant changes in the life of their schools. The process of writing of the report is continuing. In 2017, it made a further advance by developing a concrete plan of action to contribute meaningfully to the fields of teaching and learning, overall school development, community participation, and school and community health.

The main approach to taking the movement forward is active deliberation. On one hand, members of *Siksha Alochana* are engaged in creating, gathering, and sharing positive experiences, and in creatively applying them in their own fields. At the same time, efforts are on to extend discussions on education to a larger public—intellectuals, media, government officials—and to draw policy attention to some basic issues concerning the delivery of education. Experiences show that the promises (or perils) in the reach of the initiative are connected to many other aspects than just commitment of teachers and zeal of the communities, though they can and do play undeniably a central role in the exercise of transformation of schools. The stumbling blocks related with school transformations, as experienced through the practice of change, are inseparably connected with public policies concerning the delivery of education and their implementation in particular and public delivery of services in general. They include the gap between required and provided teachers and deficiency in teachers' trainings, absence of posts of teachers to carry out pedagogic activities, such as music, drawing and sports, essential for a proper functioning of schools. But the biggest problem, perhaps, relates to the very process of designing public policies which hardly contains any space for taking into account the grass root realities in which the chief implementers work. *Siksha Alochan*'s pivotal role here is to set up the examples of positive change as well as document and discuss widely the processes of change in order to underline the policy needs.

Towards achieving the goal of making quality schooling available for all, *Siksha Alochana*'s activities follow the route of enhancing the capabilities of its members through discussion, exchange, and action. This has come from the recognition of plurality in the need for and content of the delivery of education. Children have varying inclinations and each child is different from his or her fellows; this requires the teacher to acquire the ability to address the individual needs of the children, and this ability can best be developed through interactive practices—interaction between teachers and students, and teachers and the local community, especially parents. Aside from teaching and learning, the interactive practices are central to reform the school physically—making the school ambience, classrooms, Midday Meal, sanitary facilities functional and enjoyable. Accordingly, members of *Siksha Alochana* have been carrying out a series of activities, including teachers' workshops on subject teaching, community participation, identifying the gaps, etc. on one hand and various school-based innovative activities like reading festivals, arithmetic festivals, language festivals, mothers' festivals, sports, wall magazines, annual school magazines, outdoor classes, excursions and so on.

Based on the moral imperative to ensure equal opportunity of properly functional schooling for every child, *Siksha Alochana* and Pratichi Institute aim to concentrate on transforming the publicly run schools into fully effective social institutions. This implies that a school will not only ensure the literacy and numeracy achievements of the children but will also shape effectively and meaningfully the definition of schooling in a broader way by incorporating environmental issues, health and hygiene, cultural performances, library activities, and moral practices, in its fold. The plausibility of such transformation has already been established; the task in hand is to expand the movement by organizing teachers, parents, and other segments of society.

12

Social Movement and Education

Medha Patkar

Society is supposed to be a process of interaction, a process of imbibing and inculcation of not just norms but also values and progression that empowers both individuals as well as society. Unfortunately, in reality, education has often been used as a tool by a certain section to dominate over the other sections of the society, for a very long period. However, currently there is a growth of the formal institutions of education, reaching out to those sections of the population which were consciously or because of certain characteristics of education, excluded or remained on the periphery. At the same time, whether we have really achieved what as a society we wanted to achieve; and whether the state has achieved what as a state it was responsible to achieve through the educational system, is a big question mark.

Education is no more an academic subject. It is a reality to be faced, challenged, and at the same time it should also to be taken forward as an alliance of the people's movement. The challenges of the education system existed in our country from a very long period. Going back to the *Brahminical* system where caste was a barrier and therefore the *Bahujana Samaj, Dalits* and the *Mahadalits* were consciously kept out of the education system. Thus, it was very clear that there had to be not just the growth of formal education but questioning and challenging that existing system and bringing in certain political processes which alone would break the barriers. Now whether we have overcome that kind of *Brahminical* attitude within the society or whether it has erupted in the form of discrimination of different kinds and forms which is excluding a large number of our population even today, is a big question. And we all know the answer very well. Discrimination still continues in newer and newer forms and continues to infect the educational arena of the present days.

In this background, depending only on the formal educational process, which implies depending on the state, raises another pertinent question of how far should education be state-directed or the same can be asked the other way round as how far should the society be state-dependent. That question is what these movements try to answer.

Social movements feel that the spirit of education should be imparted not just as the passing on from one generation to another but within the generation and across all classes and all kinds of sections that are with or against each other but that certainly depict the diversity within the society, if not disadvantages as well. In other words, education should not be a vertical process only, but a horizontal process too. This is the agenda of the social movements so far as education is concerned. Movements want to transmit education within a certain framework of perspectives, paradigms of knowledge, skills, attitude and many other things which are not only related to economic enterprises or vocations per se, but also related to the lives, lifestyle, livelihoods and so on. Education should influence social, economic and political aspects of our lives, of our society, of all the agencies, including the state.

The movements also look at empowerment as a goal in itself. To be able to make a choice of what is good and what is not, and to empower someone to be able to make such a choice is one of the true goals of education. The movements therefore emphasize empowering those sections which have been kept at the periphery for a long period, to be able to make such important decisions for themselves. The point of view of these movements is that only the formal form of education or educational system guided or directed by the state would not be able to ignite such a spirit of empowerment.

Education should be seen as a learning process through a variety of means, and not only through the formal form of education. Society and state, despite working and performing together, have many conflicts. Keeping this in focus, movements try to frame their own agenda of implementation of education or imparting skills and empowerment through education. These movements are not only restricted to implementing the agenda of socio-political establishments, their prime focus lies in bringing forth a complete change in the society in terms of empowerment and the realization of the need of its implementation. After all, there can never be any movement without momentum; therefore these movements aim at bringing awareness not only among individuals but also the surrounding of every individual, in order to involve each and everyone in the learning process. The entire learning process should comprise of realization and analysis to make people capable of articulation. This is what these movements aim at.

The learning processes as initiated and aimed at by the movements are not similar to what usually several non-governmental organizations (NGOs) and other similar organizations emphasise. Mere workshops or trainings followed by some tasks or exercise in hand, is not what these movements are looking at. Rather these movements believe that if any of them is not self-fulfilled with experiences, then it cannot run long with its campaign. These movements then fail disastrously to empower people or make people aware of the advantages of education, of the benefits of the learning process. Then, for sure, the main objective of making people empowered and build an articulate society would also fail.

The lack of such features is evident in all the movements which have failed to achieve their goals so far. In order to achieve the goal and its eventual implementation, these movements seek vivid mediums, forms and formats to address the existing challenges. The notion of *Janashakti* or manpower which forms the base of any movement, should be used in a better way. The heterogeneity of manpower, which is the culmination of experiences of people coming from different walks of life, should be utilised judiciously as this would enhance the spirit of the movement and definitely will be of great help in achieving the movements' goals. Such amalgamation also makes the movements educative.

A movement always associates with it a global or a comprehensive approach. This is essentially why there should be people involved in it who have the experience from different walks of life. The movement would then become the stage, the platform where the interaction, the intermingling of such a wide variety of experiences takes place, thus enriching and enhancing the spirit of the movement on the whole. A movement should always have the learning process as its integral part rather than mere rallies and *dharnas*. The definition of a movement should be beyond the boundaries such as a mere protest march. Rallies and *dharnas* are of course a part of it but definitely not an essential part and the spirit of a movement should never be confined to such events.

There are several issues which need the attention of movements while framing their own agenda for education. Prime among them is education itself, which has witnessed rapid changes in a very brief period of time. The various parameters, the various mediums of education have experienced such rapid and significant changes that without addressing and analysing these one can never solve the current challenges.

The *Narmada Bachao Andolan* experience which lasted for 28 years, witnessed transitions of many things, ranging from generations, the spirit and many other things associated with the movement. The new age saw an inflation of the virtual world with new windows opening towards the global arena. This global stage was there also at the time of the previous generations but lay beyond the conscious boundaries of those people. The previous generation used to watch the movement as something new of its kind, something unique. But the new generation coming from the same families of farmers, *Adivasis* and working class reflect upon the movements as something not lying beyond, but as yet another part of the huge avenue of the virtually enhanced and inter-dependent global world.

To keep the spirit ignited throughout the generations is indeed a challenging task. *Narmada Bachao Andolan* started with people whose maximum educational qualification was primary education, but today their children have spread their wings far beyond with many of them going abroad, some of them captains of state sports team, some advocates and so on. This new generation has a global world lying right in front of them. Moreover it is also accessible. So there is a kind of a mismatch with the activists like me who do not know how to use computers or Facebook, features which have become a quintessential part of human existence.

There is a vast generation gap that has developed within the movements. Call it a gap or diversity. It is not that there are conflicts and irreconcilable differences emerging because of this, but this is what the present scenario is like. We are not sure how much we can resolve or if there is at all any need to resolve. During my stay in Manibeli village with Sadgopalji, Krishna Kumarji, I remember there was a debate as to the extent to which we can accept the formal form of education for the upliftment of the villagers. The debate spread out rapidly because the state thought that by putting up two-three land acquisition notices they were 'successful' in educating the *Adivasis* about their land rights as they became aware of such provisions. But at the same time, we were all forced to think as to the extent to which just memorizing facts would actually educate people.

While talking about self-dependency or environment conservation how much good can be extracted from the formal system of education is what our concern was. For example, thanks to Krishna Kumarji, who is responsible for some of the significant changes that were incorporated in the National Council of Educational Research and Training (NCERT) syllabus which earlier taught that tractors and motors are new and 'advanced' means of farming while bullock carts are the old means. To what extent this kind of representation is acceptable is the core question to address while discussing the formal form being the prime and only means of education.

The *Adivasis*, and the *Dalits*, in a very subtle manner pointed out the loopholes in our vision as they clearly stated why they had to choose between formal and informal forms of education, why they could not have both the systems as the means of education. I believe that they have the full right to demand both forms of education. Education as a constitutional right is not being accepted because there is no equity. There have been debates on the fact whether the Right of Children to the Free and Compulsory Education Act, 2009 (RTE) is actually encouraging equity. The facts that it is actually perpetuating inequality even though it is promising some meagre percentage of reservations in big private schools. If we actually want equity, then we should stress *saman shiksha*, that is the same level of education for all. The Kothari Commission Report talks about the Common School System with the neighbourhood concept, which is important from the perspective of movements. Funding is indeed important, but should not be a dominating factor.

When we are talking of achieving equity there are various mediums through which it could be accomplished. The prime among them is equity in diversity, i.e. equity between different sections of society, which we have not yet been unable to achieve. The natural resource-based movements or the ecological movements are the most organized. They advocate the most utopian form of lifestyle and working pattern. This is what is needed and is not reflected in the education movements.

What is needed is the incorporation in the curriculum which is read by all including the elite child, of the culture and lifestyles of those lying in the periphery. Unfortunately, this is not yet achieved. Providing a quota for slum children in private schools is not enough, what is needed is for children of the elite to spend some time at least in the slums so that an intermingling of these two different backgrounds can take place. And this can be achieved only by conscious efforts of the parents, teachers, activists and state. For example, *Anganwadi* which started as a small individual set up was later taken up by the government.

Privatization is yet another issue which needs attention. The role of privatization and its links with various aspects of education is what needs to be analysed. In an era where everything is being privatized, there is a need to decide what is good or bad for oneself, what is the aim of education which is not reflected in schools run by the state. Since most of the municipal schools have been shut down, how can we accommodate the slum children of those women who are willing to take their children, including girl children to schools out of their meagre income of Rs. 3000 or so? This is where the real challenge lies.

13
Comments on the Right to Education Campaign

Ambarish Rai

There is an urgent need of coordination among various movements being carried out in the country today. The movement for school education has to be linked with other movements, because the education movement cannot work in isolation. Moreover, movements have to act in concert. For this, a common vision is needed. While carrying out the education movement, we should remember that unlike various schemes of government like the National Rural Health Mission or Mahatma Gandhi National Rural Employment Guarantee Act, the movement for universalizing school education is a tool for social transformation.

We have witnessed since the early 1990s how privatization is capturing each and every aspect of the national life. In the education sector also, privatization and commercialization have spread rapidly. 75 per cent of the higher education institutions, 65 per cent of secondary schools and 22 per cent of elementary schools are run privately. Privatization, thus, is a rapidly increasing phenomenon in the sphere of education. This process of handing over the education system to the exploitative private operators and the eventual transformation of education into a commodity is a serious impending danger for our nation.

In earlier times, we had witnessed the opening of several private schools, but they were all of a charitable type. However, private schools operating currently are mostly in order to extract profits. The private players today are not only extracting profits from the schools and other institutions of learning operated by them but are also busy rationalizing and justifying the idea of commercialization and privatization on the basis of false arguments and distorted facts and figures. They are doing this in a concerted manner. In a democracy, it is essentially the function of the state to provide quality education to the children of the nation. But in India today the state has miserably failed in this regard since independence and currently, in order to make amends by privatizing education it is desperately trying to get rid of its responsibility to provide quality education to all the children of the country. Thereby they are lamentably failing in the discharge of a function which constitutes their very *raison d'* étre. That is why they seem to be in a hurry to hand over the schools and other institutions run by the government to the private sector.

Connecting Gandhi's philosophy of relating the world of knowledge to the world of work and Tagore's notion of education being essentially a source of creativity, I think and believe that this idealism has been left far behind. In the present condition this bold and value-based notion of education has been virtually wiped out from the educational system and we have come to depend completely on the market. Therefore, in the present situation even to talk about the revival of these value-based systems appears unrealistic.

When the Bill on the Right to Education was being debated in the Parliament and in the country as a whole, I was not in favour of it because I truly and strongly believed in the Common School System. I do so even today. For, among its other unique features, the Common School System is particularly relevant in a country like India with its segregated society. The Common School System can lay the foundation for national cohesion and integration. Unfortunately the RTE Act has only legitimized the multi-layered school system in the country. We have schools for the rich and schools for the marginalized. The RTE Act has failed to bridge this gap—a gap which persists even when in the Act education is supposed to be universalized and become accessible to all.

It is an irony that the RTE Act is not embedded either in the Nehruvian or Gandhian or Ambedkarian ideas but is an outcome of the policy of privatization and globalization dominant today. Initially, we thought the Act to be a great achievement. But very soon we came to realize that this is not the outcome or the entitlement which we fought for long. This is not the expected fruit of the struggle that took place from Gokhale till today. This is because equity was at the core of the objective of that struggle, the quintessential part of it. But RTE instead of leading to the realization of this objective, perpetuates inequality and may even aggravate it.

However, despite all the limitations the RTE Act generated a new wave of enthusiasm. It was the closest that we could find to the foundation on which we could establish the Common School System. That is why we established the RTE Forum, mainly designed to help in the creation of the environment and generation of the political will for its implementation. We have associated with the Forum a large number of experts and academics. But above all, we have made painstaking efforts in taking the teachers along our journey. For, without their cooperation the Act can never be implemented. They are at the same time the most pathetically neglected section constituting the school education system. The RTE Forum is, therefore, trying to build a bridge between the teachers and the civil society.

Part V

Impact on Education of Globalization and Neoliberal Economic Policies

14

The Story of Dismantling of Higher Education in India: The Unfolding Crisis*

G. Haragopal

The higher education in India, which was laboriously built during the first four decades after independence, is systematically being dismantled by both the neoliberal forces from outside and educational business entrepreneurs from within, with the connivance of the political class in power and also in opposition. The convincing example is the recent assault on Delhi University, one of the largest educational establishments providing not only education to a very large number but providing quality education at the undergraduate level. Some of the colleges of this University can not only compare with the finest colleges in the Western world but surpass several of their counterparts in most parts of the developing world. This University is not only known for jealously safeguarding its institutional autonomy but for its militant struggles for improving the freedoms and service conditions of the teaching community. The Indian state for almost four decades respected the academic community of this University and positively responded not only to its demands but looked up for advice and direction to some of its world class faculty.

The former Prime Minister Manmohan Singh and Nobel Laureate Amartya Sen along with several other distinguished personalities belonged to this academic fraternity. Notwithstanding all its democratic traditions, academic accomplishments, illustrious history, neoliberal forces chose this University for attack precisely for its strengths, in the belief that if they succeed here, the rest of the educational system in the country will fall in line. This well designed orchestrated attack aimed at the system, caught the entire University community by shock and surprise. The forces of resistance were left with no time to organize themselves in encountering this academic affront. Given the internal academic structures, its well laid down procedures and institutionalized norms of the university, nobody ever imagined that it could be thrown out of gear so suddenly and so easily. But it is happening.

The problem arose when the new Vice-Chancellor of the University decided to go ahead with unprecedented haste to change the 10+2+3 system prescribed in the National Eduicat9on Policy, to 10+2+4 system. He pushed through his decision and bulldozed the formal decision-making bodies like the Academic Council, ignoring the age-old, time-tested policy of formulating and changing the curriculum through the departmental faculty involvement and after vetting by several academic boards that normally discuss, debate the pros and cons of the changes. In fact, it is this latter process that ensures accommodation of several viewpoints, world-views, ideological stand points and enlarging frontiers of knowledge. New changes proposed earlier involved prolonged debate and discussions. In the present case, these processes have been thwarted and the new curriculum prepared by a chosen few, and imposed from above.

The introduction of the Four-Year Undergraduate Programme (FYUP) was never in active public debate. This was not demanded either by the students, teachers or parents. The only reason as stated by the Vice-Chancellor, is the international mobility of the students. Since American Universities have a Four Year Undergraduate Programme (FYUP), Indian Universities are being forced to create conditions for smooth entry of foreign universities into the Indian educational market. The Kothari Commission took more than two years to formulate its recommendations. This involved nationwide debate and also critical examination of global experience and experimentation. This policy started getting tampered from the mid-1980s after Indian rulers opted for the Structural Adjustment Programme of the international financial agencies like the IMF and World Bank. The 1986 Education Policy was put to public debate for two years. Although the final policy did not adequately reflect the concerns expressed in the public debate, at least the formality required by the democratic process was completed. This was perhaps the last democratic academic gesture of the Indian state towards higher education.

As the integration of the Indian economy with the global economy proceeded further by the 1990s, the educational system, particularly higher education, started experiencing severe jolts. The Knowledge Commission headed by Sam Pitroda was requested to provide direction to the Indian knowledge system. While the Kothari Commission viewed education as a "conscience of the nation" and "critical assessor of the way of life of a society", Pitroda took a totally utilitarian view, regarding knowledge as a catalyst of production and consumption. While the Kothari Commission envisaged education to respond to social needs and not wants, to Pitroda, every want was a need. Given this distorted view, the subordination of knowledge to market forces was taken by this Commission to higher levels. This was clear in the very functioning of the Commission; Sam Pitroda did not care to consult his own members and ignored them to the extent that the Vice-Chairman of the Commission, Dr. P.M. Bhargava, a renowned scientist, had to resign from the Commission in protest. Pitroda started sending dispatches (like Wood's Dispatches during the colonial period) to the Government of India, which formed the basis for some of the policy choices. Never in independent India had the policy-making process been so trivialized.

The Vice-Chancellor of Delhi University took the Pitrodian approach further. In this whole episode, the major causality has been the Constitutional commitments, the transformative agenda, and the commitment to uplift the millions of Indian citizens who are stuck in the morass of poverty, illiteracy and inegalitarian social structure. The shift in the Delhi University curriculum was also considered anti-poor, clearly visible in the anxieties expressed on behalf of marginalized sections. The Four Year Undergraduate Programme permitted two stages of dropouts, one, at the end of two years when the successful students get Associate Baccalaureate degrees and the other, at the end of three years when they get the Baccalaureate degree. (At the end of four years, they get the Baccalaureate with Honours degree). Opening these outlets for drop out midway of the course raises the question as to who would drop out in the middle of the undergraduate programme. It would certainly be the first generation boys and girls mainly from the rural areas, who struggle hard to enter the system with great difficulties and diffidence. It will be they who will be the victims. For, these students do take time to cope with the very culture of institutions of higher learning. The new policy provides the existing option without any concern about the future of those who drop out, as completion of a degree is the minimum prescribed qualification for entry into public employment or pursuit of postgraduate education or for other forms of mobility to higher levels of public spaces. One can safely assume that no boy or girl from upper castes, upper classes and higher income groups would ever drop out or opt out prematurely from higher education. It is obvious that the system contrives to eject the disadvantaged boys and girls so that the job market at the higher level does not get crowded for the privileged and powerful.

The proposed curriculum contents are unacademic, sub-standard and devoid of imagination. A simple example is, introduction of a compulsory course on Gandhain thought. This does not include the Gandhian world-view, his critique of industrial civilization nor his radical views on power and state, nor even the Gandhian secular outlook as against the fundamentalist forces, which could be relevant to fighting the growing communalism. Instead of these broader Gandhian thought forming the substance of the course, Gandhism has been brought into the stream of moral education which includes a lesson on the Satya Harishchandra story pertaining to the pre-feudal stage of history. It relates to selling of his wife by Harishchandra to keep his word. Selling and buying of persons smacks of slave trade. Another episode is of Gandhi's promise to his mother that he would not take to non-vegetarian food. Another instance included is that of the theft that Gandhi committed as a child. One wonders what moral lessons could be drawn from such episodes and what moral values could be imparted? Given the growing feminist consciousness, the story of Harishchandra could be very repulsive. Apart from these broader issues, how can these stories which should be narrated to kindergarten children, be taught to undergraduate level students who ought to be asking far more fundamental questions at that stage of the pursuit of knowledge?

A note circulated by the physics department of St. Stephens College of Delhi University on FYUP stated that this reform is ham-handed and that all the justification cited in favour of the introduction of FYUP, like permitting flexibility, being more inter-disciplinary and more in tune with worldwide practices, are misleading. The note maintains that none of these claims are built into the scheme at all. The Vice-Chancellor rejected all the experience of other institutions and designed an utterly rigid programme which was in no way an improvement on the existing scheme.

II

The Delhi University episode fits very well into the larger picture of what is happening to higher education and how a concerted attempt is being made by the Indian ruling class to bring foreign capital into the service sector, including education. The global capital, particularly the American capital is in search of avenues for investment in the service sector, as the American economy is services driven. Two-thirds of its economy is service economy. America which emerged as a super power in the post-Second World War period has seen a decline of its manufacturing sector. Its agricultural share in the country's GDP is less than two per cent. Its vulnerable economy received a rude shock in 1973 when oil-exporting nations decided to increase their oil prices at a time when the American share in the international trade in oil was marginal. Not having many options to cope with the new situation, the US triggered wars in the oil belt and using its international clout, decided to export services to other countries which influenced the US effort in the Uruguay Round of Trade Negotiations to restructure GATT and establish the wider umbrella organization, the World Trade Organization (WTO). One of the major multilateral agreements under WTO is the General Agreement on Trade in Services (GATS). The GATS Council recognized 161 services as tradable under twelve heads that included education, health and culture. By being a party to this multilateral agreement, India has agreed in principle to open up for penetration its most socially needed services, by powerful multilateral corporations in the services sector. In order to facilitate this process, the Government of India prepared more than half a dozen legislations in higher education designed to replace some of the existing institutions and set up new institutions.

The corporate profit hunting approach has not only impacted the countries outside the US, but also deeply disturbed the health and educational services within US. A telling note "How the

American University was Killed, in Five Easy Steps", circulated on internet, presents a graphic account of the destruction of publicly funded universities in US. The country had a fairly enlightened education policy in the 1950s, based on affordability, easy access to universities, passionate learning and vocal citizen involvement in the issues of the times. "The Liberal Arts stood at the centre of the college education and students were exposed to philosophy, anthropology, literature, history, sociology, world religions, foreign languages and culture". "This led", the note observes, "to the uprisings and growing number of citizens taking part in popular dissent against the Vietnam War, against racism, against the destruction of the environment in a growing corporatized culture, against misogyny, against homophobia". The American corporate sector did realize that these revolts were incubated in the university campuses and would have liked nothing more than to shut down the universities—"Destroy them outright".

The corporate world chose five easy steps: one, defund public higher education; two, de-professionalize and impoverish the professors and create unemployment and under-employment of PhDs; three, managerial class taking over university governance; four, moving in corporate culture and corporate money in the campuses and five, destroying the students. The note adds "Within one generation, in five easy steps, not only have the scholars and intellectuals of the country been silenced and nearly wiped out, but the entire institution has been hijacked, and recreated as a machine through which future generations will be impoverished, indebted and silenced". It adds "Now, low wage migrant professors teach repetitive courses they did not design for students who travel through on a kind of conveyor belt, only to be spit out, indebted and desperate into a jobless economy". The note laments that: "The real winners, the only people truly benefiting from the big-picture meltdown of the American university are those people who, in the 1960s, saw those vibrant college campuses as a threat to their established power. They are the same people now working feverishly to dismantle other social structures, everything from Medicare and Social Security to the Post Office". Looking at this wreckage of American academia, the note acknowledges:"They have won". They won in the sense that the vibrant dissent of the 60s is missing. US could easily invade Iraq and Afghanistan; enact undemocratic laws; and strengthen surveillance mechanisms against its own citizens, without any internal resistance.

This is fast becoming the story of Indian Higher Education also. In fact, the Indian case may prove far worse than the American one. The rise of fascist forces in the recent past is a clear indicator. A large section of academics either have reconciled or subjugated to these forces.

III

The dismantling of Indian higher education that began in the 1980s gathered momentum in the 1990s all over India. The disinclination to promote publicly-funded higher education has, to start with, been manifested in the gradual collapse of state universities. Here, the experience of the state of Andhra Pradesh from South India is worth recounting. This state is one of the top six developed states of India and a rising hub for the IT industry. This is also the state that has been facing radical left movements, particularly in the 1970s and 80s. The World Bank chose this state as its laboratory. The World Bank loans came with a number of conditionalities. One of them could have been the defunding of higher education. To start with, recruitment of the faculty to universities and colleges was stopped from the late 1980s to a point of abolishing the College Service Commission that was in charge of the recruitment of college teachers. The outstanding universities of the state like Osmania and Andhra Universities, with a national standing have been downgraded because of the cutting of the block grants which has adversely affected the quality of the libraries, laboratories and infrastructure. The universities were asked to raise their own funds through self-financing courses like management professional and vocational courses. The Science faculty was incentivized to go for consultancy and patenting. And disciplines like arts, humanities, social sciences and basic sciences were underfunded and the number of faculty in each discipline was reduced to the bare minimum.

In the place of permanent faculty, the institutions started employing part-time, purely temporary under-paid under-qualified faculty whose tenure was permanently temporary. This temporary and insecure faculty for decades together could neither commit to teaching nor passionate research. The neoliberal forces, both domestic and global, succeeded in hitting at the image of the publicity funded universities by starving them of grants and seeing to it that they were pushed to the verge of collapse. For the better off sections and the newly emerging lumpen class, education in the private sector was opened. The private institutions sprouted like poultry farms in every nook and corner of the state. The number of private medical and engineering colleges went up phenomenally. The rise of deemed for private universities, particularly in professional education was a spectacle unbelievable. Thus, the private sector professional education for those who could afford it, and the choice of softer disciplines with poorer quality, for the poor first generation students, completed the circle of class polarization.

The Government of India has now been pressurized to enact new legislations and amend existing national laws for the smooth entry of foreign capital in this critical service sector. It has prepared more than half a dozen bills, placed or to be placed before the Indian Parliament, to legalize and legitimize privatization and globalization of education. These bills include: The Foreign Educational Institutions (Regulations of Entry and Operations) Bill, 2010; the Universities Research and Innovation Bill, 2012; the Higher Education and Research Bill, 2011; the Educational Tribunals Bill 2010; the National Accreditation Regulatory Authority for Higher Educational Institutions Bill, 2010; the Prohibition of Unfair Practices in Technical Educational Institutions, Medical Educational Institutions and Universities Bill, 2010; and National Commission for Minority Educational Institutions (Amendment) Bill, 2009. None of these bills, nor their contents, have ever been publicly debated in any part of India, nor were demands for these ever raised by any section of people. This makes it clear how the Indian state has come to circumvent the internal democratic process in order to sub-serve the needs and demands of the global capital. Since an analysis of all these bills is not possible, a few of them are taken up in this discussion to bring out the trends in higher education at the present juncture and the efforts underway to dismantle publicly funded higher education.

IV

The Higher Education and Research Bill is aimed at dismantling the University Grants Commission that was established through an Act of Parliament on the recommendations of the Radhakrishna Commission in 1956. This Act has been and with slight modifications, continues to be in effect till today. While the functioning of the UGC is not beyond controversy, the changes that were contemplated to replace this body are to be pondered over. As a damage control, the government appointed a committee under the Chairmanship of Yashpal who commanded respect and credibility among the Indian academia. This committee which looked into the state of Higher Education felt that different agencies that have been set up from time to time to oversee the technical, medical and legal education need to be integrated to ensure a holistic approach to education. On seeing the way the Ministry of Human Resource Development was proceeding in the name of his committee, Yashpal went on record that what was proposed by the Ministry was not in spirit with the committee's recommendations.

The UGC Act of 1956 was a simple Act which reposed enormous trust in the Commission and its wisdom to guide the destiny of higher education with least intervention from the government. The mandate of the Commission was "to take all steps as it might think fit for the promotion and coordination of University Education and for the determination and maintenance of standards of teaching, examination and research in universities with full involvement and participation of the universities and its faculty". The UGC was required to assess the overall financial needs and provide the finances for the development of universities. The Commission was also to advise the central and state governments on the allocation of grants and establishment of new universities.

The UGC all said and done earned an image and invoking its name, always worked with the academic community. The community by and large respected its stand and direction. Such institutions nurtured over a period of time normally are protected and improvised, but the neoliberal agenda is out to dismantle them and bring in new structures without any legacy and historical traditions. Supplanting institutions is the major thrust of the neoliberal agenda.

An examination of the Higher Education and Research Bill, 2011, suggests a fundamental deviation from the established norms, values and structures. The preamble of the bill, of course, states that "its aim is to promote autonomy of higher education institutions and universities for free pursuit of knowledge and innovations and to provide for comprehensive and integrated growth of higher education and research keeping in view global standards of educational and research practices". It is in pursuance of these objectives that the Ministry proposed the establishment of the National Commission for Higher Education. Obviously, the terms like creativity and socially relevant knowledge are replaced by terms like innovation and global standards.

The provisions in the Bill are in total contrast with the stated objectives of autonomy and free pursuit of knowledge. In place of the UGC, a cumbersome organizational structure with one chairman, three whole-time members and three part-time members will be established. The selection committee for the chairman of the new Commission consists of the Prime Minister, the Speaker of the Lok Sabha., the leader of the Opposition in the Lok Sabha and two Ministers. Thus, the committee is completely political replacing the search committee consisting of three reputed academics.

As far as autonomy is concerned, some of the provisions in the new Bill are totally a negation of freedom of educational institutions including that of the apex body. Look at some of the clauses: the Commission shall prepare annually an evidence-based statement on the status of higher education and report on the activities of the Commission. The President of India will constitute a committee to evaluate and review the performance of the Commission which includes the extent of fulfilment of the objectives of the Commission, future directions of the Commission along with corrective measures and to see whether it has been able to promote effective academic linkages, inter-institutional linkages and public private partnership in higher education.

The dreadful clause 67 says that, if at anytime the central government is of the opinion

"(a) that, on account of circumstances beyond the control of the Commission, General Council, Board or Corporation, as the case may be, it is unable to discharge the functions or perform the duties imposed on it by or under the provisions of this Act; or

(b) This body as the case may be, has persistently defaulted in complying with any direction given by the central government under this Act or in the discharge of the functions or performance of the duties imposed on it by or under the provisions of this Act and as a result of such default the financial position of the Commission, General Council, Board or Corporation, as the case may be, or the administration of the Commission has suffered; or

(c) That circumstances exist which render it necessary in the public interest so to do. It may by notification, supersede the Commission, General Council, Board, the Board of Directors of the Corporation, as the case may be, appoint a person or persons as the Chairperson or the President, as the case may be, to exercise powers and discharge functions of the Commission, General Council, Board or Corporation, as the case may be, under this Act.

The central government has appropriated so much power to itself that all the office bearers, statutory functionaries can be superseded. It includes a clause "public interest" which gives sweeping powers to remove any functionary. This is something which the UGC Act did not ever remotely imagine. There are instances where chairpersons of UGC, of high integrity and academic standing, questioned and challenged the Ministries, if they felt that its intervention was unwarranted. In the present Act, functionaries of courage of conviction would lose their jobs at the whims and fancies of the MHD. The rulers are ignorant of the fact that autonomy is always rooted in the philosophy of self-governance with internal checks and balances, without any external intervention. A belief that all the wisdom lies with the central government is a negation of the culture of plurality of institutions and deconcentration of power. The authoritarian culture which has inspired the bill is the greater enemy of democracy, which promotes despotism.

Another innovation of the ongoing reforms is the Universities for Research and Innovation Bill (2012).This is a misleading title. In fact, the bill is nothing but an attempt to set up private universities. This is amply clear from all the provisions of the bill. The objects and reasons for setting up these universities are: "If India has to achieve a leadership role in the future global knowledge economy, mere public expenditure on higher education is not going to be sufficient and a substantial part of funding must flow into the education sector through not-for-profit private participation". The bill states that "it aims to lay down an enabling legislative framework for setting up universities in both the private and public sectors". It adds "presently there is no central law which provides for this framework, hence the need for a central legislation". The bill contemplates different modes of establishment of universities; they can be either fully public funded or fully private funded or based on public private partnership (PPP).

The clause on admissions is so vague that while the bill says that "Universities not publicly funded shall specify by statutes such criteria in the matters of admission as would account for diversities. Another clause says, "the percentage of reservation shall be determined taking into account the total number of seats available". It incorporates provision of self-disclosure of affirmative action towards members of socially and economically disadvantaged groups. The questions that arise are: what happens to constitutionally guaranteed reservations? Why should they be left to the universities concerned? Does it mean that not being publicly funded, more frankly the private universities need not follow the nationally accepted reservation policy?

Yet another bill "The Foreign Educational Institutions (Regulation of Entry and Operation) Bill" opens the high road for foreign capital into higher education. The bill provides for some regulations and restrictions for the entry of foreign universities. However, there is a clause which says "notwithstanding anything contained in the Act, the Central Government by notification, on the recommendation of the Advisory Board constituted, having regard to the reputation and international standing of foreign educational institutions, can exempt them from operation of any of the foregoing provisions of the Act." It also adds that all the matters including the penalties leviable shall be adjudicated by the National Educational Tribunal.

The idea of the National Educational Tribunal is mainly to remove some of the items including education, from the jurisdiction of the regular judiciary which is bound by constitutional morality and may not have as much of manoeuvrability that tribunals will have. The proliferation of tribunals is a fall out of globalization. A group of High Court Judges in one of their interactions at the Bhopal Judicial Academy expressed their concern about tribunalization of justice. A look at the constitution of the National Educational Tribunal indicates how such tribunals are bureaucratized. Out of its eight members, six are non-judicial members appointed by the Ministry and three are ex-officio members.

The other bills are also aimed at promoting the privatization of some of the services which were legitimately provided by the state agencies or public institutions. Since nations and nation-states operate within their legal and constitutional boundaries, they are now required to go beyond their boundaries and recast their legal systems and institutions to meet the requirements of corporate and global interests.

The spate of legislations waiting for enactment by the Parliament is the pointer to the future direction of higher education. All these bills directly or indirectly negate the constitutional mandate and its egalitarian vision. Thus a clear indicator of the fact that the force and power of the global interests have acquired such a dimension that there is no alternative to paving the way for the subordination of popular interests, larger national interest and democratic culture to the power of global interests. If the academic community and democratic sections of the civil society do not see the unfolding of this phenomenon, the sixty years of educational endeavours of the Indian society would be in vain, leaving behind a major man-made tragedy for posterity to encounter and suffer.

ENDNOTES

* Editors' Footnote:

This paper brings out the various facets of the neoliberal attack on higher education in India. For this purpose, it analyses, in particular two initiatives taken by the Government of India. These are the move to introduce a Four-Year Undergraduate Programme (FYUP) and tabling in the Indian Parliament, a number of bills to facilitate the entry of foreign providers of educational services. In the face of stiff opposition from the students' and teachers' community and a large section of other public opinion, the University Grants Commission did not give its clearance for the introduction of the FYUP. As a result, the status quo has continued to prevail so far as the undergraduate degree programme is concerned. The Higher Education and Research Bill, Universities for Research and Innovation Bill, and the Foreign Educational Institutions (Regulation of Entry and Operation) Bill, were also not pursued vigorously by the government due to the widespread opposition they evoked. These bills lapsed after the new Parliament was constituted following the general elections in 2014. Though the FYUP has been folded back and the Bills have lapsed, the effort of the neoliberal forces to change the character of higher education in India has continued in different forms. The present government is doing so mainly by executive orders issued from time to time. The analysis in this paper of the FYUP and the lapsed Bills is still very relevant and important because of the light they throw on the ongoing effort to commercialize higher education and open this sector to entry by foreign operators.

REFERENCES

1. Universities for Research and Innovation Bill, 2012, as Introduced in the Lok Sabha, Bill No. 61 of 2012.
2. The Higher Education and Research Bill, 2011, to be Introduced in the Rajya Sabha, Bill No. LX of 2011.
3. Educational Tribunal Bill, 2010, to be Introduced in the Lok Sabha, Bill No. 55 of 2010.
4. Foreign Educational Institutions Regulation of Entry and Operations Bill 2010, as Introduced in the Lok Sabha, Bill No. 57 of 2010.
5. Academy of Scientific and Innovative Research Bill 2010, to be Introduced in the Lok Sabha, Bill No. 73 of 2010.
6. The National Accreditation Regulatory Authority for Higher Educational Institutions Bill, 2010, to be Introduced in Lok Sabha, Bill No. 54 of 2010.
7. How the American University was Killed, in Five Easy Steps—Mayraj Fahim fmayraj@yahoo.com, Date: June 17, 2013 7:08:41 PM EDT

   http://junctrebellion.wordpress.com/2012/08/12/how-the-american-university-was-klled-in-five-easy-steps/How the American University was Killed, in Five Easy Steps.
8. How Not to Modernize a University, Dinesh Singh's Ham-Handed Efforts at Reform, St Stephen's College Physics Department.

9. Education as a Tradable Service Under the GATS-WTO Regime by Ramesh Patnaik, A Note Circulated to AIFRTE, Hyderabad.

Acknowledgements

Thanks are due to the Centre for the Study of Social Exclusion and Inclusive Policy and its faculty members, particularly S. Japhet, for providing a conducive climate for work, and Shashikala for negotiating my cumbersome handwritten drafts.

15

The Commoditization of Education

Prabhat Patnaik

Commoditization of Education: The New Trend

The analysis in this paper pertains to mainly higher education, although it holds for education in general. While discussing a vision of education for India it is best to start by stating the current trend. The most fundamental trend that is occurring in the sphere of education is a process of commoditization of education. The products of the education system are essentially meant to be sold as a commodity in the market.

Looking for a Job vs Commoditization of Education

People who are educated are always there in the labour market and look for a job. So in a sense they are always offering themselves on the job market. So what is specifically new at this moment? There is a fundamental difference between looking for a job in the market and becoming a commodity. Commodity is one such thing which, for its producer, does not hold any utility or provide any satisfaction or any pleasure, but is only a pure source of money. Education is now seen merely as an input or source which can provide its recipient or the student with a value that is an income package. It is a source of making money rather than a source of knowledge or grandeur of thoughts. Students are induced to look into education in this very way not only when they come to higher education but right from the school stage. A source of making money and nothing beyond. This has become the exclusive definition of education.

What is Wrong with this Notion or Concept?

Actually, there is a lot wrong with this concept of education which can be explained as follows:

1. A commodity is a package thing. If education is a commodity then it has to be in a finished package. The more finished manner it is presented in, the better recognition it gets as education. The better the package one can get hold of, the better education one is getting. However, in the process, education as a source of questioning, rationalizing, and articulating—which defines its fundamental purpose—is lost sight of. Unfortunately, this process starts at the school level itself, when parents cry for their children getting 99 per cent marks because without it they cannot get admission in good places. Education is seen as a package and what matters is who has the better package. This packaging instead of opening up the students' minds, destroys all creativity.
2. Education has a major role in nation building. It has a social role, a role to inculcate social sensitivities in those who are being educated. And if education gets commoditized then this notion of social role disappears altogether.
3. Education makes us realize the importance of being sensitive towards fellow human beings. On the other hand, in commoditization this objective does not come into reckoning.
4. Commoditization of education fundamentally stands in the way of equality of opportunity. Equality of opportunity is inclusive of affirmative action. The realization of equality of opportunity can be seen in a state of affairs where the social composition of those, let us say, in a profession, in a job, reflects the social composition of the population as a whole. In other words, the more the social composition of the population as a whole is reflected in whatever sample one takes, say, scientist, educationist or others, the closer we are to realizing equality of opportunity. Anything which is conducive towards a movement in this direction is something which promises equality of opportunity. To the extent education gets commoditized or privatized

or becomes a business, it comes in the way of realizing equality of opportunity.

5. The current trend of education is such that it is producing dualism. There is an enormous gap that has opened up between universities such as the Delhi University and provincial universities such as the Utkal University. The Economics Department of the Utkal University which was once quite reputed is run by only three faculty members for a large number of students.

Outcome of Commoditization of Education

Education can be seen in two alternative ways. Education in which individual agents of society go to somewhere known as schools or universities and receive something known as education, and pay for it. It seems like a transaction: you pay for something you receive. It is like a market where business is happening. And increasingly we are looking at education like this only. The alternative way in which education can be viewed as an activity in which society maintains a number of people in order to take forward the frontiers of knowledge which are essential for social progress.

We should keep the second option as our essential vision for education. But unfortunately, due to commoditization of education, it is the business aspect of education which is dominant in the current period. Hence, those who get education demand a higher share of money or salary as compared to those who have not invested in education.

If we go back to Adam Smith, the quintessential capitalist, then the process can be described as one where each one of us is looking at our own self-interest. Of course, we should be allowed to do so, but according to Adam Smith, there should be a social counterpoint to it. There should be state intervention in order to ensure that the society as a whole is functioning well.

If the state is an embodiment of social rationality then there have to be institutions to impart that social rationality. Education then cannot become a commodity but a space where people can sit and think what is good for society. The social role of education is an essential ingredient for every society, even for a capitalist society. Hence, the direction we are moving in is fundamentally inimical to the direction we should be moving.

Reversing the Commoditization of Education

If education is to serve a social purpose then it should fundamentally be socially financed and socially maintained. The larger part for education must be state-funded or funded by charitable organizations, but definitely not based on the privatized profit-making model. And if we already have a large number of institutions which exist to make profits, then it becomes essential for society to regulate them with respect to their curriculum, fees and others, in order to ensure that the fundamental social goals are not threatened by their existence.

Education being funded by the state and by charitable organizations is essential, not only desirable. And since education is essential for achieving social goals then there should be a proper schooling system which supports the goal of equality of opportunity where everybody gets a chance to educate himself. Even in the United States, the bulk of education is funded by either the state or by charitable organizations and not by private profit-making organizations.

There should be a universal neighbourhood school system. Even in US., there is a system of sending the ward to the nearest school to get education. The compulsory system of sending the child to a school funded by the state is what we lack in India. Moreover, in our country even the best of schools which are sympathetic towards the poor have taken for granted practices which militate against equality of opportunity. For example, tuitions have become a must since a perception has developed that remaining confined to the classroom study is getting students nowhere.

Part VI
RTE Act and its Implementation

16
The Policy Crisis in Education

Jandhyala B.G. Tilak

The Current Crisis in the Education Policy

Education in India is in a state of crisis. The crisis in education is, however, not new. Ever since J.P. Naik identified long ago, the crisis in Indian education, it has been a 'continuing crisis.' But there is also a difference in the nature of the crisis. The current crisis is not in terms of student explosion, or finances or learning deficit, or underachievement or quality and relevance or employability or lack of teachers, or teacher absenteeism or woeful infrastructure or the decline of institutions. The present crisis includes all these, but is much more; it is, essentially in terms of policy. It is a policy crisis in education.

Historical Journey of Policy Crisis

This policy crisis has several aspects. The current education policy reflects an absence of a long-term coherent policy for educational development. Instead, what we have is executive orders and some quick-fix solutions to manage the system without having any serious direction of how to go ahead. The government, both the state and the central, does not effectively intervene and lets the system evolve under the dictates of the market. Such non-intervention, which can be described as *laissez-faireism* is the root cause of the present crisis. Basically the government lacks a coherent set of policies. There is very little seriousness in the policy statements that are being made and their eventual implementation. This point can be explained by the following examples:

First, the Constitution of India of 1950 set a time-bound target which clearly stated that India should universalize elementary education within a period of ten years. However, there was no seriousness either in the 1950s or in the present period about this goal. We have been repeatedly stating that we would achieve it. In the 1950s and 60s, we also debated heatedly over the issue whether five years of primary education was actually needed or three years would be sufficient or two years of non-formal education could be treated as equivalent to five years of formal primary education. Instead of seriously pursuing the goal to universalize elementary education, we kept debating such issues, diluting and derailing the resolve to universalize elementary education. As a result, even after six decades after independence, and more than half a century after the date set by the Constitution, universalization of elementary education could not be accomplished. We only went on repeating the goal and we are still repeating it.

Second, after a series of serious deliberations based on high quality research, the Education Commission chaired by D.S. Kothari, recommended in 1966 that we should be spending at least six per cent of the national income on education by 1986. This proposal was among the few of those accepted by the Parliament and it was included in the National Policy on Education 1968. However, we have not been serious again with this too. We never had any financial plan for education to realize this goal, but went on promising repeatedly that we would realize this goal "soon". Even today we are spending only something around four per cent of the national income on education; the growth was also not steady and smooth; and we keep reiterating the goal. In between we also raised awkward questions on the six per cent of national income, and the need to achieve the goal.

Third, quite interestingly even after the National Policy on Education that promised to raise the allocation to education gradually to six per cent, was formulated in 1968, in the Fifth and Sixth Five Year Plans, the allocation to education was much less than what it was in the previous Plans. So when the policy was to increase the allocation to education, we followed the opposite trend. Had we been serious about the goal we set at that time, many of today's problems would not have arisen in the first place and some of the existing problems would probably have completely disappeared by today. Certainly finances would not have been a serious constraint in the development of education in the country. But unfortunately we were never serious.

Fourth, we introduced in 2002 with great fervour the *Sarva Shiksha Abhiyan (SSA)* as a grand programme of universalizing elementary education in the country in a mission mode and in a time-bound manner. But we never worked in a mission mode, nor did we realize the importance of a time-bound nature of action that is required. Among many ill effects, what it has actually done is that it has created parallel structures, sidelining the whole government machinery. By the side of the normal educational administration, we have created parallel structures separately for implementation of SSA. As the SSA is, after all, borne out of the District Primary Education Project (DPEP) of the 1990s, it also inherited the feature of being a parallel structure as created under the DPEP. Finally, under SSA, we have actually formalized what we today condemn as non-formal educational guarantee scheme, para-teachers, etc., and diluted and weakened the noble mission of universal elementary education. All these have now become acceptable policies for the development of elementary education. So again, we were never serous about the spirit in which we conceived universalization of elementary education.

Finally, we enacted the Right to Free and Compulsory Education (RTE) Act, in 2009, after about 17 years of debate following the Supreme Court verdict (1992) that right to education is a part of the fundamental right to life as provided in the Indian Constitution. The Act was enacted seven years after the Constitutional amendment was made in 2002, while everyone expected the Act to follow the amendment immediately. Given the long time it has taken to evolve, many expected an Act with excellent provisions. Everyone expected the Act to provide for equitable quality education for all. But what has the Act given us? First, the Act did not provide for anything resembling a Common School System, which the Education Commission recommended and is in practice in many other countries. There is no concern regarding equitable quality of education in the Act. On the other hand, it very clearly stimulates growth of private education at all levels. Providing encouragement for the growth of private schools under different provisions in the Act, it actually promotes accentuation of inequalities in education. The government is prepared to provide more and more funds to private schools under various provisions, specifically promising reimbursement of fees for 25 per cent of the students of the disadvantaged sections of the society admitted in private schools. Moreover, by providing 25 per cent reservation for weaker sections in the private schools, the government admitted the low quality of government schools, and in a sense, got reconciled to the helplessness in improving the quality of government schools. Further, some scholars have argued that this Act conceived to be making education a justiciable right is not so in reality and that it defeats the very purpose for which it was enacted. All this shows that once again we are not serious towards the goals we set. When the Act was enacted in 2009, the government had very clearly accepted that within a period of three years, most of its provisions would be implemented. But during the first three years nothing was done and at the end of the period the government woke up to the fact that "there are no trained teachers. There are no teachers—trained or untrained." Even after realizing this, nothing was done to create the infrastructure to produce more and more teachers, and to train the huge numbers of the then existing untrained teachers. With respect to the provision of other infrastructure, as specified in the Act, the picture is no better. Now we have reached a point where we have come to believe that this non-seriousness in education policy would go on for an indefinite period and policy implementation would continue to be postponed interminably.

The Recent Policy Crisis

Lack of seriousness about policy pronouncements is true, not only with respect to school education, but we find the same thing with respect to higher education as well. In the Eleventh and the Twelfth Five Year Plans, we have the clearly stated objective of inclusive growth. 'Inclusive growth' in nature, definition and scope may not be the same as the long cherished goal of 'equitable development;' they might even be contradictory. After all, *development* is much wider than *growth*. Ignoring the fine distinction between the two for a while, many expect that inclusive growth will aim at reducing inequalities in society. Inclusive economic growth requires inclusive education. But interestingly, according to the government, the inclusive growth in higher education would be pursued through the increasing role of the private sector. In fact, the government has stated very clearly that it would be allowing all kinds of privatization of higher education, including profit-making higher education, and different models of public private partnerships' (PPPs). This is in addition to increased reliance on cost recovery measures such as student fees and educational loans.

In the Eleventh Five Year Plan, the government launched a massive plan in higher education of building new central universities and new central institutions like Indian Institutes of Technology and Indian Institutes of Management. In the same context, the Planning Commission understood that the central government allocation for education left a huge gap of 88 per cent between the allocation and requirements, and expected that it would probably be filled by some "benevolent" private player directly or through yet-to-emerge innovative models of PPP. This massive expansion was planned without realizing that there were no teachers. One-third of the teaching positions in the existing universities and other institutions of higher education, including central universities and Indian Institutes of Technology, had been vacant. The degree of shortage of teachers is, of course, much worse in state universities and undergraduate colleges. Further the system is increasingly characterized by declining quality and standards in higher education, poor and ineffective governance, rampant corruption, etc. Suddenly the government considered that many of these problems could be best solved by legislative policies. So it proposed a package of legislative policies which are right now pending in the Parliament.

If one looks at many of these bills pending before the Parliament, one would realize that there is a complete new understanding on the part of the government about higher education and also on the role of the state in higher education. The new understanding is higher education is important, but it can be left to the private sector. Commoditization of higher education has been very clearly accepted, and education packages are allowed to be sold very easily in the market like most other common goods and services. It is strongly believed that if profits are allowed to be made, then more and more private organizations would come up in the higher education sector to take over the entire responsibility of higher education in such a way that the government would not have to bother about it any more, even with respect to planning, financing and delivery of higher education. The responsibility of the government could be kept to a bare minimum. At best some legislative framework would need to be provided, which is hoped to be done by the bills introduced in the Parliament. The pending bills also clearly show that we are more concerned with global needs and global developments rather than our national development. In all, these bills are highly inadequate to solve the intense problems that the government itself has identified, forget about the others, many of which have not been recognized or identified by the government.

Root Causes of the Policy Crisis

It is universally recognized that education, including higher education, is a public good. The public good is of a very different nature. It has a very special social role attached to it. We tend to forget, rather refuse to recognize the very public good nature of higher education, and tend to ask awkward questions such as: what is wrong if education is treated as a private good like many other goods and services? What is wrong if people purchase it, and if suppliers provide it or sell it at market rates? What is wrong if the suppliers make profits, even exorbitant profits? What is wrong if market forces are allowed to operate in education, after all, education is a 'business'? We ask these questions essentially because we overlook the public good nature of education, which has been recognized for centuries. Public goods need to be treated differently from other goods and services. But we tend to equate them, which would be very costly in the long run.

In the context of formulation of educational policies, we identify some 'stakeholders'—essentially students, parents, teachers and employers (industry), overlooking the fact that the entire society is the stakeholder. This is because of a very narrow understanding of the interrelationship between education and the society and the externalities that education produces, which are recognized as a legion. The whole society that comprises of everyone, not just the students or the parents, but the entire society has stakes in educational development. Not only the present society, but also the future society has a stake in educational development.

The non-recognition of the public good nature of education is the source of all the problems, and everything that is going wrong in the field of education. If, on the other hand, we recognize that education, including higher education is a public good, and we are sincere about it, we approach to solve many of the existing problems in different, desirable and effective ways. Society needs to be very firm towards its commitment to the development of education, not only in terms of policy statements but also in terms of follow-up actions and finances. Once we recognize it as a public good producing valuable externalities for generations to come, we would have a long-term plan for the development of education.

We do not feel the need of a vision and of a long-term plan for educational development because we fail to recognize the invaluable contribution of education to socio-economic and political transformation of the nations. Rather we do not recognize education as of any importance at all. There is a lot of evidence that shows that public education is actually the foundation for the development of a nation and its prosperity. The fact that a high-quality public formal education produces wide-ranging benefits for individuals and societies has been demonstrated, time and again in many countries of the world. There is no scope for a large private sector—that too profit-seeking private sector, in the education edifice of a nation. Involvement of the private sector, particularly non-philanthropy based private sector, in education will pose a serious deterrent in providing education as a human right. The private sector and the PPPs may be good in infrastructure and other projects, but not in education. Therefore, we should, at least make an effort to check the growth of the private sector, and if possible shut down some of the existing private institutions, which are working on commercial principles.

Thus the present crisis in education also reflects a crisis in our attitudes to education. It is time to think and recall what is meant by education, and what is meant by a university and higher education. It has to be realized that public education is fundamental to the development of an equitable society. Good quality, value-based education equips children and youth with the knowledge, skills, values, and attitudes that will help in producing responsible citizens who in turn will help in building a strong society based on human values. Today market models of higher education are growing rapidly, and the classical models of universities are going into oblivion. We need schools, colleges and universities which serve the social purposes of education.

Universities, for instance, must be multi-faculty and not single-faculty institutions; universities should have all levels of higher education—under graduate, postgraduate and research, and not just the undergraduate level, as suggested by the Yashpal Committee. We need to nurture the educational institutions in such a way that they essentially emphasize common universal human values for the development of a humane society, and not just produce skilled technical manpower, robots and machines.

Way Forward

With vast, diverse and rich historical and contemporary experience, we do ot have to search for new models. We already have the models—schools based on the philosophy of Jiddu Krishnamurthy, Sathya Sai Baba and other philosophers and social reformers, and universities like the *Shanti Niketan* set by Rabindanath Tagore and *Vidyapeeth*s moulded on the Gandhian philosophy in the contemporary period. We also have well-functioning *Kendriya Vidyalayas, Navodaya Vidyalayas* and the like. We also have knowledge of some of our world famous universities of the ancient period, like *Nalanda, Takshashila* and *Vikramashila*. As such models are still relevant for modern society, we need to revive and multiplicate such models, along with modern, socially desirable and innovative approaches in our present education system. Basically, it is important to understand what is meant by education and what these educational institutions are meant for and certainly not to equate education with other products of the market. It has to be internalized that education is a public good and a human right. Both these features are being ignored. In that particular sense, a drastic change in the attitude of the government, the people and the society at large towards education is needed in today's rapidly changing environment.

17

RTE Act from the Viewpoint of the Right to Education and Law

Archana Mehendale

The Right of Children to Free and Compulsory Education Act, 2009 (RTE) is supposed to be a reference point and all issues and policy matters pertaining to education should be seen in the light of this statute. All issues and policy matters pertaining to education are in fact being increasingly seen in the light of this statute. Actions are being demanded as well as justified in the name of RTE. Even the acronym RTE has entered conversations in middle class homes. The Saikia Committee that was constituted to look into the financial, administrative and legal feasibility of making education a fundamental right had recommended that by doing so, 'it would demonstrate the political will and the administrative resolve of the country for achieving the education for all (EFA) goals by 2000 AD' and that it would send the 'right signals to the international community and donors regarding India's commitment' (Government of India, 1997:8).

An amendment of the Constitution, particularly PART III on Fundamental Rights which is part of the basic structure of the Constitution, certainly needs to go beyond such tokenistic and demonstrative value. The strategy of law gives us opportunities to firstly, approach the High Courts and the Supreme Court for claiming and restoring this right and secondly, to mobilize and empower right-holders to assert their rights.

Internationally, the recognition of the right to education and provision of free and compulsory primary education has been justified by economic arguments wherein economic and social benefits that education is instrumental in generating, is held important by human rights and ethical arguments. Although both sets of arguments would still advocate for recognition of education as a right, the manner in which education is envisioned and the nature in which education systems in societies are organized would be influenced by the line of argument that is adopted. Whether right to education would be achieved through the principle of equality or through the principle of efficiency or rather how would the government negotiate between these two competing principles, remains a moot question.

Despite the long history of the recognition of education as a human right in international law such as the Universal Declaration on Human Rights (1948), International Convention on Economic, Social and Cultural Rights (1966), Convention for Elimination of Discrimination Against Women (1979) and the United Nations Convention on Rights of the Child (1989), the provision remained largely on paper. Fernandez and Jenkner (1995) listed over 40 international conventions and declarations that refer to education as a human right, although the formulations, content and corresponding obligations varied across these.

The set of rights which are usually classified as economic, social and cultural rights, are generally subject to maximum availability of state resources. General Comment 13 of the United Nations Committee on Economic, Social and Cultural Rights emphasizes that states must use their available resources to the maximum and lack of resources can be no defence to a failure to take appropriate measures.

The poor response by countries is especially evident with regard to the requirements under Article 14 of the International Convention on Economic, Social and Cultural Rights wherein governments were required to submit within two years a detailed Plan of Action for the progressive implementation of the principle of free and compulsory education within a reasonable number of years. Even after the Committee on Economic, Social and Cultural Rights emphasized that this submission was not a discretionary provision but binding on governments. Plans of Action were not submitted by several governments. Interestingly, governments were by and large indifferent to these provisions in internationally binding treaties until the political compacts starting with the Jomtien Declaration on Education for All (1990), Dakar Framework of Action (2000) and Millennium Development Goals (2000) made it an agenda of the international community and a responsibility shared by donor agencies, private enterprises, communities, civil society, besides the governments.

The past decade has witnessed both an expansion of legally assured human rights in India such as the right to education and right to work, and also people's movements and struggles to get statutory cover for other rights such as right to food, right to housing and right to health, among others. Interestingly, the general mood to get these codified into a legislation is upbeat—the political class sees this populist bait helpful to win over their constituencies, the judiciary has been benevolent in reading these rights into the Fundamental Rights particularly right to life and civil society organizations have this as an important agenda for mobilizing people and for lobbying with policy makers. This rights-based approach to development, particularly the juridification of welfare rights during times of privatization and globalization, needs to be closely examined. In the context of the right of children to free and compulsory education from Grade I to Grade VIII, the questions that must be asked are:

1. What are the implications of recognizing this right when governments are unable to bear the costs of education on their own, when governments have not appointed the required number of elementary school teachers, when the educational outcomes show poor achievement results and when private schools are thriving without having met the basic statutory norms and standards?
2. Does the fact that this is a Fundamental Right and a statutory right, provides a platform to bring course correction of the rapidly deteriorating public school system and in the governmental apathy towards it?
3. Or has it only paved the way for the government to dilute the right itself and what it assures, while simultaneously expanding the set of duty bearers to non-state actors such as private schools, teachers, and parents by a horizontal application of the Fundamental Right?

RTE is a departure from the erstwhile provincial 'free and compulsory education' legislation that was modelled on the British truancy legislation, which as Myron Weiner (1991) and Nalini Juneja (1997) have shown, remained unimplemented. Weiner gave an insightful explanation of the indifference towards free and compulsory legislation. He said, 'India's low per capita income and economic situation is less relevant as an explanation than the belief systems of the state bureaucracy, a set of beliefs that are widely shared by educators, social activists, trade unionists, academic researchers, and, more broadly, by members of the Indian middle class. At the core of these beliefs is the Indian view of the social order, notions concerning the respective roles of upper and lower social strata, the role of education as a means of maintaining differentiations among social classes, and concerns that 'excessive' and 'inappropriate' education for the poor would disrupt existing social arrangements' (Weiner, 1991:5).

What kind of education system is envisaged under the RTE? Does RTE itself provide a vision of education or is it one of the instruments that the government is using to move towards a larger overall vision? Or one may ask if there is indeed any official articulation of an education vision (post-1992 revised National Policy on Education) or plural visions on education and if so, where are they articulated? I would argue that RTE is not a vision document but reflects only a constricted politically negotiated consensus that satisfies the lowest common denominator. This is evidenced from a review of the draft Bills, responses of state governments to the Bills and the 213th report of the Parliamentary Standing Committee (2009).

In the context of globalization and education, Roger Dale (2000) raises an important question that needs to be addressed with regard to the education system—"who gets taught what, how, by whom and under what conditions and circumstances?" Regarding RTE, I would like to examine these five questions in some detail.

1. Who Gets Taught?

International legal treaties recognize education as a human right. In Mohini Jain versus State of Karnataka (1992), the Supreme Court held that education is a fundamental right without restricting it to a particular age group. However, the RTE Act, as we know, is applicable only to children between 6 and 14 years of age. Although the extension of this right to early childhood and secondary levels of education is being considered by the Central Advisory Board of Education (CABE), the political decision of selecting a group of children seems to be influenced primarily by economic considerations of what constitutes a better investment vis-à-vis their productive potential and thereby slicing the same pie differently rather than asking for a bigger pie.

2. What is Taught?

This relates to crucial questions of the aims of education, relevance and subject matter, 'tensions' in the curriculum and language. At the policy level, two divergent strands are evident; one which looks at education as an investment in developing the human potential and public good functions. This is reflected in the National Policy on Education, revised formulations of 1992 which held education as a unique investment in the present and future as its cardinal principle. The Ministry of Human Resource Development's (MHRD's) Report to the People on Education (2012) states: "Our vision is to realize India's human resource potential to its fullest in the education sector, with equity and inclusion". The second strand sees education for its intrinsic value, reflected in the National Curriculum Framework (NCF 2005) Position Paper on 'Aims of Education' wherein education is referred to as a liberating experience freeing from the shackles of exploitation and injustice, enabling respect for cultural diversity and a curriculum which changes the centre-periphery perspective. The RTE only partially addresses this through its Chapter 5 on Curriculum and Evaluation because its rhetoric is not supported by shared understanding and consensus. For instance, the 'no detention' clause has not only been contentious, it is also poorly understood as also the provision of Continuous Comprehensive Evaluation. This can even be traced in the 213th Parliamentary Standing Committee Report on the Bill which observed that the provision would be counter-productive and "there needs to be an element of fear through a proper evaluation lest the non-performers may become a liability for society at large" (Para 9.1).

3. How is Education to be Delivered?

The RTE primarily focuses on prescribing the administrative/managerial aspects of the delivery chain from the central government to state government, the local authority, and the School Management Committees. Apart from prescribing broad pedagogical principles related to preserving children's dignity, rights and enhancing their potentials, it does not enter the arena of prescribing minutely how education should actually happen in schools and classrooms and what outcomes the teachers or schools are bound to deliver. In my view, this should be welcome because, legislation, no matter how progressively written should not compromise on teachers' professional autonomy to handle a diverse set of learners.

4. By Whom Should Education be Provided?

What kind of an education system does the RTE envisage? The two key issues that emerge from RTE in this regard are: first, the silence of the RTE on the appointments of para-teachers by state governments, and second, bringing in private unaided schools under the obligation of providing free education to children from disadvantaged and weaker sections. This is not only inconsistent with the state's professed objective of investing in education with equity and inclusion but it also does not provide any impetus for radically reforming and upgrading the public education system. The RTE also plants another framework for regulation of private educational institutions, that's also a central one, without much critical review of the dysfunctional regulatory systems at the state level and the ensuring mushrooming of unrecognized and unregulated private schools. In what manner does such an education system then serve the public goods function or become a liberating experience?

5. Under What Conditions and Circumstances is Education Provided?

Is it adequate to bring the 8.1 million out-of-school children into schools and retain them through the cycle of eight years of elementary schooling? The normative framework prescribed by RTE tries to ensure basic physical infrastructure, curriculum and evaluation practices and protection against discrimination, physical punishment and mental abuse. However, it is beyond the scope of the RTE to ensure that the home and community conditions which the child negotiates with in order to participate in schooling are conducive to the child's completion of education. In other words, RTE views the school-going child in a decontextualized manner. It does not acknowledge the conditions of poverty, abuse, social hierarchies, displacement, family breakdowns, loss of livelihoods, ill-health, natural calamities that the child brings along to the classroom. Even though RTE itself cannot address these larger questions, the delays and lack of political will to amend other related legislation including the Child Labour (Prohibition and Regulation) Act, 1986 reflects an incoherent policy vision about children and childhood. Furthermore, the notion of non-discrimination, especially with reference to inclusion of disadvantaged children in private schools is handled more at the nominal than at a substantive level.

Conclusion

To conclude, RTE has only legislated upon a constricted vision of education within the constraints of federal dynamics, financial deficits, and political compulsions towards incrementalism. A search for a coherent vision and its formulation is essential because our articulated policy vision documents address policy concerns of a different time. But more so, because political and executive actions lack consistency with what was proclaimed. Articulation of a policy vision would force the policy choices to be put on the table, rather than remain discrete, opaque and tentative. One can only hope that with time we move nearer to this objective.

REFERENCES

Dale, R. (2000). Globalization and Education: Demonstrating a "Common World Educational Culture" or Locating a "Globally Structured Educational Agenda"? A Comparative Approach. Educational Theory, 50(4), 21-43.

Fernandez, Alfred and Siegfried Jenkner. 1995 (edited). International Declarations and Conventions on the Right to Education and the Freedom of Education. Frankfurt am Main: Info3 – Verlag.

Government of India (1997). Report of the Committee of State Education Ministers on Implications of the Proposal to Make

Elementary Education a Fundamental Right. New Delhi: Department of Education, Ministry of Human Resource Development, Government of India.

Juneja, Nalini. (1997). Right of the Child to Education and Issues in Implementation of Compulsory Education: Perceptions of Education Administrators. *New Frontiers in Education*, 27(1).

Rajya Sabha Secretariat (2009). Department Related Parliamentary Standing Committee on Human Resource Development, 213th Report on Right of Children to Free and Compulsory Education Bill, 2008. New Delhi. Accessed at http://www.prsindia.org/uploads/media/1229341892/scr1235039268_Right_to_Education_bill_2008.pdf on July 14, 2013.

Weiner, Myron (1991). *The Child and the State in India: Child Labor and Education Policy in Comparative Perspective*. Princeton: Princeton University Press.

18

Pre-School Children and the Education System in India

Razia Ismail

The government has not found a suitable box to put in early childhood. It is put in the same box as women, namely in the Ministry of Women and Child Development. And there it is not related to human rights as a larger question. We need to start looking at education as a foundational investment. We often tend to forget the learning setting in early childhood. Architects design foundation before they design the rest of the building. But in education we do not seem to look at foundation. We do not realize that learning begins at birth if not before. We, thus, miss out a critical phase of the development journey or the enlightenment journey that a child should undertake. If the mother lacks iodine, at a certain point the baby's brain gets affected, and even if you soak the child in iodine thereafter, it will make no difference. This is what is happening in early childhood.

What children learn in programmes undertaken by the state is how to clap hands, how to sit in a circle, how to memorize rhymes and how not to step out of the line or the circle in which they are put. Is that education? The Integrated Child Development Services (ICDS) is one of the largest programmes in the world. The ICDS has been criticized by the Planning Commission and by experts for neglecting one of its very important components, i.e. early learning stimulation. The learning stimulation generally ends up even before the age group of 3-6 when the children enter into an *Anganwadi* programme. At the age of 0-3 years, learning is left to chance, to an attentive mother or grandmother of the family who may or may not know the distinction between stimulation and disciplining. If the state is the guardian of the child then what is the state's role at these very initial as well as crucial ages?

Education is not an issue of law. It is an issue of justice. And, there is a big difference between the two. The Right of Children to Free and Compulsory Education Act, 2009 (RTE) which has been constantly cited as being the be-all and end-all to all situations is at best an expression of national vision. However, it has a limited vision. If the vision is impaired then the resolve to express it is also going to be affected. The youngest child at the first threshold of learning has no less right than the child of 6 years. The responsibility to pre-school education is still not firmly assigned in the Government of India. The RTE limitation of the fundamental right leaves out the 3-6 age group, and the way we look at learning leaves out the below 3 age group.

The right to early learning opportunity can be very critical. It is as serious and pivotal as any other right to a child. In those first years, children learn to trust, to fear, to hope, to accept, to resist, a sense of identity, confidence or surrender, words, songs, games, expressions and they carry that to the next stage. Whatever is delivered to the child formally or informally is learning and hence it is education. What is the state's role in that, in guiding it, in making it possible? Underinvestment in the early age group affects the child's ability to move readily to the phase of primary education. The majority of our children who do enter the primary school come into the classroom without the dividend of that first investment. Certainly the school enrolment has increased over time, but enrolment is not education. We have to decide some criteria for measuring education, i.e. who is getting what, at which age and how?

If we decide to make some criteria then the obvious one which comes is **'who'**.Before and after the age group of 6 years, who has the right to have learning opportunity from the state and the society? Within that age frame, where does the duty of the state begin and to whom does it extend? Before, during and after the 6-14 phase, who are the children coming to school? What are the disparities among those coming to school at that phase? The related criterion refers to **'when'**. When does the child come under the benevolent possibilities of learning? A further related criterion is **'what'**. The Act talks about the key transactions that a school and a class must ensure. But it does not have much to say about what is the substance that has been passed on from the teachers to learners, from institutions to individuals. The issue of quality and standards is related to this criterion. Another linked criterion is **'how'**. Every Indian school today makes children learn how to memorize. The little ones learn to recite and the older ones learn to write down what they memorize. But remembering is not the same as understanding, and memorizing is not the same as knowing.

The current learning process does not offer much space for questioning. The young scholar is supposed to learn to wonder, to imagine and to ask. In the average school, setting this goal may well be seen as daydreaming or disrupting the class. Years ago there was a UNESCO/UNICEF experiment to engage with the science teachers across the nation, and interestingly it was found that most of them were afraid of their pupils asking questions. They were also afraid to ask questions to the children because they were not confident of how they would answer and whether their answers would be right or wrong. Some of the teachers were found to be willing to ask questions but not to receive questions.

If a school is a learning space, it offers both formal and non-formal transfer of information, of ideas and hopefully of knowledge as well; but the question is in what way, what manner, and with what sensitivity? The child's right to be respected is a critical factor and the right of any and every child to enjoy this right is a vital concern. If information conveyed is as insensitive as the way they are taught, it makes its own negative contribution to that transfer process. Here, a few real examples are provided:

1. A primary school textbook in social studies contains the following lesson on manual scavenging:

   'In your home, there would be a person who comes to sweep and clean the house, probably it is a woman'. Then there is a picture of the woman wearing a salwar-kameez. The child is told that this woman may belong to the class of manual scavengers. The lesson does not mention what a manual scavenging is. The lesson hints that the learner is a middle class child whose home employs servants. But the child reading this lesson could himself/herself be from such a group. What then? The lesson hurts the dignity of such children. At the end of the chapter, the child is then asked what manual scavenging is. Moreover, the last question is who you think should do it. The lesson designers do not seem to be worried about their taking for granted the unjust and unlawful fact of manual scavenging. This then is an unacceptable lesson which is being taught to children. Teachers from a larger non-governmental organizations (NGOs) school network serving children of poor communities in the Delhi area have confided that they found this lesson very irksome to teach. What does the National Council of Educational Research and Training (NCERT) or the National University of Educational Planning and Administration (NUEPA) have to say about the lesson? The book is still being used.

2. An English grammar textbook gives an example to teach the word "although". The example given is "Although Hari is only a carpenter he is generally truthful". This implies that carpenters are not always truthful. Would being only generally truthful be all right? How, something judgmental for a carpenter is seeped unnoticed into the children's minds. Who approved this grammar book to be used in our school system? But it is in wide use.

When we try to juxtapose the concept of unity and diversity, which is what education should be promoting, we come up against a difficult problem. To illustrate this, an Adivasi child is to unlearn and relinquish its persona and become another one in order to be brought to the national mainstream. Nobody calculates the cost that the child has to pay in the process. Further, it has been found that in the North East, the history that is taught is not of that region but that of the heartland of India. The curriculum includes lessons on Ashoka, Chandragupta and Akbar and not on the history of the state and the region to which the child belongs. On the other hand, the children in the heartland of India do not learn anything other than the history of the heartland. This by no means can be called an inclusive teaching or learning. There is very little Indian or just about such a system.

19

A Teachers' Movement Perspective

Ram Pal Singh

1. Backdrop

The All India Primary Teachers' Federation (AIPTF) envisions quality education for all and child labour free India. Each child irrespective of her/his caste, creed, situation in which she/he lives and parents' financial status, receives quality education to reach the fullest potential of her/his capacities. She/he contributes to her/his own economic progress and that of the country too. However, presently there exist certain roadblocks in the path of this vision.

Since independence there has been a quantitative expansion of educational facilities in the country. This has increased access to education at different levels particularly for school education. About 90 per cent of children in the age of 6 plus are enrolling themselves in schools. However, the quality of education has not kept pace with the quantitative expansion of education. About one-fifth of the children who seek admission in Class-I drop out before completing primary education. Very few among those who complete primary education acquire the requisite knowledge and skills which are essential for a citizen of the 21st century. UNESCO EFA Global Monitoring Report (2014) highlights that 90 per cent of children from poorer households remain illiterate even after four years of schooling. This also holds good for poor children in India. The report further specifies that there is a learning crisis in India.

Thus children from poorer households are worst hit by this low quality of education. The report also warns that the learning crisis would affect generations of children if no corrective steps are taken. The report further highlights that ten per cent of the global funding is wasted on primary education on account of its poor quality.

Another indicator of the low quality of education in India is that India stood at 71st position out of 73 countries on the Programme of International Student Assessment (PISA) in 2012. This reflects poorly on the efficacy of the school education system in India. The reason behind the low quality of education in India is that the country is still entrapped in the old paradigm of teaching content. This is contributing to the low quality of education. Over the last two to three decades, brain research has brought a significant shift in our thinking about the nature of human learning, i.e. how people learn. As a consequence, there is a need for a paradigm shift in designing instruction from behaviourism to cognitivism and now to constructivism. Constructivism emphasizes knowledge acquisition through construction. Each child constructs knowledge on her/his own by experiencing things and by reflecting on those experiences. Collaborative learning and environmental interaction facilitate the knowledge construction process. The role of the teacher is to support his/her students in the construction of knowledge rather than to provide information himself/herself. Learning is a constructive activity. It has to be carried out by learners themselves.

2. Quality of Education Needs a Paradigm Shift

Access to quality education is the right of every child. Without quality education, education for all cannot be achieved. For example, how well pupils are taught and how much they learn, can have a crucial impact on how long they stay in school and how regularly they attend. Furthermore, whether parents send their children to school at all is likely to depend on judgement they make about the quality of teaching and learning provided—upon whether attending school is worth the time and cost for their children and for themselves.

It is unfortunate that the school education system in India puts emphasis mainly on the ability to memorize and the ability to reproduce. Teachers teach content and ask their students to memorize it. They test through examination whether the students have memorized the content. Besides, people perceive a school to be of a good quality when students of the school secure very good marks. But securing high marks hardly reflects the quality of education. It simply reflects that students have memorized the taught content very well.

While in India teachers are teaching content in our schools, teachers in developed countries are helping students to construct knowledge themselves and to develop thinking skills such as creative and critical thinking and problem solving. An indicator of quality education is to foster among children thinking skills. It is important to underline that cognitive development is identified as a major explicit objective of all education systems. The degree to which systems actually achieve this is one indicator of its quality. The second indicator is education's role in encouraging learners' creative and emotional development; in supporting objectives of peace, citizenship and security; in promoting equality and in passing global and local cultural values down to future generations.

2.1 Some Prerequisites of Quality Education

(a) Overhauling the Objectives of Education

There is a need to overhaul the education system – its objectives, curriculum, and transactional process. The emphasis should be on critical and creative thinking, problem solving and drawing inferences. The evaluation process should be such that instead of only testing knowledge, logical and creative thinking abilities of children are also evaluated/assessed.

(b) Creation of Enabling Learning Environment

India is a signatory to the Dakar Convention of 2000. India had agreed to achieve Quality Education for All by 2015. Right of Children to Free and Compulsory Education Act, 2009 came into force from April 1, 2010. The All India Primary Teachers' Federation has been pressurizing the Government of India since then to implement the Act in letter and spirit so that the country is able to achieve quality education for all by 2015. The country has not succeeded in achieving quality education by 2015 due to various road blocks.

Quality education cannot be achieved unless an enabling learning environment exists in schools. Learning happens only when the learning environment is conducive to it. Adequate infrastructure and teaching workforce contribute a lot towards creating an enabling learning environment in schools. The providers of education must create an enabling learning environment in schools.

(c) Quality of Teachers

There is a proliferation of private colleges of education in the country both at the elementary and secondary level. The majority of these colleges are sub-standard. As a result, many of them are producing teachers who do not possess the requisite knowledge and skills to be good performers in schools. The National Council for Teacher Education Curriculum Framework (2009) also highlights that ill-trained teachers are being produced by many colleges of education.

Therefore, the quality of teacher education needs to be improved first to ensure the quality of education in schools. The content and process of teacher education has to undergo a drastic change to produce professionally well-trained teachers. In this regard, the training of teachers should be based on the principle of Andragogy (Art and Science of teaching adults). This is because the learning behaviour of adults is different from those of children. For teaching children, we make use of pedagogy (Art and Science of teaching children). Transactional approaches based on Andragogy are problem-centred learning, collaborative learning and providing time for reflection, follow-up, etc. Teacher educators in colleges of education should therefore, use these instructional approaches in order to improve learning outcomes of their student-teachers.

A few instructional strategies have been developed by scholars working in the field of teacher education. These instructional strategies such as cooperative learning, differentiated instruction, theory of multiple intelligences, constructivism, mind mapping, etc. should form part of the teacher education curriculum. Moreover, student-teachers should be provided intensive training in remedial teaching.

The teaching practice programme needs to be strengthened substantially. Student-teachers should opt for practice teaching or internship for two to three days per week throughout the year. They should attend theory classes during the remaining two to three days per week. This innovation may go a long way in producing quality teachers.

The AIPTF welcomes the decision of the National Council for Teacher Education (NCTE) to increase the duration of the Bachelor in Education programme from one to two years from the academic session 2015-16. The curriculum of secondary teacher education programme has undergone a substantial change. Some of the instructional strategies referred to above such as the theory of multiple intelligences, constructivism and reflective teaching now find place in the revised curriculum. This has taken place at the instance of the AIPTF.

3. Improving Professional Development of Teachers

Professional development of teachers is a complex and challenging task. It is recognized that professional development of teachers has a direct and positive influence on increasing students' achievement. But not all professional initiatives for example, strict content delivery which is often known as sit and get approach have the same effect on students' achievement.

It is unfortunate that the quality of professional development programmes being implemented in India under the Sarva Shiksha Abhiyan (SSA) is very poor. A research study titled Effectiveness of In-service Education of Teachers conducted in 2009 by the AIPTF revealed that 28 per cent of primary teachers in Tamil Nadu and 25 per cent in Bihar perceived that the training was not at all relevant to their learning needs.

Of those who perceived that training to be effective, 93 per cent said that the training was useful to them only to some extent. Observations of some of the teachers are highlighted below:

- *Training programmes must be conducted by well-equipped and skilled persons in the concerned subject or else these are useless.*
- *In rural areas, two teachers are working in primary schools. The learning of students is affected adversely by the time devoted by teachers for in-service trainings. So it is better to reduce training days.*

- *What we are learning in the training programmes is not possible to use in the school situation.*

These responses of teachers reflect that the enormous resources both human and material being invested in the professional development of teachers are not yielding the desired dividends. It would not be wrong to say that the national resources are being squandered on this programme.

The AIPTF feels that the government should impart training after undertaking needs assessment of teachers working in different contexts through research studies. There should be a differential curriculum for training of teachers based on their learning needs. Further, besides training of teachers at the cluster, block and district levels, the government should launch school-based training programmes.

4. Free and Compulsory Early Childhood Education to Achieve Quality Education

Learning begins at birth and continues throughout life. It is now being recognized that the period of the first five to six years of a child's life is of enormous importance. This is because 90 per cent of a child's brain is developed by the age of 5 years. High quality of early childhood education results in cognition, and social and emotional gains in children, particularly from underprivileged sections of society. Since there is a remarkable brain growth during the early childhood period, these years lay the foundation for subsequent learning and development.

There are empirical evidences that exposing young children to interesting sources of information for very brief periods each day stimulates the development of brain cells during the early years and fosters a spontaneous curiosity and love for learning. The early childhood education also produces better citizens. In Michigan, it was found that 3 and 4 year olds, from low income families who did not receive pre-school education, were five times more likely to have become chronic law breakers by the age of 27 than those who did receive it. In view of the gains flowing from early childhood education, there is a need for making bold investment in young children to help them to gain the best start in life. UNESCO also advocates for Early Childhood Care and Education (ECCE) programmes which attend to health, nutrition, security and learning needs of children and which provide for children's holistic development. It organized the first World Conference on ECCE in September 2010, which culminated in the adoption of a global action agenda for ECCE called the Moscow Framework for Action and Cooperation: Harnessing the Wealth of Nations. The Dakar Framework for Action (2000) also affirmed the importance of early childhood by including development, care and education as the first of its six millennium development goals.

Clause 18 of the Right of Children to Free and Compulsory Education Act-2009 highlights that with a view to preparing children above the age of three years for elementary education and to provide early childhood care and education for all children till they complete the age of six years, the appropriate government may make necessary arrangement for providing free pre-school education for such children. Hardly any state has taken action to treat pre-school education as free and compulsory. The Government of India should also amend the RTE 2009 to cover pre-school education. This would improve the quality of education at all levels. We understand that some efforts are underway in this regard.

5. Sustainable Development Goals

In September 2015, at the United Nations General Assembly, all the 193 member countries of the world assembled, agreed and signed the Sustainable Development Goals 2030 as an Universal Development Agenda to end poverty, hunger, ensure quality education and health, gender equality and decent work for all. The Agenda 2030 includes 17 Sustainable Development Goals and 169 targets. Out of the Goals, SDG-4 relates to Education. Of 7 targets of SDG-4, targets 4.1 and 4.2 are highlighted below:

Target 4.1

By 2030, ensure that all girls and boys complete free, equitable and quality primary and secondary education and effective learning outcomes.

Target 4.2

By 2030, ensure that all girls and boys have access to quality early childhood development care and pre-primary education so that they are ready for primary education.

6. The Way Forward

Over the period, the All India Primary Teachers' Federation (AIPTF) has re-invented itself. If has transformed itself from teachers' union into teachers' professional organization. The primary objective of the AIPTF is to extend support to achieve the long cherished goal—Quality Elementary Education for All. It is making relentless efforts in this regard.

India is struggling with a host of issues/problems in the country. Of these, the most significant are: poverty, hunger, high rate of population growth, depleting water table, indiscriminate exploitation of natural resources, quality education and health, gender equality, unemployment and underemployment. Successive governments in India have made endeavours to address these issues. But these endeavours have yielded only very limited results. As such, the problems continue to persist in more or less the same intensity.

In India, not less than 30 per cent people still live below the poverty line. They are leading a very miserable life. India ranked 100th among 119 developing countries as per the Global Hunger Index (GHI). The country's hunger problem is driven by high child malnutrition. Regarding high population growth, according to the UN Population Division, India's population currently estimated at 1.34 billion is projected to rise to 1.51 billion by 2030 and further to 1.66 billion by 2050 before declining to 1.52 billion by the end of the century.

The AIPTF strongly feels that the only remedy to address and cure the current ailments of Indian society is through the achievement of quality school secondary education for all. The AIPTF is presently engaged in exerting pressure on the government to undertake the necessary legislation to render free and compulsory education from pre-school to secondary level as the fundamental right of a child. The AIPTF would continue to struggle till this is achieved.

About the Contributors

Prabhat Patnaik is Professor Emeritus of Economics, Centre for Economic Studies and Planning in the School of Social Sciences, Jawaharlal Nehru University, and Editor, *Social Scientist*. His specialization is macroeconomics and political economy. His recent publications include the book *Demonetisation Decoded: A Critique of India's Currency Experiment*, Routledge India, 2017 (with Jayati Ghosh, and C.P. Chandrasekhar). Email: prabhatptnk@ yahoo.co.in

Jandhyala B.G. Tilak is former Vice-Chancellor, National University of Educational Planning and Administration (NUEPA), and Editor, *Journal of Educational Planning and Administration*. His specialization is Economics of Education. His recent publications include the book *Education and Development in India: Critical Issues in Public Policy and Development*, Springer Verlag, Singapor, 2018. Email: jtilak@nuepa.org

Sudarshan Iyengar is former Vice-Chancellor, Gujarat Vidyapith. He is a lifelong Gandhian and his recent publications include 'Financing Education in Gandhi's Thought Perspective', in *Issues in Indian Public Policies* (2018, pp. 19-36) Springer, Singapore (with Nimisha Shukla). Email: sudarshan54@gmail.com

Ananta Kumar Giri is former Professor, Madras Institute of Development Studies. His specialization is Sociology and Anthropology. His recent publications include the book *Beyond Sociology*, Springer Nature Singapore Pvt. Limited, 2018 (with Crowley-Vigneau). Emails: aumkrishna@hotmail.com / aumkrishna@gmail.com

G. Haragopal is former Professor of Political Science, University of Hyderabad. Apart from being an eminent social scientist, he is an activist and educationist. His recent publications include 'Kidnap of the Collector in Odisha: the Question of Tribal Exclusion' in *Adivasi Rights and Exclusion in India*, Routledge, 2018. Email: profharagopal@gmail.com

Sadhna Saxena is former Professor, Department of Education, University of Delhi. Her specialization is Education. Her publications include 'Is Equality an Outdated Concern in Education?' *Economic and Political Weekly* (2012). Email: sadhna1954@gmail.com

(Late) Vinay Kantha was former Professor of Mathematics, Patna University, and Founder Director, East and West Educational Society. His publications include 'Influence of Socio-Economic Background and Cultural Practices on Mathematics Education in India: a Contemporary Overview in Historical Perspective' Zentralblatt für Didaktik der Mathematik (ZDM) *Mathematics Education*, 2014 (with Arindam Bose).

Muchkund Dubey is the President, Council for Social Development. His areas of specialization are Disarmament and Security, International Relations, Foreign Policy and India's Economic and Social Development. His recent publications include the book *India's Foreign Policy: Coping with the Changing World: Updated Edition with a New Chapter on Pakistan*, Orient BlackSwan, 2017. Email: csdnd@del2.vsnl.net.in

Archana Mehandale is Professor, Tata Institute of Social Sciences, Mumbai and leads the research programme, Connected Learning Initiative. Her specialization is Law and Education. Her recent publications include the coedited volume *School Education in India: Market, State and Quality*, Taylor & Francis, 2018, (with Manish Jain, Rahul Mukhopadhyay, Padma M. Sarangapani, and Christopher Winch). Email: arch_mehendale@yahoo.com

Poornima M. is Assistant Professor, Council for Social Development. Her specialization is educational reforms. Her recent publications include 'Right to Education in BRICS Countries: Ensuring Equity, Equality and Social Justice" in Islam and Iftekar (eds.) *International Perspectives on Comparative Education*

Policy (2015), Bloomsbury Publication, ISBN: 978-93-84898-82-3 (with Susmita Mitra). Email: nima.poori@gmail.com

Susmita Mitra is Assistant Professor, Council for Social Development. Her specialization is Environmental Economics and Education. Her recent publications include, *'Chhattisgarh Rajya mein Prathamik Shiksha ki Sthiti evang Chunautiyyon ka ek Vishleshan'* (An Analysis of Status of and Barriers to School Education in Chhattisgarh) (Hindi), in *Bhartiya Samajshastra Sameeksha* (2018), Vol. 5, Issue 1, pp: 22-41, Indian Sociological Society, Sage Publications, (with Prof. Ashok Pankaj). Email: susmita.mitra81@gmail.com

Razia Ismail is the co-founder and former co-Convenor of the Indian Alliance for Child Rights (IACR). Email: iacrindia@gmail.com

Medha Patkar is an eminent social activist and the founder member of the people's movement called Narmada Bachao Andolan (NBA). Email: nba.medha@gmail.com

Annie Namala is Director, Centre for Social Equity and Inclusion. She is a social activist and has been working for Dalit rights. Email: annie.namala@gmail.com

Ambarish Rai is founder and National Convenor of Right to Education (RTE) Forum, New Delhi. Email: amb1857@gmail.com

Rampal Singh is President, All India Primary Teachers' Federation. Email: aiptfindia@yahoo.com

Kumar Rana is Project Director, Pratichi Trust, Kolkata. Email: kumar@pratichi.org

